E.T.A. Hoffmann's Orient

Romantic Aesthetics and the German Imagination

LEGENDA

LEGENDA is the Modern Humanities Research Association's book imprint for new research in the Humanities. Founded in 1995 by Malcolm Bowie and others within the University of Oxford, Legenda has always been a collaborative publishing enterprise, directly governed by scholars. The Modern Humanities Research Association (MHRA) joined this collaboration in 1998, became half-owner in 2004, in partnership with Maney Publishing and then Routledge, and has since 2016 been sole owner. Titles range from medieval texts to contemporary cinema and form a widely comparative view of the modern humanities, including works on Arabic, Catalan, English, French, German, Greek, Italian, Portuguese, Russian, Spanish, and Yiddish literature. Editorial boards and committees of more than 60 leading academic specialists work in collaboration with bodies such as the Society for French Studies, the British Comparative Literature Association and the Association of Hispanists of Great Britain & Ireland.

The MHRA encourages and promotes advanced study and research in the field of the modern humanities, especially modern European languages and literature, including English, and also cinema. It aims to break down the barriers between scholars working in different disciplines and to maintain the unity of humanistic scholarship. The Association fulfils this purpose through the publication of journals, bibliographies, monographs, critical editions, and the MHRA Style Guide, and by making grants in support of research. Membership is open to all who work in the Humanities, whether independent or in a University post, and the participation of younger colleagues entering the field is especially welcomed.

ALSO PUBLISHED BY THE ASSOCIATION

Critical Texts
Tudor and Stuart Translations • *New Translations* • *European Translations*
MHRA Library of Medieval Welsh Literature

MHRA Bibliographies
Publications of the Modern Humanities Research Association

The Annual Bibliography of English Language & Literature
Austrian Studies
Modern Language Review
Portuguese Studies
The Slavonic and East European Review
Working Papers in the Humanities
The Yearbook of English Studies

www.mhra.org.uk
www.legendabooks.com

GERMANIC LITERATURES

Germanic Literatures includes monographs and essay collections on literature originally written not only in German, but also in Dutch and the Scandinavian languages. Within the German-speaking area, it seeks also to publish studies of other national literatures such as those of Austria and Switzerland. The chronological scope of the series extends from the early Middle Ages down to the present day.

APPEARING IN THIS SERIES

1. *Yvan Goll: The Thwarted Pursuit of the Whole*, by Robert Vilain
2. *Sebald's Bachelors: Queer Resistance and the Unconforming Life*, by Helen Finch
3. *Goethe's Visual World*, by Pamela Currie
4. *German Narratives of Belonging: Writing Generation and Place in the Twenty-First Century*, by Linda Shortt
5. *The Very Late Goethe: Self-Consciousness and the Art of Ageing*, by Charlotte Lee
6. *Women, Emancipation and the German Novel 1871-1910: Protest Fiction in its Cultural Context*, by Charlotte Woodford
7. *Goethe's Poetry and the Philosophy of Nature: Gott und Welt 1798–1827*, by Regina Sachers
8. *Fontane and Cultural Mediation: Translation and Reception in Nineteenth-Century German Literature*, edited by Ritchie Robertson and Michael White
9. *Metamorphosis in Modern German Literature: Transforming Bodies, Identities and Affects*, by Tara Beaney
10. *Comedy and Trauma in Germany and Austria after 1945: The Inner Side of Mourning*, by Stephanie Bird
11. *E.T.A. Hoffmann's Orient: Romantic Aesthetics and the German Imagination*, by Joanna Neilly
12. *Structures of Subjugation in Dutch Literature*, by Judit Gera

Managing Editor
Dr Graham Nelson, 41 Wellington Square, Oxford OX1 2JF, UK
www.legendabooks.com

E.T.A. Hoffmann's Orient

Romantic Aesthetics and the German Imagination

JOANNA NEILLY

Germanic Literatures 11
Modern Humanities Research Association
2016

Published by Legenda
An imprint of the Modern Humanities Research Association
Salisbury House, Station Road, Cambridge CB1 2LA

ISBN 978-1-909662-98-8 (HB)
ISBN 978-1-781883-09-9 (PB)

First published 2016

Copy-Editor: Nigel Hope

CONTENTS

For Shiona Beatty and Tina Richardson

ACKNOWLEDGEMENTS

This book began as a PhD thesis at the University of Edinburgh. Words cannot express my gratitude to Eleoma Bodammer, who was a wonderful doctoral supervisor. Without her encouragement and insightful readings of my work through several stages, and without our many inspiring conversations, the book would not have been written. I would also like to thank Howard Gaskill for his valuable input, his many useful suggestions, and his infectious enthusiasm for all things Hoffmann-related. Thanks are due to Ritchie Robertson three times over: for introducing me to Hoffmann when I was an undergraduate student; for making the PhD viva a genuinely enjoyable experience; and for being such an efficient and helpful editor. Frauke Matthes was likewise equally supportive and inspiring as an examiner, and thanks to her I have been able to think about my work from new perspectives. More generally, I am grateful to members of the German Department at the University of Edinburgh for providing a friendly and constructive work environment. I shared the highs and lows of the writing process with good friends and would like to thank in particular Lizzie Stewart, Marianne Zwicker, Corinna Häger, and Mary Cosgrove for being sources of both constant encouragement and welcome distraction. My PhD was funded by the Arts and Humanities Research Council, who also provided an additional grant for a fellowship at the John W. Kluge Center at the Library of Congress. Parts of Chapter 5 arose as a direct result of my time in Washington, and I would like to thank the librarians and staff at the Kluge Center for their support.

I finished this book while teaching at the University of Oxford. The Queen's College gave generous support towards publication costs. Both Wadham College and Queen's have provided congenial atmospheres in which to work: thanks are due particularly to Carolin Duttlinger and Charlie Louth, not to mention the students who have engaged with — and often enriched — my love of Hoffmann.

I am grateful to Nigel Hope, who was a meticulous copy-editor, to Graham Nelson for his efficiency in the final stages of the project, and also to the anonymous reader whose constructive suggestions helped me improve the final product.

My book is dedicated to Shiona Beatty and Tina Richardson, two brilliant teachers who made language learning a delight. I am lucky to have found my way into literature with the help of two more great teachers and now dear friends, Michael Hawcroft and Tony Phelan. Thank you for the wisdom, the fun, and (Tony) the books!

Finally, I want to thank my family — Neilly, Hunton, and Tuffnell — for their love and support, and above all Steve, for patiently listening to my many tales of Hoffmann.

J.N., Oxford, November 2016

ABBREVIATIONS

The following abbreviations are used to refer to academic journals in the footnotes and bibliography:

DVjs	*Deutsche Vierteljahresschrift für Literaturwissenschaft und Geistesgeschichte*
EGY	*Edinburgh German Yearbook*
FMLS	*Forum for Modern Language Studies*
GLL	*German Life and Letters*
GQ	*The German Quarterly*
HJb	*E.T.A. Hoffmann-Jahrbuch*
MHG	*Mitteilungen der E.T.A. Hoffmann-Gesellschaft*
MLR	*Modern Language Review*
NGC	*New German Critique*
PMLA	*Publications of the Modern Language Association of America*

NOTE ON EDITIONS, TRANSLATIONS, AND PERMISSIONS

The edition used here is E.T.A. Hoffmann, *Sämtliche Werke*, ed. by Hartmut Steinecke and Wulf Segebrecht, 6 vols (Frankfurt am Main: Deutscher Klassiker Verlag, 1985–2004).

English translations of quotations from *The Golden Pot*, *The Sandman*, *Princess Brambilla*, *Master Flea*, and *My Cousin's Corner Window* are taken from E.T.A. Hoffmann, *The Golden Pot and Other Tales*, trans. by Ritchie Robertson (Oxford: Oxford University Press, 1992), referenced as *GP* in the text. Translations from Hegel's *Vorlesungen über die Ästhetik* are from G. W. F. Hegel, *Aesthetics: Lectures on Fine Art*, trans. by T. M. Knox, 2 vols (Oxford: Oxford University Press, 1975). Translations from Kant's *Kritik der reinen Vernunft* are from Immanuel Kant, *Critique of Pure Reason*, trans. and ed. by Paul Guyer and Allen W. Wood (Cambridge: Cambridge University Press, 1998, repr. 2000).

All other translations from German and French are my own, unless otherwise indicated.

Parts of Chapter 3 appeared in an earlier form in the volume *Bonds and Borders: Identity, Imagination and Transformation in Literature*, ed. by Rebecca DeWald and Dorette Sobolewski (Newcastle: Cambridge Scholars Publishing, 2011). Substantial parts of Chapter 4 appeared in the April 2014 issue of *German Life and Letters* in my article '*Alla Turca* versus the Romantic East: E.T.A. Hoffmann and Oriental-Style Music'. I am grateful to Cambridge Scholars Publishing and to the editors of *German Life and Letters* for granting permission to reproduce this material here.

The cover image of this book is a copperplate print by Ulrich Ludwig Friedrich Wolf (1772–1832), produced as an illustration for Hoffmann's story *Die Irrungen*. The illustration appeared in the 1822 edition of the *Berlinischer Taschenkalender*, and portrays the characters Baron Theodor von S., the Greek princess, and Schnüspelpold in front of the Brandenburg Gate. I am grateful to the Klassik Stiftung Weimar for granting me permission to use this image.

INTRODUCTION

In 1950, the French scholar Raymond Schwab wondered, 'Will it still be possible to speak of Romanticism, of the nineteenth century, of the modern soul, without recording the consequences of the Oriental Renaissance in all provinces of the mind?'[1] With this rhetorical question, Schwab identified an issue which even today continues to preoccupy scholars of German Romanticism. As Suzanne L. Marchand has noted, 'The German romantics became some of the Orient's biggest champions in the period between about 1800 and 1820.'[2] The strong link between the Romantic movement and studies of the Orient is far from a recently discovered area of enquiry. Almost thirty years before Edward W. Said was to admit his failure to address in detail the German preoccupation with the East in his seminal work, *Orientalism* (1978), Schwab had begun this very process. Fourteen years after Schwab, A. Leslie Willson added to the field a literary history of what he termed the 'mythical image' of India and its reception in Romantic-era Germany.[3] While Willson identifies earlier, incomplete, works in the field, these two stand out as comprehensive studies of the important relations between Romanticism and Orientalism, and the uses the former made of the latter. Written before post-colonial theory came into vogue, these works engage with the processes of Romantic Orientalism from the ground up. For this reason they provide a fitting point of departure for this study, which aims to define the place of the writer E.T.A. Hoffmann within Romantic Orientalism, by shedding light on his response to the scholarly and literary Orientalism of his time, and demonstrating how he both related it to the Romantic project and used it as a lens through which to examine his contemporary Germany.

For scholars of German Orientalism, the Romantic period is particularly pertinent, as Schwab insistently claims. *The Oriental Renaissance* is a meticulously researched study of the historical coincidence of Romanticism and Orientalism, and Schwab concludes that these two scholarly and literary movements were not merely temporally linked but functioned as interlocutors in a great shift in European thought which characterized the tumultuous post-Enlightenment period.[4] Focusing on England, France and Germany, with a nod to Russia, Schwab demonstrates how Orientalism and Romanticism worked in tandem to revitalize a Europe 'which had had enough of the rationalizations of reason'.[5] The intellectual fomentation around the turn of the nineteenth century added up to no less than a second Renaissance, with Romanticism and the Orient challenging norms in literature and thought from within and without, respectively. For Schwab, the key date is 1771, representing a linguistic breakthrough when Anquetil-Duperron translated and published the *Zend Avesta*, breaking down language barriers between

East and West and beginning a new practice of 'approach[ing] [...] Asian text[s] totally independent of the biblical and classical traditions'.[6] Equally important was the discovery and translation of Sanskrit in the 1780s, an event that, in Schwab's reading, made the world truly global by expanding the definition of 'oriental languages' to include more than simply Semitic languages. The study of languages, optimistically described as 'a means of taking revenge against Babel', dovetailed nicely with theories of Romantic universalism.[7] Furthermore, both Romanticism and Orientalism posed a challenge to the Classical Age, the former by looking to the medieval era for artistic inspiration, and the latter by widening the scholarly gaze beyond the boundaries of Europe, and uncovering an ancient mythology that preceded even that of the Greeks. In this respect, too, Romanticism found an ally in Asia, as a significant part of the universalism project was the aim to find the common origins of mankind. Schwab's view on the whole, then, is a favourable one, linking Romanticism to a cosmopolitan Orientalism and demonstrating rather convincingly that the 'Oriental Renaissance' was much more outward-looking than the Renaissance of the sixteenth century. The Classical Renaissance affirmed the primacy of European culture, but the second Renaissance challenged Europeans to look beyond their geographical and cultural borders.[8]

Willson looks more specifically at the relationship between German Romanticism and India, or rather, an imaginatively constructed image of India. While his assessment of the use of a 'mythical image' by Romantic authors is on the whole positive, his work nonetheless hints at a more introspective Romanticism. Not quite embracing a true cosmopolitanism, the Romantics, in Willson's view, were interested in a 'mythical image', an India that was 'unreal', even if it was 'true in [the Romanticist's] ideal world and in his imaginative projection of that world through his art'.[9] As he charts the rise and fall of the Indic ideal, Willson analyses a certain type of Orientalism whose practitioners take their inspiration from eastern mythology and distort it to advance their own artistic ambition. In the case of German Romanticism, this ambition was the creation of a new mythology. Willson closely connects the imagined India to this project:

> A restatement of Western values embossed with the stamp of the mythical image, in the symbolism of a new mythology, meant a deeper understanding of man's place in the cosmos. Friedrich Schlegel's definition of a historian as a retrospective prophet, a conjurer of the past, found an extension in the Romantic author, whose ideal assimilation of mythic reality vivified an immediate poetic present.[10]

From this observation it is only a short step to Said's later complaint that the Romantics were interested in India only in so far as it would provide a means by which to breathe life into modern Europe.[11] This view is borne out by Willson's conclusion that the mythical image of India crumbled under the scrutiny of scientific investigation, in the form of Friedrich Schlegel's study of the Sanskrit language.[12] Far from an accurate portrayal of Indian life and customs, the image served to elevate and further mythologize India as 'a land where poetry permeated every aspect of human wisdom', and this vision could not withstand the weight of scientific study.[13]

From the very inception of post-colonial studies of German Romanticism, writers of the movement have therefore both faced charges of self-interest, and been defended as cosmopolitan where the Orient is concerned. Scholars have congregated on both sides of the fence ever since. In addition, Willson's study provides an early and rare consideration of Hoffmann's position. His claim that the inspiring mythical image had more or less dissipated by 1808 following Schlegel's *Über die Sprache und Weisheit der Indier* [*On the Language and Wisdom of the Indians*] does not preclude the identification of later examples of the image in the work of the authors who followed the Early Romantics. According to Willson, Johann Gottfried Herder, the forerunner to Romanticism, was the chief promulgator of the image, and Novalis its best practitioner, particularly in *Heinrich von Ofterdingen* (1802). This work is credited with assimilating and transfiguring the Indic image into a 'mythology of poesy'.[14] Willson falls in line with many critics in his view of an optimistic Early Romanticism and a later, more cynical period, but he concedes that fragments of the mythical image remained after 1808. If Novalis and the Schlegel brothers, along with other prominent Romantic writers Jean Paul, Wilhelm Heinrich Wackenroder, Ludwig Tieck, Friedrich Hölderlin, and Karoline von Günderrode take part in the 'projection of the image', those who come after them hold up its 'reflection'.[15] Hoffmann is grouped along with Heinrich Heine and, unusually, Adalbert Stifter in this latter category. Willson references Hoffmann's *Meister Floh* [*Master Flea*] (1822) in passing, but devotes his energies to revealing the use made of the image in *Der goldene Topf* [*The Golden Pot*] (1814). In this work, the mythical image of India is reflected in Lindhorst's exotic home; moreover, the new mythology project comes close to achieving its goal in the tale of an orientalized Atlantis where man returns to primordial harmony. While praising this tale as second only to Novalis's unfinished novel as an example of new mythology in fiction, Willson nonetheless asserts that Hoffmann's India is a 'never-never land', and that he does not create an image, but simply picks up fragments of the image formed by his predecessors, after its heyday has passed.[16]

Schwab's heavy emphasis on Sanskrit and Willson's exploration of the Indic ideal point to an extremely influential facet of German Orientalism: the Romantic longing for India. In doing so, however, they imply certain limitations. If the progression from the study of Semitic languages to Sanskrit on the one hand broadens the Orient to include India, identifying a complete shift in focus to India risks the exclusion of a range of geographical areas and cultural groups that also constituted the Orient for nineteenth-century Germans. Srinivas Aravamudan's recent study of the Enlightenment affirms that the Orient, as it is imagined in any given period, cannot be reduced to one key area, even if that area is prominent. Instead, Aravamudan describes a 'geographical gamut of cultures, races, and religions that the construct of Orientalism addresses, from southern Europe to North Africa and from West, South and East Asia to indigenous America'.[17] Likewise, Andrea Polaschegg's comprehensive work on nineteenth-century German Orientalism demonstrates how apparently disparate areas and cultures were subsumed into one overarching concept of the Orient, whose various composite parts retained a certain cohesion by way of their shared characteristics and geographical borders.[18]

Polaschegg's starting point is that of the earlier Orientalists: the Bible. Specifically, in identifying where the Orient might have been said to exist, Polaschegg references the Book of Matthew, in which the wise men came 'vom Morgenland' to visit Christ. As Polaschegg rightly points out, the concept of 'Morgenland' is a subjective one. If one takes its literal meaning, i.e. the land where the sun rises, then the 'Morgenland' might move west as its observer does, and indeed this is precisely what happened as Christianity spread westwards into Europe.[19] Eventually, for nineteenth-century observers, travel to the Orient did not even require a trip outside Europe, indeed one barely needed to go east of Vienna.[20] With the Ottoman influence reaching out from Turkey over the south-east of the continent, including the Greek peninsula, the Orient could be encountered, in reality as well as the imagination, not far from home. Europe was also linked to the Orient via Spain's Islamic history. Furthermore, Polaschegg identifies a common factor linking southern Europe to northern Africa: the Mediterranean. This large shared natural border connected Europeans to the 'Moors', another semantically broad term used to cover the inhabitants of northern Africa and even Ethiopia, as well as providing a seemingly interchangeable term for 'Muslims'.[21] The Mediterranean was also the province of piracy, and the perceived threat of the 'barbarians' from northern Africa and Arab states was diffused in Europe by a string of popular comic operas in the late eighteenth century, taking as their theme the abduction of westerners by Barbary pirates. Furthermore, the Arabian peninsula connected Africa to Asia, the focus of linguistic and anthropological studies around 1800. The latter category of intellectual enquiry provides yet another point of overlap between Africa and Asia, for the nineteenth-century and particularly Romantic search for the origins of mankind had two focal points: Egypt and India.[22] Friedrich Creuzer's sustained attention to both Egypt and India, alongside Greece, in his history of ancient mythology, published from 1810, is testimony to this trend.[23] Finally, although the eighteenth-century fascination with China was waning, it lived on in the popular imagination, and so the Orient of the Romantic period stretched from southern Spain to the Far East.[24] Relationships, whether real or imaginary, between diverse parts of the wider Orient meant that they stood in a representative relationship to each other: 'Die Janitscharenmusik, die chinesischen Schriftzeichen, der Koran, die Pyramiden, der Sari oder ein persisches Ghasel — sie alle können den *gesamten* Orient aufrufen und repräsentieren' [Janissary music, Chinese characters, the Qur'an, the pyramids, saris, a Persian ghazal — all these things can summon up and represent the *whole of* the Orient].[25] Thus, not only was the Orient a mutable and often subjective construct, it was also formed in such a way that an imaginative leap from Turkey to India, or China to Egypt, did not require any great degree of mental elasticity.

It is in this tradition that Hoffmann's understanding of the Orient, and that of his contemporaries, must be considered. Hoffmann was surrounded by a literary culture in which the Orient, if it were defined at all, could signify anywhere from Spain to China. Ludwig Tieck's story, *Liebesgeschichte der schönen Magelone und des Grafen Peter von Provence* [*Love Story of the Fair Magelone and Count Peter of Provence*] (1797), details an encounter between the German Peter and an oriental woman whose exact provenance is never clear: her father is a sultan and she is referred to simply as 'die Heidin Sulima' [the heathen Sulima].[26] His 1799 epic play, *Leben und Tod der heiligen Genoveva* [*The Life and Death of Saint Genevieve*], deals briefly with the Islamic invasion of Europe as far north as Tours in the year 732, displaying contemporary remnants of a cultural fear of the Islamic Other, long after the Habsburg victory over the Ottomans at the 1683 Siege of Vienna. At the same time, Novalis was looking to Egypt and the ever-mysterious Isis for the elusive answer to Romantic longing in *Die Lehrlinge zu Sais* [*The Apprentices of Sais*] (1797), but turned his critical eye towards Jerusalem in *Heinrich von Ofterdingen* (1802), which explicitly denounces the violence of the Crusades through the voice of the captive Muslim girl Zulima. Meanwhile, Friedrich Schiller brought China to the German stage, with an adaptation of Gozzi's play *Turandot* in 1801. Achim von Arnim did not venture so far east, but like Tieck played on the fear of the Other with the introduction of Turkish pirates to the south of France in the 1812 story *Melück Maria Blainville, die Hausprophetin aus Arabien* [*Melück Maria Blainville, the House Prophet from Arabia*]. The fact that Arnim's eponymous heroine is specifically referred to as Turkish in the story, but described in broader terms as 'aus Arabien' [from Arabia] in the title, exemplifies the use of sweeping terms to designate specific parts of the wider Orient. Finally, Goethe's *West-Östlicher Divan* [*West-Eastern Divan*] (1819) is famed as proof of his love affair with Persia.

It is within this climate that Hoffmann responded to both the Romantic tradition of the Indic ideal, and to the contemporary fascination with the Orient in its widest possible sense. The mythical image of India, as described by Willson, is certainly key to *Der goldene Topf*, *Meister Floh*, and, arguably, *Prinzessin Brambilla* [*Princess Brambilla*] (1820). Hoffmann's Orient (or more precisely, Orients) covers much wider ground than this, however, and he focuses on many of the geographical and cultural areas that had captured the attention of his predecessors and contemporaries, while also responding to the very process of imagining the Orient from within the German-speaking lands. *Das Sanctus* [*The Sanctus*] (1816) is partly set in fifteenth-century Moorish Granada, with a plot driven by an incidence of Christian–Muslim conflict. Also from the *Nachtstücke* [*Night Pieces*] collection, *Das steinerne Herz* [*The Stone Heart*] (1817) features Baron Exter, a former ambassador to Turkey who cherishes memories of his time in Constantinople to the point of ludicrous obsession. Likewise focusing on Turkish imagery, *Die Automate* [*The Automata*] (1814) studies the effects of the imagined mystery of the Orient on an impressionable public, with the arrival of a Turkish fortune-telling automaton in a German marketplace. Furthermore, different aspects of the sprawling Orient might come together in one character. This is true in the case of Prosper Alpanus, the magus in *Klein Zaches genannt Zinnober* [*Little Zaches, Called Cinnabar*] (1819) who was raised in India but nevertheless appears 'beinahe Chinesisch gekleidet' [dressed in an almost Chinese style] (III, 583). A more complex example is the unnamed Greek princess of *Die Irrungen* [*The Errors*] (1821) and its sequel *Die Geheimnisse* [*The Secrets*] (1822), who comes from a modern Greece blighted by the barbarism of Ottoman rule, and who is compared to both the Chinese Turandot and the Egyptian Isis.

Turning closer to home, Hoffmann's work is also influenced by European interpretations of the Orient in literature and music. His earliest published work of fiction, *Ritter Gluck* [*Ritter Gluck/The Knight Gluck*] (1809), describes two performances of Christoph Willibald Gluck's opera *Armide* (1777), the story of a sorceress from Damascus who falls tragically in love with a Christian knight. In *Das steinerne Herz*, characters who dress up for a costume ball feel oddly foreign and look at each other with all the wonder reserved for the Orient: 'mich dünkt [...] ich hätte dich schon in der asiatischen Banise erblickt' [it seems to me [...] that I've seen you before, in the Asian Banise] (III, 324). The reference is to *Asiatische Banise* [*The Asian Banise*], a novel written in 1689 by Heinrich Anselm von Zigler und Kliphausen (1663–97). The novel's action unfolds in mixed oriental settings — Japan, Siam, and Burma — and follows the adventures of Prince Balacin as he attempts to rescue the Princess Banise in a land suffering under tyrannical rule. The novel remained popular for almost a century after its first publication, with fifteen editions published between 1689 and 1764. It also influenced later literary works — the figure of the oriental despot, Chaumigram, who appears in the *Banise*, is also found in the puppet theatre in Goethe's *Wilhelm Meisters Lehrjahre* [*Wilhelm Meister's Apprenticeship*] (1795–96). The continued popularity of the novel into the 1760s is of note here because the theme of the costume party in Hoffmann's tale is 1760s dress, perhaps explaining the identification of old-fashioned clothing with the Orient.[27] Finally, the magical fairies in *Klein Zaches genannt Zinnober* hail from Dschinnistan, referenced in the text as the land of the *Arabian Nights* (III, 544). Antoine Galland's translation of this work into French, published between 1704 and 1717, had a much-documented influence on European literature and culture.[28] Christoph Martin Wieland's collection of fairy tales *Dschinnistan* (1786–89) provided the source for the libretto of Mozart's opera *Die Zauberflöte* [*The Magic Flute*, 1791], and a variant on the name, Ginnistan, was used by Novalis for Klingsohr's fairy tale in *Heinrich von Ofterdingen*.[29] Its continued relevance as inspiration for Romantic poetry and art is exemplified in Hoffmann's *Don Juan* (1811), when the enraptured narrator calls out to the singer who has captured his imagination, 'du Dschinnistan voller Herrlichkeit' [you magnificent Dschinnistan] (I, 708). Hoffmann's Orients are thus far-reaching and yet founded in the contemporary cultural imagination, projecting outwards from Germany.

As the above examples demonstrate, scholars of German Romantic Orientalism are faced with a breathtaking array of cultures that are nevertheless swallowed up by broad terms intended to define them as parts of one more or less homogeneous group. Ever since Said's ground-breaking study, it has proved impossible to ignore the more negative aspects of such a grouping-together of disparate regions and peoples. Said's overarching theory is that such practices are designed to emphasize the superiority of the West by reducing the Orient to a set of clichés, defining it not on an empirical basis but solely in relation to Europe. This theory is indeed evident in one of the Grimms' definitions of 'Morgenland' [the Orient] as 'gegensatz zu Abendland' [the opposite of the Occident].[30] Furthermore, each composite part of the constructed Orient gains what Said terms 'distributive currency' in orientalist discourse, meaning that once an idea about one part of the Orient becomes accepted, it can be broadly applied to any so-called oriental area or culture, regardless of factual evidence or religious and cultural differences.[31] In this sense, at least, the German Romantics are surely guilty of a process Said describes as 'orientalizing the Oriental'.[32] Furthermore, the Orient became a function in the service of self-definition. Understood in terms of its opposition to Europe, the Orient was constructed imaginatively to fit a European need for self-definition; therefore it was also held up as a comparison to western religion and culture, from which it inevitably suffered. Reinforcing this picture is the fact that the birth of Romanticism, and the early days of German Orientalism, coincided with the growth of German nationalism. Nicholas Saul's study of gypsies, another group subjected to orientalist discourse due to their mysterious but certainly eastern heritage, reveals how Germany functionalized the oriental Other during its 'slow transition to nation- and statehood':[33]

> The Romantic Gypsy is presented not only in a relatively authentic light, but also as aestheticized and politicized, both as the ideal of the Romantic artist and also, in their capacity as Gypsy other, the touchstone of authentic *German* national identity.[34]

It was not uncommon for writers who made the Orient the subject of their literary work also to take part in programmatic nationalist projects: Achim von Arnim's work in collecting German folk songs is a case in point. Scholars since the 1970s, then, have been forced to grapple with the key question: was Romantic Orientalism cosmopolitan, or part of an inward-looking, and at worst chauvinistic, project seeking to define what it meant to be German? This question has been a defining one for studies of German Romantic Orientalism in recent decades.

On the whole, the answer has pointed to an inherent ambivalence on the part of Romantic authors. As Carl Niekerk writes, 'It is one of the paradoxes of Romanticism that the movement is perceived simultaneously as committed to pluralism and yet also as the birthplace of modern German nationalism.'[35] Michael Hofmann likewise weighs up Herder's alleged humanism and finds in it a claim for the superiority of both Christianity as a religious basis for modern life, and Greco-Roman antiquity as a cultural model.[36] Herder's call to accord all cultures equal respect might be laudably progressive for his time, but his view on the progression of history, in which all cultures have a transitory period of prominence, means that the great achievements of, for example, India, are firmly consigned to the past.[37] Perhaps the most considered study, in terms of breadth, of this characteristic ambiguity is Todd Kontje's 2004 *German Orientalisms*, which charts the fortunes of the Orient within the context of German nationalism.[38] While Kontje gives a balanced view of major figures in eighteenth- and nineteenth-century Orientalism, including Herder, Novalis, Friedrich Schlegel, and Goethe, he acknowledges their contribution to a nationalist project via their interest in the East. In essence, the depiction of the Orient by Germans, in Kontje's view, largely depends on the status of the nation. As the threat of the Ottoman Empire receded, German-speaking dramatists and librettists could afford to be more playful in their depictions of the East, but an apparent drive towards cosmopolitanism was also a thinly veiled effort at one-upmanship over the empire-building French in an era when Germans were far from achieving a coherent national identity, never mind domination overseas.

The cosmopolitan tradition fostered by the Romantics and their contemporaries is therefore a manifestation of nationalist pride, and Kontje argues, for example, that Goethe's pioneering concept of *Weltliteratur* [World Literature], an initiative that was to be spearheaded by none other than the Germans themselves, was as much a promotion of a new German literary movement as a sign of Goethe's enthusiasm for non-European literature in the wake of the *Divan*.[39]

Some assessments of the motivation for the intellectual curiosity characterizing the arguably one-way relationship between West and East have been more generous. Said's work has been criticized for its essentialist treatment of western engagement with the Orient, with critics claiming that it is possible, and indeed necessary, to interpret so-called orientalist works more sympathetically in the context of their time.[40] With such an approach in mind, Mohammed Sharafuddin argues that Orientalism does not necessarily preclude the possibility of a true discovery of the East, and may instead, to some extent, encourage real engagement.[41] Goer and Hofmann take this stance in regard to German Orientalism in the eighteenth and nineteenth centuries, claiming that the discourse surrounding the Orient was not shaped by a disdain for the Other, but rather by 'Neugier und Respekt sowie Achtung vor dem Gegenüber, das in einer ungeahnten Weise anregen und bereichern konnte' [curiosity and respect, as well as esteem for otherness, which could, in unexpected ways, stimulate and enrich].[42] In this strain of thought, Aravamudan attempts to acquit eastwards-looking Enlightenment writers of the most unsavoury of the charges directed at them ever since *Orientalism* appeared. Providing a nuanced reading that importantly acknowledges the temporal and cultural context — and limits — in which eighteenth-century authors operated, Aravamudan praises the utopian aspirations of Enlightenment Orientalism. The East might be, on the whole, a construct imagined within Europe, but the mode in which it was expressed was 'experimental, prospective, and antifoundationalist'.[43] The famous tradition of self-criticism that developed in the Enlightenment period is bolstered by an Orientalism motivated by the desire to reflect on, and improve, European attitudes as much as it fostered feelings of superiority.

The Scope of this Study

The following work on Hoffmann takes place within this critical debate and is guided by its central question. One common thread connecting Hoffmann's numerous fictional works is the issue of his inherent ambiguity: his stories have been recognized many times over not only as open-ended, but also as bringing seemingly irreconcilable opposites inexplicably together. I have aimed to uncover whether Hoffmann's fictional treatment of the Orient has the same double nature. Did Hoffmann incorporate oriental themes and elements into so many of his works in order to enliven a German tradition of Romantic writing, thus falling into the category of self-interested writers maligned by Said and his followers? Or did he turn his critical gaze inwards?

Given his sustained engagement with the Orient and its reception in Germany throughout his authorial career, from the earliest work (*Ritter Gluck*) to those written in the year of his death (*Meister Floh*, *Die Geheimnisse*), Hoffmann becomes conspicuous by his near absence in scholarship on Romantic Orientalism. With the exception of very few short studies, most notably Birgit Röder's recent article,[44] this aspect of his work has suffered from critical neglect, particularly considered alongside the numerous pages devoted to his predecessors and contemporaries, Herder, Novalis, and Friedrich Schlegel.[45] The reasons for this considerable oversight have not been addressed, although Röder does suggest that Hoffmann's more famous treatment of Italy has proved a greater draw for his critics.[46] One might add to this that Hoffmann was not a student of oriental languages, nor did he make programmatic statements, as did Schlegel, about the future of Romantic literature — at least not overtly, although his views can certainly be found embedded in his fiction. Where he did advance theories about art, they were more likely to relate to music, his passion for which is evident in his many published reviews. His vast, four-volume collection of stories, *Die Serapionsbrüder* [*The Serapion Brethren*] (1819–21), is the closest Hoffmann comes to making statements about literary practice, and these are present in the frame narrative of the Serapion brothers' discussions, largely untreated by critics until Hilda Meldrum Brown insisted upon their significance in her 2006 work.[47] In short, then, Hoffmann is not generally famed as a theorist of Romantic art, as his aesthetic programme is presented in a rather less direct manner than those of his contemporaries, and he rarely makes overt statements connecting his fictional Orients to a longed-for literary rejuvenation.

Perhaps even more significantly, Hoffmann is not regarded as a key figure in the literary nationalist project which blossomed during the Age of Goethe. Victoria Dutchman-Smith advances a highly plausible reason for this, noting the importance of early Hoffmann reception both outside and within Germany.[48] At a time when German nationalists needed literary heroes to boost their cause, Dutchman-Smith argues, Hoffmann was not deemed an appropriate figure for emulation.[49] Walter Scott's famous criticism of Hoffmann was approved by no less eminent a writer than Goethe, who, along with Joseph von Eichendorff, denounced Hoffmann's artistic approach as one to be avoided. This criticism hinged on the prevalence of madness in Hoffmann's fiction, as well as his reputation as a drinker and his tendency to engage with national politics only indirectly.[50] Furthermore, while Hoffmann draws on the German medieval tradition revered by the Romantics in *Der Kampf der Sänger* [*The Singers' Contest*] (1817) and *Meister Martin der Küfner und seine Gesellen* [*Master Martin the Cooper and his Journeymen*] (1818), he did not follow in the footsteps of Clemens Brentano, Achim von Arnim, and the Grimms, who hoped to awaken German nationalist sentiment by reviving the medieval oral tradition of storytelling. As folklorists, the editors of *Des Knaben Wunderhorn* [*The Boy's Magic Horn*] (1805, 1808) and the *Kinder- und Hausmärchen* [*Fairy Tales for Household and Nursery*] (1812–15) were keen to preserve in writing the voice of the common people by collecting popular German folk songs and tales. Intended partly as a means of loosening the hold of foreign cultural influences in Germany, such as French neo-classicism and Italian opera, this project served a nationalist agenda. Ethel Matala de Mazza explains the self-proclaimed national literature of the period as an attempt to achieve a coherent identity: not only would texts produce a sense of a shared cultural past, but they would promote this unity for a German future.[51] De Mazza notes that Hoffmann endorsed the concept of the literary circle with his 'Serapion Brotherhood', but in terms of politicizing cultural exchange, the Heidelberg circle of Romantics, which included Arnim and Brentano, were eminently more engaged.[52] Indeed, this distinction informs Scott's criticism. After praising the Grimm brothers for their interest in popular tradition, Scott admits that Hoffmann was 'also a high-spirited patriot', before castigating him for a failure to translate this sentiment into written form.[53] If critics, with justification, wish to read literary Orientalism as one way of constructing German identity, Hoffmann — an unlikely mouthpiece for German nationalism — is therefore not the most obvious writer to consult.

Nevertheless, the claim of this study is that Hoffmann is a key voice in Romantic Orientalism, and the fact that he was not as entrenched in debates about national identity as some of his fellow Romantics provides several new angles from which to view the practices of Orientalism. The following chapters consider both sides of Romantic Orientalism, and weigh up its alleged ambivalence by examining two major strands in Hoffmann's work: the presentation of his views on Romantic aesthetics, and his criticism of modern German culture and society. Was the Orient used for self-definition and the promotion of a literary programme? In Hoffmann's case, this does not necessarily mean an exploration of German identity, but can be related to the progression of specifically Romantic ambitions. Or does Hoffmann's construction of the Orient become more of a critical tool, employed in order to question German social and literary customs and, more importantly, to criticize the European enthusiasm for a generic East?

In responding to the first question, Hoffmann's aesthetic aims must be reviewed. Hoffmann sustained a keen interest in the position of the artist in modern society.[54] When this interest is coupled with oriental imagery, he begins to develop and change the practice of Romantic Orientalism rather than simply replicate stereotypes. He advocates certain approaches to the Orient to help artists overcome the painful schism occasioned by their existence among the 'philistines' of modern society. Hoffmann's tales often feature artists, or characters receptive to creative impulses, who seek solace in a world other than that which they inhabit in order to compensate for their unhappiness on earth. The examples of Nathanael in *Der Sandmann* (1816) and Elis Fröbom in *Die Bergwerke zu Falun* [*The Mines at Falun*] (1819) reveal how this can be a dangerous undertaking when the imagined world eclipses the everyday, threatening both physical and mental well-being. Whenever the creative impulse is ignited by visions of an oriental world, however, the effect is often a positive one, both for artistic production, as in *Der goldene Topf*, and for re-establishing the position of protagonists in their own societies, for example in *Prinzessin Brambilla* and *Meister Floh*. The following chapters argue that Hoffmann does not simply promote the image of the Indic ideal, however, but reveals the limits of this approach. His ambivalence regarding the uses of a Romantically constructed Orient is linked not only to his reputation as a cynic, but also to his creation of an aesthetic guide for artists who must remain part of modern society. His failure to embrace wholesale the notion of a poetic utopia does not amount to a rejection of the Romantic East. Instead, Hoffmann's fiction engages with Romantic

Orientalism in a way that usefully suggests its relevance, and the limits thereof, for modern creativity.

The second major aspect of Hoffmann's work considered here relates to his critical responses to the society surrounding him, and to the actual processes by which Romantic and popular art is created. Hoffmann was a very self-aware author, keeping one eye constantly on the mechanisms of cultural production. For example, frequent appeals to the reader on the part of the fictional narrators of his stories reflect an ongoing interest in the process of writing for an audience. It is highly implausible that such a self-conscious writer would use oriental tropes unthinkingly. As the following chapters reveal, his literary work is shaped and influenced by both the scholarly and popular orientalist discourses of his time, a fact of which he is clearly aware. Hoffmann's Orients are situated in the imagination and in the German market; they arise from both aesthetic aspirations and real intellectual enquiry among German scholars. His acknowledgement of this allows him to indulge in parodies, often thinly disguised, of the very same orientalist practices in which he takes part. Additionally, Hoffmann is famous for critical observations of social interaction, for example at fashionable tea parties or between young women and their potential bridegrooms.[55] Such criticism of nineteenth-century society is enhanced by comparison of German and oriental characters, with the latter often coming out more favourably. As a critical tool, the Orient doubles up as a lens through which to examine not only artistic production, but social customs in Hoffmann's Germany. His famous self-reflection therefore provides material for a new interpretation of the nineteenth-century artistic treatment of the East.

The following chapters, each one a discussion of a particular thematic aspect of Hoffmann's work, seek to respond to these major areas of enquiry. The study can be broadly divided into two sections, the first (Chapters 1–3) dealing with Hoffmann's employment of oriental imagery and figures as a means of commenting on Romantic practices, and the second (Chapters 4 and 5) showing how Hoffmann uses the Orient as a tool for understanding processes of cultural production in his contemporary Germany. There are, however, inevitable overlaps between the two, not least because Hoffmann's discussions of aesthetic practice are often set against the prevailing social and cultural norms of the time. Chapter 1 examines Hoffmann's oriental spaces, identifying their alleged geographical location and, more importantly, their imagined position in relation to the starkly contrasted modern, and objectively real, world in which Hoffmann's protagonists originate. In doing so, the chapter questions traditional critical approaches to Hoffmann's treatment of the rational and the fantastic, and looks to a school of thought which, instead of emphasizing an oppositional dualism, notes that reductive analyses overlook Hoffmann's subtle integration of literal and imaginary spaces. According to Friedrich Schlegel, the Orient is the location of 'das höchste Romantische' [the highest Romanticism], and yet in Hoffmann's tales it is not neatly separated from modern German settings but rather encroaches upon and mingles with everyday European life, by way of the mythical characters that infiltrate modern Germany.[56] This suggests that far from setting the fantastic and the rational in binary opposition to one another, Hoffmann establishes a rapprochement of the two spheres, a move which enables poets to achieve genuinely creative engagement with the inspiring elements of the East, whilst remaining firmly rooted in modern life. By bringing the Orient closer to modern everyday life rather than setting up a distant utopian vision, Hoffmann begins to resolve the dilemma of the marginalized Romantic artist, according the imagination a place in a world which initially appears hostile to artistic production. The chapter also argues that rather than operating as merely fantasy worlds, Hoffmann's wide-ranging oriental spaces reflect cultural, economic, political, and intellectual concerns of Germany at the time, as his texts dealing with oriental themes often contain elements of realism. Examples are to be found in *Meister Floh*, which references trade with India, and *Die Irrungen* and *Die Geheimnisse*, in which a modern orientalized Greece is linked to the German philhellenism that shaped popular support for the revolutionary Greek wars of the 1820s. These significant details strengthen the ties anchoring the imagined Orient to a physically real, and accurately portrayed, Germany.

Chapter 2 deals with a philosophical problem that troubled the Romantics and considers its impact on Hoffmann's fiction and its attempted resolution therein. The issue of the subjective self dominates Hoffmann's writing, and the problems this subjectivity raises are at least partially resolved in an oriental context. In the aftermath of Immanuel Kant's 1781 *Kritik der reinen Vernunft* [*Critique of Pure Reason*], in which the mind becomes the creator of the outside world, the disjuncture between the disembodied, thinking subject and the material world is problematized by Romantic philosophers who wish to overcome this division and restore harmony between mankind and nature. The way forward, according to the *Naturphilosophie* [philosophy of nature] of Friedrich Wilhelm Joseph Schelling (1775–1854) and Gotthilf Heinrich Schubert (1780–1860), is a new mythology inspired by the concept of original harmony. In Hoffmann's work, the Orient is the locus of this mythological harmony, providing a cure for the schism between the spiritual and the material which has occasioned the Romantic condition of *Zerrissenheit* [inner conflict]. The chapter reveals that even the Nordic mythology that serves to inspire conflicted artists in *Prinzessin Brambilla* is in fact very much orientalized, and Romantic universalism is promoted within oriental spaces. The issue is underscored by the fluidity of identity, as characters visibly transform according to their viewers' perspectives. In particular, oriental characters reveal their mythological forms only when they are observed by receptive Romantic characters. Hence Hoffmann both criticizes the subjective position as an unreliable means of understanding the world, and makes the Orient key to promoting instinctive intuition over empiricism. On the other hand, in *Das Sanctus* (1816) and *Die Automate* (1814), stereotypes about the Orient cause the oriental body to be misunderstood and misappropriated. In *Das Sanctus*, colonial ambition means a captive female Muslim is viewed exclusively in terms of her symbolic value in a struggle between Islam and Christianity, with little attention paid to the identity she attempts to claim for herself. *Die Automate*, meanwhile, reveals the inherent problems encountered when would-be Romantics search for spiritual connections in a mechanized world. The focus of these ambitions is a mechanical fortune-telling Turk, and stereotypes of oriental mystery lead to the fatally misdirected belief that the Turk, a body without a mind, can provide insight into the spiritual world. Thus Hoffmann's treatment of the mind/body problem and its resolution in the Orient is shown to be ambiguous, and an absence of the mythological context renders the Romantic project void.

Chapter 3 shows how Hoffmann's portrayals of oriental women serve a double purpose, as they appear spirited and independent in contrast both to bourgeois girls on the marriage market, and the passive muses who inspire would-be Romantic artists. A close consideration of Hoffmann's oriental female characters thus uncovers his views on both artistic practice and the social norms of his time. In his depictions of women, Hoffmann frequently reveals how they are victims of two models of patriarchy, as the mother/wife figure, and as the voiceless muse who merely reflects male desire. The latter is famously parodied in *Der Sandmann* (1816), in which the poet Nathanael is so enraptured with his own poetic creations that he cannot differentiate between a living woman and the lifeless doll which appears to inspire him. The flawless but insipid bourgeois wife, another male-constructed role, is likewise exposed to parody throughout Hoffmann's oeuvre. Oriental women in Hoffmann's fiction do not fit comfortably into these categories, however, and instead act as triggers to provoke criticism of gender relations in nineteenth-century Germany, with regard to the practices of the Romantic artist as well as the socially constructed ideal of femininity. Hoffmann's oriental women are surprisingly vocal at a time when the threat of the Other was often overcome by processes of distancing and silencing. With reference to Gayatri Spivak's thesis on the subaltern as powerless over even her own identity, I argue that this terminology is less appropriate for Hoffmann's oriental women than for his German girls, and thus his criticism of his contemporary Germany, and of the practices of male artists, is made clear. Typically of Hoffmann's writing, an ambiguity emerges: his oriental women are often mythical figures who inspire male-authored poetry by dint of their mysterious provenance, and so the stereotype of exotic difference is not eradicated, but they do resist subordination to male control. This apparent contradiction, by which Hoffmann affirms some prevalent views about the East but undermines others, is proof that his engagement with the Orient is not primarily an effort to reform received ideas about eastern culture. He is concerned rather with examining the effect of orientalism on art at home.

The final two chapters shift the main focus from Hoffmann's views on the ideal practice of Romantic art to his criticism of cultural production in his contemporary society. In producing this criticism, Hoffmann both praises art which, in his view, successfully incorporates eastern elements into a western context, and satirizes orientalists who wish to appear learned among their fellow Germans. Chapter 4 turns to Hoffmann's most enduring interest, music, and considers his response to the production of oriental-style music within the German-speaking lands as part of a wider debate on Romantic musical aesthetics. Hoffmann's persistent interest in the *alla turca* style popularized by Christoph Willibald Gluck, Joseph Haydn, and Wolfgang Amadeus Mozart in the later eighteenth century can be traced through his musical reviews, and is expressed in his own attempt to write a libretto based on Mozart's 1782 *Die Entführung aus dem Serail* [*The Abduction from the Seraglio*]. Finally, Hoffmann explores this interest via his fictional composers who aim to create operas with an oriental theme. Alongside this, the chapter considers his lesser-documented engagement with Indian-style music, culminating in his composition of music for Julius von Soden's 'Indian Melodrama', *Dirna* (1809). The chapter argues for a surprising ambivalence on Hoffmann's part with regard to oriental-style music, perhaps an unexpected conclusion given that both the Orient and music occupied a prominent place in debates about the truly Romantic. It is the important relation between artistic form and content that ultimately determines Hoffmann's response to oriental-style music as a means of accessing the Romantic ideal through art. For Hoffmann, and contemporaries including Wilhelm Heinrich Wackenroder, music was the art that could bring one closest to the Absolute. In order to achieve this transformative potential, an overriding impression must be created, so that particular passages of music become part of the overall whole, just as the listener enters into the all-encompassing experience. This explains Hoffmann's aversion to virtuoso trills in music, as they distract from powerful overall impressions. While the Orient provides a fitting musical theme for those seeking Romantic inspiration, the *alla turca* effect created by specific instruments can therefore undermine the impression created by the orchestra, particularly if it is used for decorative effect alone. Hoffmann's composers in *Ritter Gluck* and *Das Sanctus* are distinguished by their efforts to create a Romantic style inspired by the Orient on the one hand, and oriental-style trills employed for exotic effect in popular music on the other.

Chapter 5 brings together the history of scholarly study of the Orient in Germany in the period immediately prior to the Romantic era, and Hoffmann's literary reception of European scholars with such interests. I argue that the close relationship between real-life scholars of oriental languages and myth and Romantic writers of fiction leads to the creation of a hybrid scholar/magus figure in Hoffmann's work. This figure arises partly in response to the activities of Hoffmann's contemporaries, for example Heinrich Friedrich von Diez (1751–1817), an esteemed but in later years somewhat eccentric orientalist who attempted to take on an oriental appearance in his home city of Berlin. Hoffmann's magus figures are predominantly, although not exclusively, scholars of the Cabbala, who attempt to practise eastern magic in a German setting, and to explain their learning to a German audience. Overlooking their audiences' limits, imposed by an exclusively German frame of reference, Hoffmann's scholars on the whole set themselves up for a comical failure, which can be partly explained by their own assimilation of the stereotype of the mysterious Orient as something completely foreign to their observers. The chapter also explores the significance of popular fiction in shaping German responses to the alleged mysterious wisdom of the Orient, as well as revealing the breach between knowledge that originates in the Orient, and the German ability to understand it. The surface appropriation of oriental props, as Hoffmann notes in his satirical manner, does not make a genuine oriental scholar. This final chapter therefore concludes the book by emphasizing the ambivalence characteristic of Hoffmann's work. Keen to employ the myth of the Orient to elucidate Romantic principles, Hoffmann nevertheless exposes to unmerciful parody those who show the outward signs of a fashionable infatuation with the East.

Notes to the Introduction

1. Raymond Schwab, *The Oriental Renaissance: Europe's Rediscovery of India and the East, 1680–1880*, trans. by Gene Patterson-Black and Victor Reinking (New York: Columbia University Press, 1984), p. 473. First published in French as *La Renaissance orientale* (Paris: Editions payot, 1950).
2. Suzanne L. Marchand, *German Orientalism in the Age of Empire: Religion, Race, and Scholarship* (New York: Cambridge University Press, 2009), p. 55.
3. A. Leslie Willson, *A Mythical Image: The Ideal of India in German Romanticism* (Durham, NC: Duke University Press, 1964).
4. The 'Romantic period' here designates the early 1790s until the late 1820s, the time span generally regarded by literary historians as encompassing German Romanticism. For background on differing opinions regarding what constitutes early, middle, and late Romanticism, see Ricarda Schmidt, 'From Early to Late Romanticism', in *The Cambridge Companion to German Romanticism*, ed. by Nicholas Saul (Cambridge: Cambridge University Press, 2009), pp. 21–39. Early Romanticism therefore developed approximately twenty years after the events considered by Schwab to mark the start of the 'Oriental Renaissance' (1771, see above). The important point to note, however, is that the early development of German Romantic literature and philosophy is broadly analogous to the transmission in Germany of the Indian texts discovered by William Jones and others. Georg Forster produced a German translation of the ancient Hindu play *Sakontala* in 1791, and William Jones's translations of ancient Hindu texts in the journal *Asiatic Researches* reached a German audience in the 1790s (see Schwab, p. 53 and p. 205). As Schwab notes, as early as 1792, Jean Paul created the Hindu protagonist Emanuel-Dahore in *Hesperus* (Schwab, p. 204).
5. Schwab, p. 482.
6. Ibid., p. 17
7. Ibid., p. 168.
8. Ibid., p. 475.
9. Willson, p. ix.
10. Ibid.
11. Edward W. Said, *Orientalism*, 3rd edn (London: Penguin, 2003), p. 115.
12. Willson, p. 220.
13. Ibid., p. 71.
14. Willson, p. 155.
15. Ibid., pp. 127 and 221.
16. Ibid., p. 221. See also Chapter 1 for more detail on the critical response to the notion of a Romantic 'never-never land'.
17. Srinivas Aravamudan, *Enlightenment Orientalism: Resisting the Rise of the Novel* (Chicago: University of Chicago Press, 2012), p. 5.
18. Andrea Polaschegg, *Der andere Orientalismus: Regeln deutsch–morgenländischer Imagination im 19. Jahrhundert* (Berlin and New York: Walter de Gruyter, 2005), particularly pp. 63–101.
19. Ibid., pp. 64–66.
20. Ibid., p. 70.
21. Ibid., pp. 74–75. See also the Grimm brothers' definition of 'Mohr' according to which Ethiopia is a land inhabited by Moors. Jacob Grimm and Wilhelm Grimm, *Deutsches Wörterbuch* [*German Dictionary*] <http://woerterbuchnetz.de/DWB/> [accessed 27 January 2013].
22. Polaschegg notes: 'der deutsche Orient war bis zur Mitte des 19. Jahrhunderts nicht nur ein historischer, sondern sogar ein antiker, wo nicht gar ein vorzeitlicher Raum' [until the middle of the nineteenth century, the German Orient was not only an historic space, but in fact an antique, or even prehistoric one] (Polaschegg, p. 82).
23. Friedrich Creuzer, *Symbolik und Mythologie der alten Völker, besonders der Griechen* (Leipzig and Darmstadt: Heyer & Leske, 1st edn 1810–12; 2nd edn 1819–22; 3rd edn 1837–42).
24. For a discussion of the importance of China for eighteenth-century Orientalism, see Birgit Tautz, 'From Text to Body: The Changing Image of "Chinese Teachers" in Eighteenth-Century German Literature', *EGY*, 1 (2007), 27–45. Elsewhere, Polaschegg notes that the eighteenth-

century interest in China gave way to the longing for India. See Andrea Polaschegg, 'Von chinesischen Teehäusern zu hebräischen Melodien: Parameter zu einer Gebrauchsgeschichte des deutschen Orientalismus', in *Orientdiskurse in der deutschen Literatur*, ed. by Klaus-Michael Bogdal (Bielefeld: Aisthesis, 2007), pp. 49–80 (p. 50).

25. Polaschegg, p. 100.
26. Ludwig Tieck, *Werke*, ed. by Marianne Thalmann, 4 vols (Munich: Winkler, 1963), II, 149.
27. Heinrich Anselm von Zigler und Kliphausen, *Die Asiatische Banise* (Munich: Winkler, 1965), with an informative afterword by Wolfgang Pfeiffer-Belli (pp. 473–84). See also Todd Kontje, *German Orientalisms* (Ann Arbor: The University of Michigan Press, 2004), pp. 61–62.
28. See for example Kontje, p. 61 and Lynne Thornton, *Women as Portrayed in Orientalist Painting* (Paris: ACR, 1994), p. 4. The interest in the *Arabian Nights* was so pronounced that the Austrian diplomat Joseph von Hammer-Purgstall was commissioned to find a manuscript copy in Constantinople in 1799. See Robert Irwin, *The Arabian Nights: A Companion* (London: Allen Lane, 1994; repr. London: I. B. Tauris, 2005), p. 20.
29. Ellis Shookman, 'Christoph Martin Wieland 1733–1813', in *Encyclopedia of German Literature*, ed. by Matthias Konzett, 2 vols (Chicago and London: Fitzroy Dearborn, 2000), II, 1004–1005 (p. 1004).
30. <http://woerterbuchnetz.de/DWB/> [accessed 27 January 2013].
31. Said, p. 23.
32. Ibid., p. 49.
33. Nicholas Saul, *Gypsies and Orientalism in German Literature and Anthropology of the Long Nineteenth Century* (London: Legenda, 2007), p. 2.
34. Ibid., p. 22.
35. Carl Niekerk, 'The Romantics and Other Cultures', in *The Cambridge Companion to German Romanticism*, ed. by Nicholas Saul (Cambridge, Cambridge University Press, 2009), pp. 147–61 (p. 156).
36. Michael Hofmann, 'Humanitäts-Dikurs und Orient-Diskurs um 1780: Herder, Lessing, Wieland', in *Der Deutschen Morgenland: Bilder des Orients in der deutschen Literatur und Kultur von 1770 bis 1850*, ed. by Charis Goer and Michael Hofmann (Munich: Wilhelm Fink, 2008), pp. 37–55.
37. See Kontje, pp. 78–79.
38. See particularly Chapter 2, 'Romantic Orientalism and the Absence of Empire', in Kontje, pp. 61–132.
39. Ibid., p. 131.
40. See for example John M. Mackenzie, *Orientalism: History, Theory and the Arts* (Manchester and New York: Manchester University Press, 1995).
41. Mohammed Sharafuddin, *Islam and Romantic Orientalism: Literary Encounters with the Orient* (London and New York: I. B. Tauris, 1994), p. xviii.
42. Charis Goer and Michael Hofmann, 'Einleitung', in *Der Deutschen Morgenland: Bilder des Orients in der deutschen Literatur und Kultur von 1770 bis 1850*, ed. by Charis Goer and Michael Hofmann (Munich: Wilhelm Fink, 2008), pp. 7–11 (p. 7).
43. Aravamudan, p. 4.
44. Birgit Röder, '"Fort in die Welt! — Nach Konstantinopel!": Das Orientbild im literarischen Werk E.T.A. Hoffmanns', *GLL*, 64:4 (2011), 501–20.
45. See for example Chen Tzoref-Ashkenazi, *Die indogermanische Verbindung: Friedrich Schlegels Suche nach den indischen Ursprüngen der Deutschen*, trans. by Markus Lemke (Göttingen: Wallstein, 2009) and 'India and the Identity of Europe: The Case of Friedrich Schlegel', *Journal of the History of Ideas*, 67:4 (2006), 713–34; Robert Bruce Cowan, 'Fear of Infinity: Friedrich Schlegel's Indictment of Indian Philosophy in *Über die Sprache und die Weisheit der Indier*', GQ, 81:3 (2008), 322–38; Elena Pnevmonidou, 'Veiled Narratives: Novalis' "Heinrich von Ofterdingen" as a Staging of Orientalist Discourse', GQ, 84.1 (2011), 21–40.
46. Röder, p. 505.
47. Hilda Meldrum Brown, *E.T.A. Hoffmann and the Serapiontic Principle: Critique and Creativity* (Rochester, NY: Camden House, 2006).
48. Victoria Dutchman-Smith, *E.T.A. Hoffmann and Alcohol: Biography, Reception and Art* (London: Maney Publishing, 2010), pp. 39–45.

49. 'Hoffmann, [...] in the writings of Goethe and Eichendorff, became an example not of what other Germans should become, but of the fate they should avoid' (ibid., p. 42).
50. See Walter Scott, 'On the Supernatural in Fictitious Composition; and Particularly on the Works of Ernest Theodore William Hoffmann', *The Foreign Quarterly Review*, 1 (1827), 60–98.
51. Ethel Matala de Mazza, 'Romantic Politics and Society', trans. by Julia Ng and Ladislaus Löb, in *The Cambridge Companion to German Romanticism*, ed. by Nicholas Saul (Cambridge: Cambridge University Press, 2009), pp. 191–207.
52. Ibid., p. 198.
53. Scott, p. 66 (on the Grimms), and p. 77 (on Hoffmann).
54. A very useful overview of Hoffmann's efforts to bring art into a productive relationship with society is provided in Diana Stone Peters's article, 'E.T.A. Hoffmann: The Conciliatory Satirist', *Monatshefte*, 66.1 (1974), 55–73.
55. The comical tea party scenes at the end of *Der Sandmann* provide a famous example (see Chapter 3, p. 78).
56. Friedrich Schlegel, *Kritische Friedrich-Schlegel-Ausgabe*, ed. by Ernst Behler, 35 vols (Munich: Ferdinand Schöningh/Zurich: Thomas, 1958-), II (1967), 320.

PART I

Romantic Philosophy and Aesthetics

CHAPTER 1

Romantic Realities: Oriental Spaces and the Modern German Setting

Sie war in Mainz und [...] auch in Indien gewesen
[*She had been in Mainz and also[...] in India*].[1]

Until relatively recently, consideration of the apparently irreconcilable dualism in E.T.A. Hoffmann's tales dominated the author's critical reception. Examples of Hoffmann characters who do not experience or at least witness otherworldly forces are few and far between, and these experiences are often linked to the pull of the creative impulse which eventually alienates the artist figure from the society in which he must live. This principle forms the basis for many of Hoffmann's narratives, and led to the long-standing view among critics that the author presents two eternally estranged worlds; the main factor contributing to the existential crisis suffered by so many of his protagonists. The example of the painter Berthold in *Die Jesuiterkirche in G* [*The Jesuit Church in G*] (1816) serves to support this view, as the artist spends his life searching for a glimpse of the ideal, only to commit suicide after he has achieved his creative goal. The true artist, one infers, is not meant for the objectively real, physical world, and Hoffmann's numerous Doppelgänger and the otherworldly figures which infiltrate modern German locales provide evidence of an apparent split between the prosaic bourgeois world and the realm of the supernatural, the creative, or the fantastical. Horst S. Daemmrich's unequivocally negative reading of this split provides a pessimistic evaluation of the likelihood of earthly achievement of the artistic ideal, emphasizing instead the hopeless situation of the torn artist figure.[2] Recent scholarship has, however, sought to move away from this dichotomy, a move which tallies with a shift in the reception of German Romanticism as a whole. The traditional paradigm of the Romantic–Enlightenment binary has been contested as outdated, as has the notion that the Romantics wished exclusively to live in a pre-modern world. Nicholas Saul, for example, notes the situation of the German Romantic movement 'on the cusp of the transition from tradition to modernity', but adds that 'their attitudes [...] characteristically exhibit both pre-modern and modern features'.[3] While the significance of the much-documented Romantic yearning is not to be underestimated, readings of Romantic protagonists as unfulfilled artists continually out of step with the modern world somewhat over-simplify the matter. Cynthia Chalupa tackles such reductive interpretations of Hoffmann in an article which recognizes the existence in his work of both the bourgeois and the creative worlds, but notes that the identification of an unbridgeable gap between these spheres 'leads to a simplified reading of his texts against which the author himself appears to have been working'.[4]

Hoffmann's Oriental Spaces

Among these critical revisions, the role of Hoffmann's oriental spaces has thus far been largely overlooked. In the fifty years since A. Leslie Willson made the claim that the Romantics, and specifically Hoffmann, treated the Orient as a kind of 'never-never land of magic language and paradisiac, poetic being', no sustained effort has been made to question this view.[5] This oversight is surprising, given the growing scepticism regarding the value of dualism as a key concept for understanding Hoffmann's position on the possibility of artistic attainment during earthly life. In responding to this critical turn, the mythical Orients which persistently appear in Hoffmann's literary texts in order to furnish his artist figures with new creative insights provide rich material for discussion. The orientalized mythological worlds that form the backdrop for several of the author's best-known stories include Atlantis, the original home of the salamander Lindhorst in *Der goldene Topf* (1814), Urdar, which is compared to both Memphis and the banks of the Ganges in *Prinzessin Brambilla* (1820), and Famagusta, where the protagonist Peregrinus Tyss temporarily takes on the role of an Indian King, in *Meister Floh* (1822). This Romantic engagement with an imaginatively constructed Orient can be traced back to Friedrich Schlegel's oft-quoted 1799 dictum from *Rede über die Mythologie* [*Speech on Mythology*]: 'Im Orient müssen wir das höchste Romantische suchen' [It is in the Orient that we must look for the highest Romanticism].[6]

The apparent temporal, spatial, and metaphorical distance between these oriental realms and Hoffmann's modern urban German settings is belied, however, by the many encounters between German protagonists and fantastical oriental characters in seemingly prosaic locations. Lindhorst, for example, visits a Dresden coffee house almost every evening, while Peregrinus Tyss first meets the Indian princess Gamaheh, in the guise of a Dutchwoman, Dörtje Elverdink, in a house in the Kalbächer Gasse, a street still to be found on maps of Frankfurt today. Moreover, movement between European and oriental settings, in an imaginative context, is presented as unproblematic in *Nußknacker und Mausekönig* [*The Nutcracker and the Mouse King*] (1816) and *Prinzessin Brambilla*. In the embedded tale of the former, 'Das Märchen von der harten Nuß' ['The Story of the Hard Nut'], Droßelmeier travels easily on foot from the forests of Asia to Nuremberg, while *Prinzessin Brambilla* concludes with the lovers Giglio and Giacinta claiming they can rule happily over an imagined kingdom in which the Italian towns Bergamo and Frascati neighbour Persia and India. This integration of the fantastic and the everyday sits comfortably alongside interpretations of Hoffmann's ostensibly oppositional spheres as in fact closely woven together. Indeed if Hoffmann's oriental spaces are taken to be representative of the creative Romantic spirit, as shall be demonstrated, close analysis of Hoffmann's placement of the mythical East within modern Germany reveals how this interrelation underpins his ambivalent attitude to the notion of the tragic dualism of the artist who longs to renounce the objectively real world. *Der goldene Topf*, *Meister Floh*, and the double narrative *Die Irrungen* (1821) and *Die Geheimnisse* (1822) present characters suffering the typical Romantic condition of *Zerrissenheit* as they are torn between the German spaces they physically inhabit and the oriental worlds which offer both redemption for a creative spirit and a confusion bordering on madness. Within the new critical framework, however, it becomes necessary to ask whether the opening up of an alternative world is truly responsible for the artist's crisis of identity, or whether it may in fact bring a solution by providing a bridge between apparent opposites.

The oriental worlds present in these tales can be usefully categorized according to the Foucauldian model of the utopia versus the heterotopia, and the trend in Hoffmann's writing towards reconciliation of alleged opposites can be traced in a move from the former to the latter. The case for dividing Hoffmann's fantastical oriental spaces into two types becomes clear with a definition of each. In Foucault's words:

> Utopias are sites with no real place. They are sites that have a general relation of direct or inverted analogy with the real space of Society. They present society itself in a perfected form, or else society turned upside down, but in any case these utopias are fundamentally unreal spaces.[7]

Utopias exist, therefore, on a purely imaginative plane, and arguably exacerbate the ongoing artistic conflict between earthly life and spiritual creativity by representing an unattainable ideal. The image of the utopia is at its strongest at the conclusion of *Der goldene Topf*, with the narrator's vision of Anselmus, who has cast off the burdens of daily life to reside in Atlantis and live 'das Leben in der Poesie' [life in poetry] (II/i, 321; *GP*, 83). Anselmus's relocation to a realm entirely cut off from nineteenth-century city life does not offer a solution for the dilemma of the would-be poet in modern Dresden but rather removes him entirely from the conflict. Utopias may serve to highlight imperfections, but ultimately do little to resolve them. Heterotopias, on the other hand, act as 'a sort of simultaneously mythic *and real* contestation of the space in which we live'.[8] As imagined spaces, they nevertheless have the power to effect positive change because of their very grounding in actual, tangible places. They are

> real places — places that do exist and that are formed in the very founding of society — which are something like counter-sites, a kind of effectively enacted utopia in which the real sites, all the other real sites that can be found within the culture, are simultaneously represented, contested, and inverted. Places like this are outside of all places, even though it may be possible to indicate their location in reality.[9]

One obvious example in Hoffmann's work is the home of Peregrinus Tyss, which is located on a Frankfurt street and houses Tyss's merchant father and mother before their deaths, but also acts as the location for Tyss's enactment of his childish fantasies, admits a host of oriental characters including the Princess Gamaheh and the eponymous Meister Floh, and serves as the backdrop for the opening out of the oriental dream-world, Famagusta. It is from this house that Peregrinus eventually emerges into the modern world as a more confident individual. Embracing the apparent contradictions of the heterotopia, therefore, appears to enact a more lasting positive change upon the protagonist who suffers a crisis of modernity.

Indeed, it is this very problem that renders the heterotopia necessary for Hoffmann's protagonists. Foucault identifies a type of space entered by those who are experiencing a transitional phase in their lives: the crisis heterotopia, which is 'reserved for individuals who are, in relation to society and to the human environment in which they live, in a state of crisis'.[10] Foucault names adolescents at boarding school and pregnant women in confinement as examples of such individuals. The point is that the heterotopias into which these individuals are moved, whether by force or of their own volition, support a state of becoming. This transition takes place in a location removed from everyday social interaction: it is both a part of society, and located on society's borders. When the period of change has passed, the individuals will generally be reintegrated into the fabric of their societies. Each of the protagonists treated in this chapter falls into the category of the individual in crisis. Anselmus in *Der goldene Topf*, the Baron Theodor von S. in *Die Irrungen* and *Die Geheimnisse* and Peregrinus Tyss are, for various reasons, living out a sort of extended adolescence at the start of the narratives. They hover on the threshold of responsible adulthood without taking the decisive step forward, and this potentially indefinite deferral of time is interrupted only when they encounter heterotopian spaces that force change upon them.

The Orient is a central component of these spaces, and for each of the characters, it reflects a part of their ambition and offers a path to fulfilment. Anselmus exists on the margins as a student awaiting his first professional appointment. His occupation as Lindhorst's scribe is understood to be a temporary measure, both by Heerbrand, who sees it as an interim solution for Anselmus's financial problems, and by Lindhorst, who uses the apprenticeship to ascertain whether the young man is a worthy suitor for his daughter Serpentina. The transitional stage of Anselmus's life takes part in Lindhorst's home, a building located on the borders of respectable Dresden society, in keeping with the model of the crisis heterotopia. Anselmus's hope of becoming a poet is represented by the oriental writing he must transcribe; likewise, the Orient mirrors his ambition of marrying Veronika by offering him her exotic double, Serpentina. While he is in the heterotopia of Lindhorst's home, all pathways remain possibilities: Anselmus may yet return to Dresden and professional life, or he may embark upon a life of poetry in Atlantis. Baron Theodor von S.'s ambitions are rather different: he seeks personal glory and admiration, and hopes to find it by becoming a hero in the 1820s Greek War of Independence. Inspiration arises when his everyday experience of Berlin becomes heterotopian, in other words, when it begins to accommodate a multitude of spaces. Again, the Orient is significant: not only does the Baron hope to fight against the Ottomans, but the elements of modern Greece that surface in Berlin and inspire him are heavily orientalized. As noted above, the imagined Orient is also superimposed onto Peregrinus Tyss's Frankfurt home in order to tempt him away from his reclusive lifestyle. These heterotopias have varying degrees of success in rehabilitating the protagonists, as each character takes a different direction upon his exit. Common to all, however, is the suspension between East and West. The combinations Dresden–Atlantis, Berlin–Greece, and Frankfurt–Famagusta all propel the protagonists into a state of flux.

Der goldene Topf

Readings such as Willson's, which conflate Hoffmann's mythical Orients with a Romantic utopia, cannot therefore do full justice to the author's complex treatment of narrative spaces and their relation to artistic production. *Der goldene Topf* in particular has been the subject of such interpretations, at the expense of a complete understanding of the critical perspective the text provides on the act of poetic creation. The denouement of the tale is problematic for Daemmrich, who reads it as an essentially pessimistic judgement on the place of the poet in society, claiming that the existential dilemma of the artist goes unresolved as Anselmus must remove himself from the sphere of bourgeois Dresden life in order to fulfil his dream of poetic creation.[11] Heinz Puknus has a more positive outlook on Hoffmann's work as a whole, arguing for a rapprochement of the fantastic and the everyday as Hoffmann's writing progressed.[12] Nevertheless, Puknus identifies *Der goldene Topf* as a work which draws an uncompromising line between the world of the artist and that of the *Bürger* [middle-class citizen].[13] Hoffmann's utopian spaces, however, are never presented without irony, and his approach in fact undermines the sort of poetic vision traditionally associated with such writers as Novalis (1772–1801), who were productive during the early phase of Romanticism and seemed to epitomize the longing for a faraway, antediluvian harmony between man and nature to repair the modern identity crisis of the artist.[14] The model of the Orient as an intangible primordial world is parodied at the end of *Klein Zaches genannt Zinnober* (1819), when Prosper Alpanus disappears over a flaming rainbow to return to his beloved, the Princess Balsamine, whom he has not seen for two thousand years and who resides '[im] fernsten Indien' [in farthest India] (III, 619). Temporal and spatial incompatibilities between this utopian world and the world Alpanus leaves behind are emphasized by the author's sly admission that the apparent happy ending for the poet Balthasar, whom Alpanus has helped to achieve his artistic and romantic ambitions, occurs only to placate the reader, masking the darker side of the tale.[15] Such cynical treatment of the theme of accession to a higher creative plane, only five years after the publication of *Der goldene Topf*, implies at the least an ambiguous attitude towards the productive value of the utopia. Indeed, Hoffmann's alleged enthusiasm for an oriental 'never-never land' must be contested on the basis that the imagined Orient functions as a catalyst for creative productivity only when it is combined with a life rooted in the realities of nineteenth-century Germany.

The heterotopia provides an alternative route for the modern poet to that offered by the utopia, even though it does contain elements of the latter. John Reddick argues convincingly that the multiplicity of settings, images, and identities characteristic of *Der goldene Topf* gives the text its central meaning, namely, that suspension between contradictory understandings of the world provides the only possible means of experiencing, albeit very briefly, a Romantic realm that transcends the emptiness of modern existence.[16] The lack of any coherent impression regarding, for example, Lindhorst's or Serpentina's true identity or Anselmus's eventual fate means that the reader cannot even be certain of Anselmus's steady artistic progress, especially as he disappears at the end of the narrative and cedes his place in Dresden to the narrator, who has thus far hovered in the background.[17] Reddick privileges neither a fully Romantic nor a realist reading, demonstrating that the apprehension of a plurality of meanings allows the artist — and the reader — to avoid the 'fixed and deadening roles' of middle-class city life while also resisting the lure of complete surrender to fantasy.[18] The identification of a German–oriental heterotopia in *Der goldene Topf* adds a new dimension to this interpretation of the text, by demonstrating how such plurality is retained even against the backdrop of an objectively real city. Hoffmann creates a hybrid Dresden–Atlantis space, physically located in the German city but within which mythical oriental figures and exotic imagery mingle with the everyday routine of official urban life. Anselmus happens upon this while his life is still firmly rooted in Dresden, as he stumbles into Lindhorst's adversary from Atlantis, the uncanny Apfelweib [apple-woman], at the Black Gate and becomes infatuated with Lindhorst's daughter, the golden-green snake Serpentina, by the river Elbe. Even Lindhorst's home, cast clearly as an oriental space which inspires creativity with its palm trees, wondrous music and chattering birds, is within hearing distance of the bells of the Church of the Holy Cross in Dresden. These spaces correspond, then, to the heterotopian model, as Anselmus's initiation into poetry takes place in an environment combining imagined elements with the familiar and real cityscape of Dresden.

Far from representing an artistic paradise unattainable in earthly life, the heterotopia is a salient example of Hoffmann's Callot principle at work. This principle is summarized thus by Stefan Bergström:

> The Callot Principle, developed in [Hoffmann's] collection *Fantasiestücke*, advocates taking the various forms of everyday life, as they appear in the writer's inner romantic world, and representing them in a strange wonderful shimmer in which they exist. The author proceeds from the outer world of everyday life to the inner world of the imagination.[19]

In keeping with this concept, the figures from the everyday world and from Atlantis who are central to Anselmus's experience mirror each other. Veronika, who harbours ambitions of becoming Anselmus's wife, finds her counterpart in the oriental Serpentina, and her father Paulmann plays a similar role to Lindhorst, in that he aims to help Anselmus progress in his career so that he can marry his daughter. Oriental imagery provides inspiration for representing the surroundings in an imaginative way, and thereby increases artistic potential. This becomes most clear in Lindhorst's home, where Anselmus undertakes the task of transcribing Arabic and Coptic scripts in order to earn money until he gains a permanent official post. The identity assumed by Lindhorst within the everyday Dresden setting is that of a rather eccentric archivist, and indeed Anselmus's role fits in with this explanation of his employer. Within the exotic surroundings of the archivist's home, however, it becomes clear to Anselmus that he is transcribing the story of Lindhorst's former life in Atlantis, and as his access to the oriental paradise increases, so does the strength of his creative visions. His most productive hour comes after Lindhorst shows him to a room explicitly associated with an epic Sanskrit poem: 'Heute kommen Sie nur hie hinein, werter Anselmus, denn wir müssen in das Zimmer, wo Bhogovotgita's Meister unser warten' ['Come in by this door today, my dear Anselmus [...] for we must go into the room where the Masters of Bhagavad-gita are awaiting us] (II/i, 284–85; *GP*, 50).[20] His imagination is fired by the exoticism of this room: the music, the birds, the rustling of the palm leaves and the mysterious crystal-like tones of Serpentina's voice all aid his intuitive understanding of Lindhorst's oriental script. The description of this environment bolsters the traditional association of oriental imagery and Romantic passion, as Serpentina slithers sensually down a palm tree and presses her body against Anselmus. Exotic imagery is also positively connected to creative production when an emerald green palm leaf is revealed to be a roll of parchment on which Lindhorst's story is inscribed. Here Hoffmann connects to the Romantic tradition, announced by Friedrich Schlegel, admired by Willson, and later famously criticized by Edward Said, of using the imagined Orient to promote a new poetic understanding of the world.[21] Central to the Callot principle, however, is the condition that the writer does not lose contact with objective reality.[22] Anselmus's imaginative visions lead to creative production — the act of writing — only as long as he remains in Dresden. This state is not a lasting one, however, as the Dresden–Orient serves as a gateway to the faraway fantasy land, Atlantis, an oriental utopia in which Anselmus no longer needs to project fantastical meanings onto the everyday because he lives a life of imagination which is uncompromised by modern-day concerns. Atlantis is, therefore, as removed from the modern world as the final home of Alpanus and Balsamine, and, one might therefore infer, of less significance than the heterotopia to the modern poet who wishes to reconcile his creative and his everyday life.

In *Der goldene Topf* the Callot principle — that is, an acceptance of the heterotopia rather than a longing for the utopia — is revealed as an antidote to the Romantic death-wish expressed by aspiring poets, such as Nathanael of *Der Sandmann* and arguably Anselmus, who cannot find their way in the modern world and consequently succumb to madness and eventually death. This can be illustrated with reference to the character who, following Anselmus's departure from earthly life, is left behind to relate his story: the first-person narrator of the Twelfth Vigil. The shift in narratorial voice in this final vigil reveals that while Hoffmann's artist protagonist has not yet developed to the point where he can live usefully and creatively in the modern world, the possibility for such an achievement remains open. The narrator's initial envy of Anselmus's life in Atlantis is ultimately undermined by a comparison of their situations in which the narrator surfaces as the true poet, capable not only of poetic vision, but also of its creative expression. Anselmus's immersion in the world of poetry is marked by an increasing distance from earthly, bodily existence, and his declaration of love to Serpentina is linked to a death-drive: 'wenn ich nur dich habe, was kümmert mich sonst alles Übrige; wenn du nur Mein bist, so will ich gern untergehen in all' dem Wunderbaren und Seltsamen, was mich befängt seit dem Augenblick, als ich dich sah' [if only I had you, what would I care about all the world besides? If only you were mine, I would gladly perish amid the strange and wondrous things in which I have been entangled since first I saw you] (II/i, 288; *GP*, 53). Indeed, this seeming longing for death is supported by the strong possibility that Anselmus, in order to ascend to a life of eternal creation, throws himself into the river Elbe. When he believes himself to be literally imprisoned in a crystal bottle — a punishment for blotting Lindhorst's scripts — the young men who jeer at him point out that he is in fact standing on a bridge over the Elbe. A simple allegorical reading of this incident suggests that Anselmus's mind is imprisoned in the constraints of earthly or indeed bodily life, freedom from which will allow him to escape the torture of the divided self. When the crystal has shattered, 'er *stürzte* in die Arme der holden lieblichen Serpentina' [he *plunged* into the arms of the fair and lovely Serpentina] (II/i, 309; *GP*, 72), an action which can be linked back to his earlier attempt to jump into the river when he believes he sees the three beautiful snakes beneath the water and executes 'eine heftige Bewegung, als wolle er sich gleich aus der Gondel in die Flut *stürzen*' [[a lunge] forward as though to *fling himself* out of the rowing-boat into the waves] (II/i, 238; *GP*, 9 (my emphases)).[23]

This position can be strengthened by a reading of Anselmus as the double not solely of Heerbrand, but also of Lindhorst.[24] Phosphorus's pronouncement to Lindhorst when he expels him from the heavenly realm of Atlantis propels him into an existence similar to that of Anselmus, who is also misunderstood by those devoid of a poetic spirit: 'sinke hinab zu den Erdgeistern', Phosphorus commands Lindhorst, 'die mögen dich necken und höhnen und gefangen halten' [sink down to the earth-spirits, and let them tease you and mock you and keep you captive] (II/i, 289; *GP*, 55). The ultimate redemption for Lindhorst will come when, like Anselmus, he can accede once more to Atlantis, a realm where poetry and nature exist side by side in blissful detachment from the tormenting constraints of everyday, common life (II/i, 290–91). The ascension to Atlantis can be understood as a 'poetic apotheosis, but factual suicide', although critics have also downplayed the latter in favour of the symbolic message of artistic fulfilment.[25] An extreme utopia–death correlation explains Anselmus's failure at modern life: he is unable to reconcile the imaginary (represented here by the oriental elements he sees in Dresden) with the outer world. Ultimately, he fails to follow the Callot principle, as the amalgamation of the real and the fantastical causes in him fits of confusion which suggest the onset of insanity. The function of the Orient as utopian ideal, therefore, is helpful only in so far as it provides an escape for the tortured poet, but it does not, for Anselmus, aid in repairing the 'shattered self'.

The Callot principle does not founder completely, however, as the visibility of the narrator in the Twelfth Vigil reminds the reader that a creative story has indeed been produced by a Dresden writer. With the first-person account of the writer's attempt to complete the story of Anselmus, the classic Romantic dilemma of the poetic mind trapped in the prosaic world surfaces once more, but its solution rescues *Der goldene Topf* from the deeply pessimistic conclusion suggested by Daemmrich. The fictionalized Hoffmann-narrator claims that he experienced Anselmus's deep happiness as he united with Serpentina, and yet could not express this feeling on paper. Here the narrator shares the pain of Hoffmann's musician characters who fail to shape their flashes of heavenly inspiration into tangible pieces of work.[26] This condition leads to a melancholic state on earth. The narrator's failure to create is likened to Anselmus's state of mind in the Fourth Vigil, described thus:

> Du schlichst mit trübem Blick umher wie ein hoffnungslos Liebender, und Alles, was du die Menschen auf allerlei Weise im bunten Gewühl durcheinander treiben sahst, erregte dir keinen Schmerz und keine Freude, als gehörtest du nicht mehr dieser Welt an.
>
> [You crept to and fro with downcast gaze like a rejected lover, and none of humanity's many and varied activities gave you either joy or pain, as though you had ceased to belong to this world.] (II/i, 251; *GP*, 20)

Towards the conclusion of the tale, therefore, dreamy ignorance of the modern world is shown to be detrimental rather than helpful to artistic production, provoking a state of artistic crisis. The solution follows, however, as the narrator loses himself in the same oriental paradise as Anselmus, but only temporarily. The narrator enters the crisis heterotopia, visiting Lindhorst's home and sitting down at the very desk at which Anselmus wrote his copies. This action provokes a vision of Atlantis, where he observes emerald palm leaves, exotic flowers, and elemental spirits. When the vision has passed, Anselmus's story is transcribed in front of the writer, in a mirroring of the Eighth Vigil, when Anselmus awakes from a dream-like state in which Serpentina told him her father's story, and finds the same story written in front of him. The Hoffmann-narrator is therefore another Anselmus double, with one crucial difference: he remains in the objectively real world. While he initially bemoans this fate, Lindhorst intervenes to reveal the advantages of temporary rather than permanent flight to Atlantis: 'Waren Sie nicht so eben selbst in Atlantis und haben Sie denn nicht auch dort wenigstens einen artigen Meierhof als poetisches Besitztum Ihres innern Sinns?' [Weren't you in Atlantis yourself a moment ago, and haven't you at least got a pretty farm there, as the poetic property of your mind?] (II/i, 321; *GP*, 83). The Hoffmann figure therefore succeeds where Anselmus does not. Visions of oriental realms inspire his creation, and he writes the fantastical into the everyday when he describes a letter delivered to his garret from the salamander Lindhorst. Atlantis and its distant oriental charms are helpful, therefore, in allowing the narrator to avail himself of the Callot principle. Unlike his protagonist, he progresses towards a rapprochement of the prosaic and imaginary worlds via the vision of an oriental space which will remain alive in his mind. He becomes capable of entering into an illusion and, more importantly, surviving the breaking of this illusion, embarking on a two-part process of imagination and reflection necessary for the creation of Romantic art.[27] The positive result of this new understanding is *Der goldene Topf* — the completed text itself.

Die Irrungen/Die Geheimnisse

Hoffmann's later work sees a shift in focus as his protagonists no longer relocate to an alternative world which is antithetical to a modern and increasingly commercialized Germany. Instead, they remain in the space also inhabited by the fictionalized Hoffmann figure, whose presence is consistently felt through narratorial intervention and, as in the final vigil of *Der goldene Topf*, occasional appearances in the stories he weaves. This move towards a life grounded in the physically objective reality of the early nineteenth century, and its associated growth of the middle classes, corresponds to a closer connection between artistic imagination and real-life concerns of the day. A case in point is the double narrative, *Die Irrungen* and *Die Geheimnisse*, which is set in a highly recognizable modern Berlin and thematizes the popular support among fashionable Berlin society for the cause of Greek independence. Such a move does not, however, indicate a fading interest in the oriental spaces which inspired Anselmus and later the poet Balthasar. On the contrary, such spaces are brought into closer contact with modern life, as visions of fantastical oriental figures abound and the transition between the worlds, as a two-way process, becomes almost seamless. The result of this change for Hoffmann's would-be Romantic protagonists differs, but the overall effect is a move away from a segregation of the practical and the imaginary even more pronounced than in his earlier work. *Die Irrungen*, *Die Geheimnisse*, and *Meister Floh* set forth a hybrid German-oriental space, in which it becomes increasingly difficult to distinguish between imagined and real events and landscapes. Paradoxically, the stronger rooting in a recognizably modern Germany serves to increase the fantastical effect, and the imagination begins to find a more significant place among the everyday. As Bergström notes, the categorization of a text as fantastic depends largely upon the 'emphasis on the reader's hesitation regarding the setting of a text in the real world or in a supernatural milieu'.[28] This contrasts with fantasy, in which the reader unquestioningly accepts the supernatural or imagined world from the outset, rather than vacillating uncertainly between two possible interpretations. An amalgamation of the two worlds therefore increases the need for imaginative engagement, and *Die Irrungen* and *Die Geheimnisse* provide such an opportunity, as the reader can never be certain whether the wondrous events truly unfold within the fictional reality of the text, or whether they represent 'das bloße Hirngespinst einer Geisteskranken' [simply the fantasies of a madman].[29]

Even if this is the case, the apparently mad delusions of the protagonist, the Baron Theodor von S., have an actual temporal connection to Hoffmann's Berlin as well as to wider cultural and political concerns. While the two texts reference a variety of locations, including imagined oriental spaces, the narratives unfold in one multi-faceted setting, as none of the characters ever leave Berlin throughout the story, although exotic locales are invoked. The subtitle of *Die Irrungen*, 'Fragment aus dem Leben eines Fantasten' [A Fragment from the Life of a Fantasist], points deceptively to a world of pure illusion. The fantasist in question, the Baron Theodor von S., is, despite his dreamy detachment from reality, very much a product of 1820s Berlin, which is clear not only from his obsession with fashion and high society, but more pertinently for this discussion, in his claimed support of the popular cause for Greek independence from the Ottoman Empire. It is here that the satirized superficial fashions of the time connect to the fantastical orientalized world observed by the Baron. A consideration of the Greek elements in the tale reveals that the worlds of *Die Irrungen* and its sequel cannot be crystallized into two clearly defined oppositional spaces, but rather that the imagined world it presents draws on a variety of popular concerns, contemporary political and aesthetic discussions, and fantasy based on an orientalized modern Greece. As part of the Baron's preparations for a journey to Greece, he reads Sonnini and Bartholdy (v, 474), mimicking the actions of his creator who did the same in order to gather details for his text. These references are to the popular travelogues read widely across Europe, C. S. Sonnini's *Travels in Greece and Turkey*, which appeared in two volumes at the turn of the nineteenth century and was translated from its original French into both English and German, and J. L. S. Bartholdy's *Bruchstücke zur nähern Kenntnis des heutigen Griechenlands* [*Fragments Providing Closer Knowledge of Modern Greece*] (1803–04). The complex Greece–Orient relation in the minds of the German public at this time was based on a tension between interpretations of modern Greeks as part of the wider 'oriental' frame of reference on the one hand, and as descendants of a classical tradition on the other, which would set them in opposition to an Orient deemed by certain scholars to be inferior, or indeed barbaric. Suzanne Marchand notes an entrenchment of cultural philhellenism in the German states, and particularly in Prussia, in the post-Napoleonic period.[30] This followed the determined efforts by Friedrich August Wolf to improve the standing of classical philology in German universities, and the educational reforms of Wilhelm von Humboldt, who introduced compulsory Greek and Latin testing at the *Gymnasien* and strove to make classical subjects the 'centrepiece' of the new University of Berlin, founded in 1810.[31] Marchand connects the strong enthusiasm for Greece to the question of German national identity, although she claims that both Germanophilia and Orientalism were 'rival tropes' to philhellenism.[32]

However, the still common understanding of the Ottoman-controlled Greek lands as 'Turkey in Europe', as well as the identification, among German supporters of Greek liberation, of the oppressive Ottoman regime with the anti-liberal German states under Metternich, served to complicate this relationship.[33] Furthermore, the construction of Greece in the Romantic imagination mirrors that of the Orient in that both were perceived as natural spaces where genius could flourish free from artificial constraints.[34] On the other hand, for some observers, belief in this image necessarily required an ignorance of the actual situation of modern Greece. Voices raised in support of Greek independence were often the result of classical education at the *Gymnasien*, and this very education was based on a tradition which not only subordinated modernity to antiquity, but which raised the ancient Greeks far above other ancient peoples, including Egyptians, Jews, Persians, and other 'Orientals'. Marchand names Wolf as a chief proponent of this school of thought, and Danny Praet and Mark Janse's identification of this real-life scholar as a character in *Die Irrungen* reveals Hoffmann's awareness of, and engagement with, the scholarship of his time.[35]

Hoffmann emphasizes the role of popular travel texts and literature in creating a demand for knowledge of peoples and landscapes which are constructed as mysterious in the public imagination, and draws attention to the role of such texts in encouraging the emergence of modern Greece, in the popular consciousness, as yet another oriental space. While classical philhellenism still reigned in fashionable intellectual Berlin circles, travelogues such as Sonnini's had an orientalist bias which influenced perceptions of Greece. Sonnini consistently refers to Greece broadly as 'the East' and disparages Greek rituals, describing the Greeks as 'a people long addicted to superstition', a trait of which he despairs throughout his account.[36] Hoffmann lifts some of these rituals directly from Sonnini's text and places them in his tales, openly citing Sonnini as a source of which the characters in his texts are aware. Furthermore, the mysterious Greek princess with whom the Baron becomes infatuated is described as having the gaze of Turandot, a reference which would not be lost on German theatregoers familiar with Schiller's 1801 adaptation of Gozzi's play.[37] Referencing the role of literature in the shaping of public opinion, *Die Geheimnisse* ironically suggests that Hoffmann's own work adds to this trend, when Schnüspelpold, the princess's malevolent protector, writes a letter of complaint to his creator in which he claims that the masses who have read *Die Irrungen* in the Berlin *Taschenkalender* now crowd at his door hoping to catch a glimpse of the princess. He complains:

> Ich weiß, wen sie suchten und manche hatten auch dessen gar kein Hehl, sondern fragten kecker unverschämter Weise geradezu nach der schönen Griechin, als sei mein himmlisches Fürstenkind ein wunderbares Naturspiel, das ich der gaffenden Menge ausstelle.
>
> [I know who they were looking for, and some of them made no secret of it, but boldly and shamelessly asked directly for the beautiful Greek girl, as if my delightful princess were a wondrous freak of nature to be exhibited before the gaping masses.] (v, 512)[38]

Schnüspelpold is himself linked to oriental mystery when he is revealed to be a practitioner of Cabbalistic magic who masquerades as a respectable retired Chancellery Assistant, and accordingly, the same crowds who seek the princess hope to observe evidence of Schnüspelpold's magical powers. Finally, modern Greece, fighting for independence, is romanticized through conflation with ancient Greece: the Baron, when preparing to travel to Greece, imagines himself 'auf klassischem Boden' [on classical soil] (v, 483).[39] This willed ignorance of modern reality, or the aesthetic preference for an ancient Greece over its allegedly wilder contemporary counterpart again mimics popular perception. Polaschegg, for example, cites August von Kotzebue's 1812 play *Die Ruinen von Athen* [*The Ruins of Athens*] as an example of this phenomenon: 'Wir finden den Parthenon in Trümmern liegend, heulende Derwische dort, wo einst der Kult der Pallas Athene gepflegt wurde' [We find the Parthenon lying in rubble, and wailing dervishes where once the cult of Athena was enshrined].[40] Hoffmann's source, Bartholdy, also expresses this attitude, claiming that an arrival in Greece naturally occasions a feeling of higher aesthetic sensibility which is linked to the land's classical heritage.[41] The apparently imagined realms in *Die Irrungen* and *Die Geheimnisse* therefore reflect several interests and opinions of the German reading public: travelogues, literature, political opinion, public curiosity, fashionable trends, and, as Praet and Janse have demonstrated, showy intellectualism are amalgamated to create an orientalized fantasy very much grounded in Hoffmann's world.

The Baron undergoes a different, and rather more comical, crisis than that of Anselmus: he is engaging in the fraught process of constructing his own social identity. As he has very little genuine Romantic potential, however, the heterotopia has a limited effect on his creative capabilities. His failure as a would-be Romantic is explained by his impulsive and superficial attachment to Greece, which is a product of the intellectual and social climate of Berlin, but which in his case amounts to nothing more than a comical blend of daydreaming and performativity. He has neither a clear intellectual understanding of, nor a creative connection to modern Greece, and glimpses only a dream Graeco-oriental landscape in fantasies and while sleeping. Initially he harbours Romantic pretensions and seems to be seeking a world outside that which he must inhabit:

> Der Baron gehörte zu den Leuten, denen nicht eben viel Besonderes im Leben begegnet, die aber alles, was ihnen in den Weg tritt, für etwas ganz Außerordentliches und sich selbst von dem Schicksal dazu bestimmt halten, das Außerordentliche, Unerhörte zu erfahren.
>
> [The Baron was one of those people whose lives go unmarked by any significant event, but who nevertheless believe everything that happens to them to be something quite extraordinary, and feel themselves fated to experience the extraordinary and outrageous] (v, 462)

Accordingly, when he finds a mysterious blue purse, he instantly feels that it will be connected to a wondrous adventure, and his intuition is proved correct when he later finds out that the purse is the property of a Greek princess who is searching for a hero to lead the Greek army to success and free her people from Ottoman rule. He is quickly exposed, however, as a pseudo-Romantic and sentimental dreamer, who meets the princess in an orientalized dream realm, climbing through the skies with her on a floral throne guarded by genies, but misses her actual visit because he is sleeping. Furthermore, he views her only when she is veiled, or reflected in a mirror in the Fuchs Konditorladen, again a real site in Hoffmann's Berlin.[42] The princess's mysterious appearance is compounded by a comparison with the Egyptian goddess Isis, and combined with the symbolic significance of the mirror as a means of viewing the self, this plays on the tradition of Romantic journeys of discovery to an imagined Orient which lead the subject back to a familiar scene and encourage inner reflection.[43] The Baron makes a declaration within this tradition: 'die blaue Brieftasche mit dem goldnen Schloß war erst der magische Spiegel, in dem ich mein Ich in Liebe zu dir erblickte!' [the blue purse with the golden clasp was simply the magic mirror, in which I first saw myself in love with you!] (v, 473–74). This claimed insight is undermined by his continuing lack of self-understanding, made clear in the satirical narration of his attempts at constructing a Romantic identity: 'Als er den letzten Bissen eines gebratenen Huhns verzehrt, rief er aus: was ist irdisches Bedürfnis, wenn der Geist das Göttliche ahnet!' [As he swallowed the last morsel of a roast chicken, he cried out, 'What are earthly needs, when the spirit is approaching the divine!'] (v, 485). His preparations to travel to Greece amount to nothing, as he does not even reach Potsdam before turning back for the city. As Polaschegg notes, however, the appearance of having travelled to Greece is of as much value to the Baron as an actual journey, for simply driving out beyond the Brandenburg Gate is enough to gain him the reputation of a committed supporter of the Greek cause, putting him in favour with fashionable circles in Berlin.[44] His main concern before leaving is to procure clothes in the modern Greek style, which, tellingly, he has made by the theatre's costume-maker. This lack of a genuine Romantic affinity for Greece bears out Schnüspelpold's observation on modern Berlin in general, when he tells the princess that if she wants to see any real nature in the city, she should go to the theatre: even the apparently natural is performed, and the fictional world of the stage is more authentic.

This implicit judgement of 1820s Berlin society also provides a critical perspective on the philhellenists who in fact contributed very little tangible aid to the Greek cause. The Baron experiences only relief when he discovers he will not have to travel to Greece to find the princess. His imagined calling as the saviour of Greece founders not only as it is comically revealed that he cannot bear the sight of blood, but when he, perhaps naturally, shows little inclination for a war that, it is claimed, is fought out in barbaric oriental style. On the authority of a (satirized) learned Professor, the Baron learns of the martyrs allegedly common in the Orient, and indeed he is surrounded by those who conflate Turks and modern Greeks. The classical Greece of his imagination is demolished in a comic episode when the Princess asks him to fight, and reveals the perils of such an undertaking:

> Schlägt es fehl, so stirbst du entweder den Heldentod des tapfern Kriegers oder bekommt dich der Pascha gefangen, so wirst du höchstens gespießt oder man streut dir Pulver in die Ohren und zündet es an, oder wählt eine andere dem wahren Helden anständige Todesart.
>
> [If it fails, you will either die the heroic death of the brave warrior, or the Pasha will take you prisoner, in which case you will be impaled, at best, or they'll throw gunpowder in your ears and set it alight, or choose for you another death suited to the true hero] (v, 505–06)

This oriental barbarity is of course painted as the work of the Turkish enemy, but its proximity to Greece shatters any illusions and the description has a physical effect on the Baron: 'auf glühende Hitze folgte eine Eiskälte' [glowing heat was followed by icy coldness] (v, 506). This reflects the switch from bold enthusiasm for a Romantically constructed space, to the cold inertia which sets in when the actuality of the situation is realized. The Baron's self-delusion and vain performance, therefore, negate the possibility of any actual or creative engagement with the Graeco-oriental space he claims to admire so much.

Nevertheless, the reader is consistently reminded of the production of a creative text within the reality of the nineteenth-century literary market. First of all, the narrative is linked to 1820s Berlin via its author, who indulges in self-parody by encouraging comparison between himself and the Baron via their shared name, Theodor. Narratorial self-awareness reaches new heights in the sequel, *Die Geheimnisse*, when a semi-fictionalized Hoffmann enters his own text in order to track down his characters so that he can complete his tale in time for publication in the Berlin *Taschenkalender* — the journal in which the stories did in fact appear in consecutive years. The texts comment, then, on the actual situation of the modern artist, who not only has a duty to fulfil his creative ambition but must write to the demands of the reading public within a market shaped by production deadlines, and who is not therefore at liberty to rely on creative inspiration as and when it may appear. Hoffmann's self-insertion into his own story is also a reminder, comically blunt at points, that an act of creation is taking place, via the author's imaginative following of his characters into their fantasy oriental worlds. As well as a double of the Baron, the Hoffmann character is also the Doppelgänger of the oriental magus, Schnüspelpold, and through this creative self-projection the narrator achieves a work of art, regardless of whether or not the protagonists themselves are capable of the same.

Meister Floh

The 1822 story *Meister Floh* presents a protagonist who begins to deal more helpfully with the problem of two seemingly oppositional worlds which nevertheless continue to intermingle in modern Germany. The realm of the Romantic imagination is here represented mainly, although not wholly, by a mythical Orient which references a lost paradise, not entirely unlike the world to which Anselmus finally ascends. Puknus identifies this text as providing a clue to Hoffmann's later assessment of the two worlds. Rather than give preference to the artistic sphere, Puknus argues, Hoffmann values the two spaces separately but equally, with artist and *Bürger* admittedly different but neither superior to the other.[45] Hoffmann does not, however, distance himself from the Romantic position, as a slight adjustment to this interpretation shall reveal. *Meister Floh* shows that the artist and the *Bürger* do not lead a mutually exclusive existence, but rather that the poetic muse is accessible to all but the most closed minds: hence the choice of a representative middle-class citizen for the protagonist.[46] Peregrinus Tyss, the son of a Frankfurt merchant, benefits from the commingling of worlds as he ultimately emerges from an unhealthily reclusive fantasy life which cushions him from the reality of his parents' deaths. By the end of the story he is happily married to Röschen Lämmerhirt, the daughter of a bookbinder to whose family Peregrinus has been kind at Christmas. This typically bourgeois conclusion is not, however, ridiculed as one might expect from Hoffmann. Instead, *Meister Floh* presents the mythical orientalized space as a mediating force which enables Tyss to harness his imagination, and to move forwards from a state of denial and a crisis of modernity into a happier existence which follows bourgeois convention while leaving room for a healthy level of Romantic fancy. The tale can therefore be read as an antithesis to *Der Sandmann* and indeed *Der goldene Topf*, as the hero, although initially out of touch, ultimately overcomes his infatuation with the sensual, elusive, and arguably Romantic figure Dörtje/Gamaheh and finds his place in the modern world while remaining open to the power of the imagination. As Ritchie Robertson puts it, 'Hoffmann affirms the Romantic view of nature but distances himself from Romantic conceptions of passion.'[47]

Tyss's universe brings together an array of concrete and imagined spaces. His Frankfurt home, where much of the action unfolds, serves as a perfect representative of yet another heterotopia, as it manages to '[juxtapose] in a single real place several spaces, several sites that are in themselves incompatible'.[48] It is not only a practical space which served the needs of his mother and merchant father, but also provides a haven where Peregrinus hides from the outside world while indulging in nostalgic fantasies, furnishes the Dutch Enlightenment scientist Swammerdamm with a room where he carries out experiments with lenses, and functions as a gateway by which the Romantic figures Meister Floh and the Indian Princess Gamaheh enter into Tyss's daily life. Indeed, the mythical oriental realm of Famagusta opens up in Tyss's home when he is induced into a delirium by Meister Floh and takes on the dream role of the Indian King Sekakis, overseeing the union of the Indian thistle Zeherit and Gamaheh. This dream provides a symbolic parallel to Tyss's own life: Zeherit and Gamaheh are the mythical incarnations of Tyss's friend Georg Pepusch and the charmingly seductive Dörtje; as their love story is resolved, Tyss in turn realizes that he loves Röschen. Famagusta is closely linked to Hoffmann's orientalized depiction of Atlantis. In an intertextual reference, Lindhorst is named as an expert on the Indian thistle (VI, 339), and moreover, this thistle is none other than the Cactus grandiflorus, a plant which blooms only once a year at midnight and subsequently dies, here symbolizing a perfect Romantic *Liebestod* which follows artistic fulfilment. In *Der goldene Topf* Lindhorst awaits the blooming of this plant as his story is transcribed, and the placement of the cactus in a distant oriental space underscores the imaginative potential of the dream realm. The lotus flower which Peregrinus/Sekakis holds is a further reference to mythical India, connecting Famagusta to both Atlantis with its lilies, and Urdar, where the princess Mystilis emerges from a lotus flower.

The Orient as portrayed in *Meister Floh*, however, resists typification as a Romantic utopia, as the tale not only points to the regenerative power of the mythical world, but also frames the Orient within a modern German setting, where it has a very actual presence and an economic and cultural value.[49] Tyss's father trades in Indian products such as pepper and indigo dye, and sends his son to the port of Hamburg, where he hopes he will develop a head for modern business which, in his case, relies on consumer products from the East. While the Indian Gamaheh is the Romantic double of the Dutchwoman Dörtje, the elder Tyss's business interests provide a more practical link between India and the Netherlands, with a nod to the Dutch East India Company, which dissolved in 1799 and would therefore have been active in Peregrinus's lifetime. Furthermore, in the infamous Knarrpanti episode, references are made to Mozart's opera, *Die Entführung aus dem Serail* (1782), which was set in Turkey and gained a lasting popularity among European audiences.[50] Finally, as a child, Peregrinus is given a model of the city of Peking, which displays in detail streets and houses, and which seems to transport him to another world whenever he looks at it. This is indicative of Peregrinus's dreamy nature, but it also calls to mind a contemporary trend which was linked to the bourgeois demand for new knowledge of foreign cultures: the panorama. Vance La Varr Byrd's recent dissertation defines the panorama as 'a European mass-medium, a late eighteenth- and nineteenth-century consumer good, and a symbolic form' which fulfilled an 'ersatz-travel function' by allowing viewers to explore distant realms without actually completing a journey.[51] Its appeal was felt largely in the burgeoning bourgeois market, where it was viewed as a means of entertainment as opposed to high art. While Tyss's panorama is not on the scale of some of the exhibits described by La Varr Byrd, it is nevertheless similar to that phenomenon in its relatively large size, the level of detail it provides, and most importantly in the effect it has on its viewer:

> So hatte er z.B. einst einen Aufriß der Stadt Pecking mit allen Straßen, Häusern u.s.w. der die ganze Wand seines Zimmers einnahm, zum Geschenk erhalten. Bei dem Anblick der märchenhaften Stadt, des wunderlichen Volks, das sich durch die Straßen zu drängen schien, fühlte Peregrinus sich wie durch einen Zauberschlag in eine andre Welt versetzt, in der er heimisch werden mußte.
>
> [Thus he once received as a present an elevation of the city of Peking, with all its streets, houses, and so on, which took up a whole wall of his room. Looking at this fairy-tale city with the extraordinary people who seemed to be thronging its streets, Peregrinus felt as though the stroke of a magic wand had transported him to another world in which he wanted to make his home.] (VI, 311; *GP*, 245–46)

Tyss's engagement with the Orient, therefore, while fantastical, is made possible by a modern environment in which foreign lands both excited the cultural imagination and exerted a very real influence on the German market. His own interpretation and use of this commonly imagined space is the crucial factor which contributes to his development, as he initially treats foreign landscapes as an imaginative means of escaping modern life. For this reason the question of whether Peregrinus has actually travelled to India instead of Hamburg, or whether this journey was merely an imagined one, is treated as a minor detail in the text (VI, 314).[52]

Tyss's home can be viewed as a microcosm of the modern world in which the poet strives to survive, and as such, his situation enables comment on the dilemma of the Romantic artist. Foucault writes:

> Heterotopias are most often linked to slices in time — which is to say that they open onto what might be termed, for the sake of symmetry, heterochronies. The heterotopia begins to function at full capacity when men arrive at a sort of absolute break with their traditional time.[53]

Following this model, the constellation of multiple spaces which exist within the house in Frankfurt is accompanied by disparate slices of time, most evidently in the opening pages when Peregrinus relives a childhood Christmas scene at the age of thirty-six. An interpretation of this episode as a manifestation of grief at his parents' deaths is not sufficient, as his refusal to engage with modern reality characterizes even the childhood years before his loss.[54] The common theme throughout this stubborn ignorance of the world is a fixation on the Orient: as a child, Tyss gazes raptly at the image of Peking and tries to fashion a Chinese-style dressing gown, and as an adult he rides joyfully upon a rocking horse declared to be 'echt arabische Rasse' [of the true Arab breed] (VI, 305; *GP*, 240).[55] The lack of specificity in Tyss's imagined Orients further underscores their generic appeal as timeless realms which function as ideal spaces for self-indulgent nostalgia. His initial stubborn rejection of modernity and the present day has parallels in the struggle of the Romantic author to find a place for his creativity in a changing world, as well as in the related Romantic veneration of the mythical Orient as a timeless space where humankind remains connected to, and inspired by, the power of nature. Gaston Bachelard's interpretation of the home as a site of subjective memory adds strength to an allegorical reading in which Peregrinus's enslavement to the past symbolizes a search for lost poetry, akin to the antediluvian harmony which became part of the Romantic cultural memory. In both cases, the truth of the memory is necessarily tempered by the subjectivity of longing:

> Memories of the outside world will never have the same tonality as those of home and, by recalling these memories, we add to our store of dreams; we are never real historians, but always near poets, and our emotion is perhaps nothing but an expression of a poetry that was lost.[56]

Tyss's home is not, however, a sealed space, in keeping with the nature of heterotopias which 'always presuppose a system of opening and closing that both isolates them and makes them penetrable'.[57] The impossible yearning for the past which characterizes Tyss's home opens it up to the Romantic imagination, which enters in the form of Meister Floh and Dörtje/Gamaheh. Meister Floh's appearance plunges Tyss into an adventure reminiscent of fairy-tale stories in which the hero is faced with a challenge. Meister Floh tells Tyss that in the mythical world Famagusta, the sleeping Princess Gamaheh was attacked by the Leech Prince, whose kisses sent her into a state close to death. While the thistle Zeherit, who loved Gamaheh, attempted to kill the Leech Prince, the spirit Thetel bore Gamaheh away, and Meister Floh travelled with her by clinging to her collar. Meister Floh was discovered by the scientist Leuwenhoek, and Swammerdamm found Gamaheh; together the scientists managed to restore her to life in the form of Dörtje, but only temporarily. In this interim state she needs periodic bites from Meister Floh to keep her alive, and so she wishes to make him captive, a fate from which Meister Floh begs Peregrinus to protect him. Tyss's infatuation with Dörtje tests his loyalty to Meister Floh. Meanwhile Swammerdamm and Leuwenhoek compete for possession of Gamaheh, but they are missing the talisman that can bring her fully to life — a red carbuncle. Despite their commitment to modern science, Swammerdamm and Leuwenhoek are seemingly conversant in the Romantic myth, as Leuwenhoek knows about Gamaheh's past life in Famagusta. These fantastical, fairy-tale elements are, however, bound up with scientific progress, as Meister Floh makes himself visible to Peregrinus with the aid of a magnifying lens. The collision of temporally and spatially incompatible realms causes in Tyss a confusion comparable to the condition of Romantic dualism: 'Dieser Kampf widersprechender Gefühle beklemmte seine Brust und erfüllte sie zugleich mit süßer nie gekannter Angst' [This conflict of opposing emotions constricted his heart, yet filled it at the same time with a delicious agitation that he had never before experienced] (VI, 349; *GP*, 277).

Ultimately, however, the dream-world Famagusta, and the elements of this world which infiltrate Tyss's Frankfurt, have a mediating and indeed curative function as Tyss learns to live with the objective reality of both his circumstances and the world which surrounds him. Continuing with the allegorical reading of Tyss's story, the denouement supports the judgement that '[f]or Hoffmann, typical bourgeois life, not to be mistaken with the philistinism that he disparaged throughout his career, provides a necessary tempering of artistic fervour that verges on the brink of sentimentalism'.[58] Tyss's transformation from an unworldly daydreamer into a responsible husband does not deny him access to his fantasy oriental realm, as evidenced by the continued presence of Meister Floh at the end of the tale. In fact, Tyss's temporary immersion in the utopian world, in which the parallel story of George Pepusch and Dörtje is resolved, allows him to return to modern life with a new outlook, no longer consumed, but rather, aided by imaginative fancy. Unlike Anselmus, Tyss does not require permanent relocation to the mythical realm, as Romantic imagination — represented by the carbuncle which proves elusive to the cold-hearted scientists — is to be found in his own heart. The carbuncle affects Tyss positively as it reawakens his latent ability to love; his temporary entrance into the oriental world is the context in which this ability is realized.[59]

This becomes clear when Tyss temporarily loses himself in a dream of Famagusta. In this dream, Peregrinus is the Indian King Sekakis, and in this role he metes out judgement. He declares that Swammerdamm and Leuwenhoek are bereft of imagination and so are incapable of finding the carbuncle. He then approves the union of Zeherit and Gamaheh, whose intense Romantic passion is the mythical counterpart to the loving but sensible relationship Peregrinus is forming with Röschen.[60] The mythical Orient merges with Tyss's own path towards maturity, and his dream is the pinnacle of this psychological journey. William H. McClain reads the dream as 'a descent into the lower regions of consciousness which allows the hero to become aware of the totality of his own personality'.[61] *Meister Floh* is therefore in the tradition of the *Erziehungsroman* [novel of education] because Tyss comes to appreciate that visions of a higher reality and everyday existence together form a coherent whole rather than a disjointed experience.[62] This ultimate truth is revealed in the dream, in which the seemingly chaotic elements of Tyss's adventures come together. At the climax of the dream, Peregrinus recognizes the love for Röschen that will keep him happy for the rest of his life. The dream is a psychological cure because Peregrinus is on some level responsible for it himself:

> Peregrinus actually reveals his own reality to himself by means of the dream symbols which are emanations of his own mind. All of the events and personal encounters which Peregrinus has recorded in his memory while in the conscious state now reappear in the guise of dream happenings through which a higher order of meanings is made manifest, and in which the fragmentary experiences of the everyday world are fused into a total experience, — total both in the sense that it is the product of the harmonious interworkings of the conscious and the subconscious mind, and that it brings to the mind recording it the total meaning underlying a series of isolated and apparently unrelated phenomena.[63]

When Peregrinus awakes to modern life he is 'cured', having learned to embrace the apparently disparate worlds rather than suffer under their conflicting pulls on him. Indeed, Hoffmann hints at this solution from the outset of *Meister Floh* by commenting on the condition of the Romantic storyteller forced into a modern setting where bourgeois consumerism dictates artistic style. The narrator, true to the Romantic veneration for tradition over modernity, disapproves of the preferences of the modern reading public, but nevertheless must bow to their demands if he wishes to continue a successful literary career. His awareness of this tension, however, allows him to subvert expectations by employing his own preferred opening formula in order to describe the modern state of affairs: 'Es war einmal — welcher Autor darf es jetzt wohl noch wagen, sein Geschichtlein also zu beginnen' [Once upon a time — what author nowadays dare begin his tale in such a way?] (VI, 303; *GP*, 239). But he *does* begin the tale in this way. The narrator's awareness of the market in which he must work paradoxically, and here ironically, allows him to remain true to his Romantic sensibilities. Similarly, Peregrinus's acceptance of the modern world enables a continued healthy level of engagement with fantasy in the form of the Famagusta native, Meister Floh. Tellingly, the other oriental elements in the tale recede, having served their purpose in revealing to Tyss the need to temper his imagination even as he embraces it.

Conclusion

In seeking to establish the relationship between the oriental and the German spaces in Hoffmann's work, it becomes clear that they are not invariably oppositional but that the fantastical oriental world may serve as a bridge between the Romantic imagination and everyday life. While some of the mythical realms may appear, in the Romantic tradition, to be lands of eternal poetry, untouched by time, they are also, paradoxically, culturally specific to an early nineteenth-century German context, as Hoffmann makes clear in his references to trade, to popular opera, and even in intertextual links. To repeat Foucault, the spaces are 'simultaneously mythic and real'.[64] A close consideration of this interrelationship advances the theory that Hoffmann is keen to emphasize 'not the antithetical quality of [...] two worlds of experience, but rather the close interpenetration of the two and the many interconnections which lead from one to the other'.[65] With the exception of the Baron Theodor von S., who provides a comic example of the vain misuse of perceived Romantic spaces for superficial reasons, the oriental spaces serve to aid the protagonists in reaching a new understanding, either of their poetic abilities, or of their place in the modern world. A constant presence throughout this process is the narrator figure, who sometimes remains relatively hidden, and sometimes reveals himself more obviously to the reader as he observes and records the other characters' forays into and out of the imagined oriental realms. The narrator figure serves to remind the reader of the key issue at stake: the challenge presented to the poet who must live in the modern world while practising his creative talents. In *Der goldene Topf* this dilemma is partially resolved as the narrator is made aware of the possibility of visiting the oriental dream-world Atlantis in his imagination whenever inspiration is lacking. *Meister Floh* presents an alternative solution, when the Orient comes to the protagonist in the guise of several characters, eventually allowing an essentially bourgeois figure to remain open to imaginative influence. Availing themselves of the heterotopia, protagonists, in one way or another, move away from a state of inertia brought on by an existential or creative crisis.

Like his Romantic predecessors, Hoffmann does fit the mould in that he constructs the oriental space as a Romantic realm. Throughout his work, however, the Orient as he presents it fulfils different functions, as demonstrated by the three examples above. The alternative oriental world may affirm a Romantic position, as in *Der goldene Topf*, or comically subvert it, as in the Greek tales. Ultimately, however, the Orient functions as a mediating force, bringing imagination into an everyday modern setting in a manner which allows for healthy development. This evidence of Hoffmann's position on Romantic dualism can be confirmed by the moral lesson of one his final tales, *Des Vetters Eckfenster* [*My Cousin's Corner Window*] (1822), in which reality proves to be the basis for a redemptive imagination. A conversation which takes place in *Die Serapionsbrüder*, finally, demonstrates Hoffmann's lack of regard for the artistic (mis)use of a purely imaginative Orient which has no relevance to either the modern German states or the Orient itself and, as a result, has minimal impact. The words of Hoffmann's alter ego, Theodor, serve to close this discussion:

> Sonst war es üblich, ja Regel, alles, was nur Märchen hieß, ins Morgenland zu verlegen und dabei die Märchen der Dschehezerade [sic] zum Muster zu nehmen. Die Sitten des Morgenlandes nur eben berührend, schuf man sich eine Welt, die haltlos in den Lüften schwebte und vor unsern Augen verschwamm. Deshalb gerieten aber jene Märchen meistens frostig, gleichgültig und vermochten nicht den innern Geist zu entzünden und die Fantasie aufzuregen.
>
> [It used to be customary, indeed the rule, for writers to set everything that might be called a fairy tale in the Orient, and to take Scheherazade's tales as a model. Barely alluding to the customs of the East, they created a rootless world that floated hazily before our eyes. For this reason such tales were on the whole only cold and mediocre and did not succeed in awakening my spirit or exciting my imagination.] (IV, 720–21)

Notes to Chapter 1

1. *Meister Floh*, VI, 403; *GP*, 322.
2. See Horst S. Daemmrich, *The Shattered Self: E.T.A. Hoffmann's Tragic Vision* (Detroit: Wayne State University Press, 1973).
3. Nicholas Saul, 'Love, Death and *Liebestod* in German Romanticism', in *The Cambridge Companion to German Romanticism*, ed. by Nicholas Saul (Cambridge: Cambridge University Press, 2009), pp. 163–74 (p. 166).
4. Cynthia Chalupa, 'Re-imaging the Fantastic: E.T.A. Hoffmann's *The Story of the Lost Reflection*', *Marvels & Tales*, 20 (2006), 11–29 (p. 15).
5. A. Leslie Willson, *A Mythical Image: The Ideal of India in German Romanticism* (Durham, NC: Duke University Press, 1964), p. 221.
6. Friedrich Schlegel, *Kritische Friedrich-Schlegel-Ausgabe*, ed. by Ernst Behler, 35 vols (Munich: Ferdinand Schöningh/Zurich: Thomas, 1958-), II (1967), 320. Schlegel's statement is supported by a fragment dedicated to Novalis, in which he wrote, 'Allen Künstlern gehört jede Lehre vom ewigen Orient' [Every teaching from the eternal Orient belongs to all artists] (ibid., II, 272), and Novalis responded to this sentiment in the work *Heinrich von Ofterdingen* (1802), in which the master poet Klingsohr refers to the Orient as 'Das Land der Poesie, das romantische Morgenland' [The land of poetry, the romantic Orient]. See Novalis, *Schriften: Die Werke Friedrich von Hardenbergs*, ed. by Paul Kluckhohn and Richard Samuel, 4 vols (Stuttgart: Kohlhammer, 1960–77), I, 283.
7. Michel Foucault, 'Of Other Spaces', trans. by Jay Miskowiec, *Diacritics*, 16 (1986), 22–27 (p. 24).
8. Ibid., p. 24 (my emphasis).
9. Ibid.
10. Ibid.
11. Daemmrich, pp. 31–32.
12. Diana Stone Peters takes a similar view: 'the degree to which one can speak of a development

in Hoffmann's fiction is not related to the quality of his work, but rather to his ever greater accommodation of the most concrete aspects of psychological and social reality'. Diana Stone Peters, 'E.T.A. Hoffmann: The Conciliatory Satirist', *Monatshefte*, 66:1 (1974), 55–73 (p. 57).

13. Heinz Puknus, 'Dualismus und versuchte Versöhnung: Hoffmanns zwei Welten vom "Goldnen Topf" bis "Meister Floh"', *Text und Kritik: Sonderband E.T.A. Hoffmann* (1992), 53–62 (p. 54).
14. Such interpretations of Novalis have also been questioned in recent years. While Ricarda Schmidt states that Novalis harboured a 'belief in the marvellous', she also advises against marking too strong a division between his philosophies and those of later Romantics such as Hoffmann. See Ricarda Schmidt, 'From Early to Late Romanticism', in *The Cambridge Companion to German Romanticism*, ed. by Nicholas Saul (Cambridge: Cambridge University Press, 2009), pp. 21–39 (pp. 24 and 36). Likewise, Todd Kontje describes two opposing schools of thought in Novalis reception. One views the poet as 'an ethereal figure who dreamed of a magical blue flower that would lead him to a world of poetry and love'. The other view, developed in the latter half of the twentieth century, recognizes in Novalis a man very much rooted in the modern world: 'a hardworking civil servant who studied geology and helped supervise the local salt distillation industry, a flirtatious aristocrat who was not above a dalliance or two with local peasant girls' (Todd Kontje, *German Orientalisms* (Ann Arbor: The University of Michigan Press, 2004), p. 84).
15. 'Eigentlich hätte die Geschichte mit dem tragischen Tode des kleinen Zinnober schließen können. Doch, ist es nicht anmutiger, wenn statt eines traurigen Leichenbegängnisses, eine fröhliche Hochzeit am Ende steht?' [Really, the story could have concluded with little Cinnabar's tragic death. But isn't it nicer when, instead of an unhappy funeral, there is a happy wedding at the end?] (III, 646).
16. John Reddick, 'E.T.A. Hoffmann's "Der Goldne Topf" and its "Durchgehaltene Ironie"', *MLR*, 71:3 (1976), 577–94. Paul Wolfgang-Wührl also examines the ambivalence of the Dresden setting: see Paul Wolfgang-Wührl, *E.T.A. Hoffmann, Der goldne Topf: Die Utopie einer ästhetischen Existenz* (Paderborn: Ferdinand Schöningh, 1988), pp. 25–33.
17. Reddick, pp. 591–92.
18. Ibid., p. 584.
19. Stefan Bergström, *Between Real and Unreal: A Thematic Study of E.T.A. Hoffmann's 'Die Serapionsbrüder'* (New York: Peter Lang, 2000), p. 29.
20. The Romantic orientalist Friedrich Majer published a German translation of the Bhagavad-Gita in Julius Klaproth's *Asiatisches Magazin* in 1802. Alongside Georg Forster's 1791 translation of the play *Sakontala* (from William Jones's 1789 English translation), this provided German enthusiasts with 'an example of the earliest expression of the Hindu intellect', which served the artistic purposes of 'Romantic enthusiast[s] ever urging the synthesis of the intellectual treasures of the Orient and the Occident'. See A. Leslie Willson, 'Friedrich Majer: Romantic Indologist', *Texas Studies in Literature and Language*, 3:1 (1961), 40–49 (p. 46).
21. Said is critical specifically of Schlegel and Novalis, who, he claims, were much less interested in Asia than 'Asia's *use to* modern Europe'. See Edward W. Said, *Orientalism*, 3rd edn. (London: Penguin Classics, 2003), p. 115.
22. See also Bergström, p. 29.
23. The theory that Anselmus commits suicide is advanced by James McGlathery, who states unequivocally that Anselmus 'quits the confines of mortal life' and suggests that Veronika is aware of his suicide. James McGlathery, 'The Suicide Motif in E.T.A. Hoffmann's "Der goldne Topf"', *Monatshefte*, 58:2 (1966), 115–23 (p. 115). See also Maria Tatar, 'Mesmerism, Madness and Death in E.T.A. Hoffmann's *Der goldne Topf*', *Studies in Romanticism*, 15 (1975), 365–89, and Anthony Harper and Oliver Norman, 'What Really Happens to Anselmus? "Impermissible" and "Irrelevant" Questions about E.T.A. Hoffmann's *Der goldne Topf*', *New German Studies*, 11 (1983), 113–22. Tatar claims that the story of Atlantis as a 'submerged mythical realm' is significant, noting that Anselmus would need to jump into the water to get there (Tatar, p. 382).
24. Bergström claims that Anselmus is 'the psychic double of Register Heerbrand, or perhaps rather a projection of the latter character since he vanishes when Heerbrand marries Veronika, ending his need to live in the world of fantasy' (p. 37).
25. McGlathery, 'The Suicide Motif', p. 121. See also Ricarda Schmidt, 'Schmerzliches Sehnen und böser Hohn: Ambivalenzen in Hoffmanns Darstellungen von Künstlern', *HJb*, 17 (2009), 20–36

(pp. 24–25).

26. The curse of creative inspiration which cannot be expressed is one which haunts Hoffmann's musicians. In *Der Dichter und der Komponist* [*The Poet and the Composer*] (1813), the composer Ludwig makes the following confession:

> Ich will dir zugestehen, daß meine Phantasie wohl lebendig genug sein mag, manches gute Opernsujet zu erfinden; ja, daß, zumal wenn Nachts ein leichter Kopfschmerz mich in jenen träumerischen Zustand versetzt, der gleichsam der Kampf zwischen Wachen und Schlafen ist, mir nicht allein recht gute, wahrhaft romantische Opern vorkommen, sondern wirklich vor mir aufgeführt werden mit meiner Musik. Was indessen die Gabe des Festhaltens und Aufschreibens betrifft, so glaube ich, daß sie mir fehlt.
>
> [Granted, my imagination may well be lively enough to come up with many a good subject for a new opera; and indeed, particularly at night when a slight headache puts me in that dreamlike state which is just like the struggle between wakefulness and sleep, not only do very good, and truly Romantic operas occur to me, but they are actually performed before me, in my own music. But as for holding on to these ideas and writing them down, well, I am a failure.] (I, 756)

Meanwhile, Hoffmann's alter ego, the choirmaster Kreisler, claims that living in modern fashionable society compromises his artistic ability. When asked to perform at a tea party, he makes the excuse that all his imaginative powers have deserted him. See *Johannes Kreislers, des Kapellmeisters, musikalische Leiden* (1810), II/I, 38.

27. See Wolfgang-Wührl, pp. 40–42.
28. Bergström, p. 7.
29. See Andrea Polaschegg's reading of *Die Irrungen* and *Die Geheimnisse* in Polaschegg, *Der andere Orientalismus: Regeln deutsch–morgenländischer Imagination im 19. Jahrhundert* (Berlin and New York: de Gruyter, 2005), p. 243.
30. Suzanne L. Marchand, *Down from Olympus: Archaeology and Philhellenism in Germany, 1750–1970* (Princeton: Princeton University Press, 2003), p. 6.
31. Ibid., p. 27.
32. Ibid., p. xxii.
33. Constanze Guthenke, *Placing Modern Greece: The Dynamics of Romantic Hellenism, 1770–1840* (Oxford: Oxford University Press, 2008), p. 20.
34. Marchand credits Johann Joachim Winckelmann with the 'association of the Greeks with nature, genius, and freedom, and of the modern world with the unnatural, the overspecialized, and the tyrannical' (p. 9).
35. Danny Praet and Mark Janse, '"Dem Namen nach": Greek and Jewish References and Word Play in the Character Names of E.T.A. Hoffmann's *Die Irrungen* and *Die Geheimnisse*', *HJb*, 13 (2005), 78–97 (p. 81).
36. C. S. Sonnini, *Travels in Greece and Turkey, undertaken by Order of Louis XVI. and with the Authority of the Ottoman Court*, 2 vols (London: T. N. Longman & O. Rees, 1801), II, 19.
37. A similar comparison is drawn between a mysterious foreign woman and an oriental figure from popular culture in *Prinzessin Brambilla*, when the enraptured Giglio Fava calls the eponymous Ethiopian princess 'Rinaldos Armida' (III, 810). The exact provenance of the woman is ignored in favour of a reference that points generally to the oriental and exotic: the Greek princess is supposedly like the Chinese Turandot, and the Ethiopian one is likened to Rinaldo's Damascan sorceress.
38. The popular appeal of orientalism in the marketplace is also reflected in the opening sentence of Hoffmann's *Die Automate*:

> Der redende Türke machte allgemeines Aufsehen, ja er brachte die ganze Stadt in Bewegung, denn Jung und Alt, Vornehm und Gering, strömte vom Morgen bis in die Nacht hinzu, um die Orakelsprüche zu vernehmen, die von den starren Lippen der wunderlichen lebendigtoten Figur den Neugierigen zugeflüstert wurden.
>
> [The speaking Turk caused a great sensation, spreading excitement through the

whole town. From the young to the old, the noble to the poor, crowds streamed from morning to night to hear the divinations whispered to curious visitors from the rigid lips of the wondrous, living-dead figure.] (IV, 396)

39. Hoffmann's wording recalls the first line of Goethe's famous 'Roman Elegy V': 'Froh empfind' ich mich nun auf klassischem Boden begeistert' [Now on classical soil I stand, inspired and elated], Johann Wolfgang von Goethe, *Werke, Hamburger Ausgabe*, 14 vols, ed. by Erich Trunz (Munich: dtv, 1998), I, 160; translation from Johann Wolfgang von Goethe, *Erotic Poems*, trans. by David Luke (Oxford: Oxford University Press, 1997; repr. 2008), p. 15.
40. Cited in Polaschegg, p. 242.
41.

> Daß sich unser auf klassischem Boden ein gewisses heiliges Gefühl bemächtigt, ist wahrlich kein bloßes Hirngespinst, und jeder Mensch, dem Wissenschaft, dem Kunst, dem Freiheit, dem Gesetzlichkeit und Originalität etwas gelten, muß mehr oder weniger in Griechenland davon ergriffen werden.
>
> [It is assuredly no mere delusion that a certain sacred feeling takes hold of us on classical soil, and anyone who holds that science, art, freedom, law, and authenticity have any meaning at all will surely experience to some extent this feeling when in Greece.] (Bartholdy, 'Brief an meinen Bruder von meiner Reise nach Griechenland', in *Bruchstücke zur nähern Kenntnis des heutigen Griechenlands* (Berlin, 1805), p. 77; cited in Guthenke, p. 57)

42. The mirror has both a utopian and a heterotopian significance for Foucault. It is a utopia because it shows a place that does not actually exist — a mere image. It is, however, also a heterotopia, because the mirror itself exists in reality, and shows a counter-image of reality (Foucault, p. 24). See also Laura Terézia Vas, 'Orbis Pictus: Intermedialität zwischen Berliner Stadtmalerei und literarischer Stadterfahrung dargestellt anhand der Werke von E.T.A. Hoffmann und Wilhelm Raabe' (unpublished doctoral thesis, University of Cincinnati, 2008), pp. 63–64, for a discussion of this scene.
43. In the embedded story of Novalis's *Die Lehrlinge zu Sais* (1797), the hero Hyazinth dares to lift the veil of Isis only to discover behind it his lost love, Rosenblütchen. Hoffmann also references Romantic self-reflection most obviously in *Prinzessin Brambilla*, when Giglio and Giacinta look at their distorted reflections in the Well of Urdar and learn to understand each other and themselves.
44. Polaschegg, p. 244.
45. Puknus, p. 57.
46. Ibid., p. 60.
47. Ritchie Robertson, 'Introduction', in E.T.A. Hoffmann, *The Golden Pot and Other Tales*, trans. by Ritchie Robertson (Oxford: Oxford University Press, 1992), pp. vii–xxxii (p. xxvii).
48. Foucault, p. 25.
49. This point does not go completely ignored in *Der goldene Topf*, as Veronika dreams of owning a Turkish shawl, a fashionable commodity which the crowds in *Die Geheimnisse* also demand. Generally speaking, however, there is very little connection made between modern Europe and the actuality of 'oriental' countries as emerging areas of trade in the earlier tale, with the Orient understood by the German bourgeois representatives as a place of pure fantasy where 'orientalischer Schwulst' [Oriental bombast] reigns (II/I, 246; *GP*, 16).
50. The reactionary Knarrpanti figure is a barely disguised parody of Karl Albert von Kamptz, the director of the police ministry and Hoffmann's superior. This led to legal action being taken against Hoffmann; he continued to defend himself even on his deathbed. See Robertson, pp. xxix–xxx.
51. Vance La Varr Byrd, 'Ausblick und Einblick: German Literary Responses to Early Panoramas (1787–1844)' (unpublished doctoral thesis, University of Pennsylvania, 2008), p. 4 and p. 5.
52. Later on, the reader finds out that Peregrinus and George Pepusch met one another in Madras, but in Peregrinus's early life the line between the imagined and the real Orient is blurred.
53. Foucault, p. 26.
54. William H. McClain rightly points out that Peregrinus has always been dreamy and unsuited

to the business world, and describes the impact of his parents' deaths as 'the climax of [a] directionless life', or the most significant factor to influence an already pronounced tendency: 'The shock of this news [the news of his parents' deaths] and the realization that the secure and comfortable world of his childhood were gone forever caused Peregrinus to lapse into a sort of apathy' (William H. McClain, 'E.T.A. Hoffmann as Psychological Realist: A Study of "Meister Floh"', *Monatshefte*, 47:2 (1955), 65–80 (p. 68)).

55. The original has 'ächt arabische Race'. I have changed the spelling to the modern variant.
56. Gaston Bachelard, *The Poetics of Space*, trans. by Maria Jolas (Boston: Beacon Press, 1994), p. 6.
57. Foucault, p. 26.
58. Chalupa, p. 14.
59. See also Robertson, p. xxviii and McClain, p. 73.
60. See Robertson, p. xxviii.
61. McClain, p. 77.
62. Ibid., p. 71.
63. Ibid., p. 77.
64. Foucault, p. 24.
65. McClain, p. 66.

CHAPTER 2

Romantic Divisions: the Mind/Body Problem and the Oriental Cure

[I]ch bin eigentlich toll geworden, weil der Ich keinen Körper hat
[I really have gone crazy, because the self has no body].[1]

When Giglio Fava cries out these words in confusion in *Prinzessin Brambilla* (1820), he represents a generation of Romantics facing an epistemological problem in the wake of Kant. Giglio's new belief that the body and the self are distinct entities assumes the separation of the thinking subject from a material world which includes the physical body. The resultant feeling of alienation from the outside world, and even from one's own body, plagues Hoffmann characters such as Nathanael, Anselmus, and Peregrinus Tyss. As Eleoma Joshua argues, the 'consciousness of the break between material and spiritual reality' is one of the major factors causing 'the Romantic maladies of Weltschmerz, melancholy and "Zerrissenheit"'.[2] After Kant, the possibility of absolute, universal knowledge of the self and the world was denied, and the Romantics were left questioning a modern state of existence which saw the thinking subject irrevocably divorced from the physical world through the act of reflection.

In his *Kritik der reinen Vernunft* [*Critique of Pure Reason*] (1781), Kant identifies sensible intuition and thought as two necessary but separate conditions for attaining knowledge of the outside world.[3] Furthermore, as we can intuit objects only through the senses, which do not have the power to conceptualize, it is impossible to achieve an absolute understanding of things in themselves. Rather, the mind produces knowledge of the appearances of objects in time and space as the only form in which we can understand them. Our understanding, then, is drawn from the appearance rather than the object itself and is necessarily subjective. This subjectivity is linked to Kant's 'Copernican Turn', which represents a major shift in epistemology. Instead of seeing our cognition as dependent on objects, Kant posits that the objects conform to the human mind.[4] This is problematic because the mind's construction of reality is always subjective and never universal. Reacting to Kant, J. G. Fichte claims that both the ego and the non-ego, i.e. the self as well as the outer realm in which the self exists, are in fact posited by the ego. In asserting both its own existence and that of the world around it, the ego becomes the transcendental ego. This notion influenced Romantic writers interested in the dissolution of 'the rigid distinction between the imaginary and real worlds'.[5] Even if Fichte unites the ego and the non-ego within the ego, however, the question of subjectivity remains. For the Romantics, a subjective crisis leads to confusion about how to view the world, and annihilates the hope of reconciling the thinking self with the natural world. This separation of mankind from nature causes a Romantic longing for a lost harmony which seems impossible to fulfil, for as Barbara Maria Stafford argues, 'In the eighteenth century, the belief finally foundered that things could still be sewn up tightly, imitating nature's unity.'[6]

Romantic philosophers respond to this problem by searching for a way to link the mind to the outside world, and question the value of the subjective position set up by Kant. Both Friedrich Wilhelm Joseph Schelling (1775–1854) and Gotthilf Heinrich Schubert (1780–1860) view the division between the thinking subject and the material world as a negative influence on the relationship between mankind and nature. Schelling and Schubert recall a primordial age when mankind had not yet objectified the material world, but existed within it as part of a greater harmony. Schelling maintains that the beginning of critical thought provided the roots for the modern fragmented condition:

> Sobald der Mensch sich selbst mit der äussern Welt in Widerspruch setzt [...] ist der erste Schritt zur Philosophie geschehen. Mit jener Trennung zuerst beginnt Reflexion, von nun an trennt er, was die Natur auf immer vereinigt hatte, trennt den Gegenstand von der Anschauung, den Begriff vom Bilde, endlich, (indem er sein eigenes Objekt wird,) sich selbst von sich selbst.[7]
>
> [As soon as man sets himself in opposition to the outside world, the first step towards philosophy is complete. With this separation begins, for the first time, reflection, from this point on he separates that which nature had united forever, he separates object from intuition, concept from image and ultimately (by becoming an object to himself), he separates himself from himself.]

In such assertions, Schelling differs from Fichte, as Brad Prager succinctly explains: 'Fichte suggested that the transcendental ego is the ground or basis for all judgments, whereas speculative Romantics such as Schelling elided this with transcendence itself.'[8] Likewise, Schubert implicitly criticizes the division between the self and the world when he specifies the difference between the primordial era and the modern age. Reversing Kant's Copernican turn, he claims: '[d]amals hat nicht der Geist des Menschen die Natur, sondern diese den Geist des Menschen lebendig erfasst' [at that time, the human spirit did not assimilate nature; rather, living nature assimilated the human spirit].[9] By making it into an object for analysis, the subject (mankind) lost its ability to access nature directly through intuition, and destroyed the harmony of its natural state.[10] A way to overcome this fragmentation is offered by the new mythology project championed by both these philosophers.

Romantic 'neue Mythologie' is inspired by the myth of the primordial state but offers a basis for the rejuvenation of modern life and a new harmony for the modern age.[11] At the start of his *Ansichten von der Nachtseite der Naturwissenschaft* [*Thoughts on the Night-Side of the Science of Nature*] (1808), Schubert sets out his aims: to describe the ancient relationship between mankind and nature, to explain the once harmonious relations between the individual and the whole, and to show how the seeds of a future progression to a higher existence are contained even within the shattered state of modernity.[12] This is the essence of his three-stage system of history, based on the myth of an ancient harmony, the disillusionment of the present, and the eventual resolution of the problem in a future accession to a new type of harmony — the third stage of history which mankind is yet to experience. The task of new mythology is to unite the spiritual and the material; only then will damaging subjectivity be overcome and mankind can rediscover original harmony.

Neue Mythologie and the Orient

Perhaps the best-known case for a new mythology is made by Friedrich Schlegel, whose *Rede über die Mythologie* [*Speech on Mythology*] (1799) culminates with his famous call to seek the highest Romanticism in the Orient. His conception of 'neue Mythologie' is that of a new source from which poets would draw, inspired by a fusion of ancient myths which ideally would become universal rather than nationally specific. Having said this, in Schlegel's view the task of reawakening this mythology falls specifically to the Germans. He speculates on the wonders that might arise from Indian poetry if only German writers had the chance to access it, as they would almost certainly have a better capacity to understand its depth and translate its meaning than the Indians themselves. For Schlegel, modern India has become dulled and brutal, and therefore incapable of carrying out this task.[13] He also expresses the hope that this new mythology will allow for a proper understanding of the world and, in keeping with the Romantic longing for harmony, stresses the significance of Romantic writing as a means of representing the whole rather than individual elements.[14] In naming India specifically as a site of poetic treasures, however, he makes a statement about the importance of the Orient as a starting point in the move towards universality.

Schubert's search for a way to reunite the material and the spiritual also takes place within the context of the new mythology project and, like Schlegel, he adopts a universalist approach while nevertheless specifying the Orient as a source of inspiration. While Schubert does not restrict his discussion of myth to a particular nation, he makes the claim that echoes of the primordial time can be found among people who are closest to the mythical 'Urvolk' [the first people on Earth].[15] The voices of these people are to be found by the temple of Isis, in the pillars of Thoth, and singing with the Egyptian priests, as well as in the Nordic *Eddas* and in Mexico.[16] Following Schlegel's precedent, Schubert also directs the German gaze towards the Orient as a source of hope for rejuvenation: 'Da ist der Blick der sterbenden alten Zeit nach dem Orient gewendet, aus welchem, wie einzelne Stimmen verkündigten, das neue Heil aufgehen wird. Endlich, siehe! ist die Stunde der Erfüllung gekommen' [The gaze of this old, dying time is fixed on the Orient, from which, just as individual voices have proclaimed, redemption will come again. Look! Finally the hour of realization is here].[17] Even those hoping to find inspiration in specifically Nordic mythology were confronted with the Orient. The *Prose Edda*, the main source of a Germanic mythology used in the eighteenth century, was believed by several prominent scholars to have Asian roots.[18] Even though Romantic universalism was based on the notion of a synthesis of various cultures, ambitions for a new mythology were therefore very much characterized by Orientalism. The Orient represented both the primordial state and the longed-for future harmony; the mythologized location where the division of the thinking subject from the world would be overcome and the natural state of unity would return to mankind.

Hoffmann's Romantic and Oriental Bodies

In Hoffmann's work, both Romantic characters and oriental bodies challenge the subjective point of view because they appear in different guises depending on the viewer, and so their identity cannot be fixed. *Der goldene Topf* (1814) presents Lindhorst as either a salamander or an eccentric archivist depending on the setting in which he finds himself, while *Klein Zaches, genannt Zinnober* (1819) portrays Rosabelverde and Alpanus in their magical forms as a fairy from Dschinnistan and an oriental magus respectively, even as they appear to the outside world as respectable bourgeois citizens of a new Enlightenment regime. The actor Giglio Fava and his beloved Giacinta Soardi are rarely sure even of their own identities as they move fluidly between the roles of Italian actors in the Roman carnival and Assyrian prince/Ethiopian princess. Oriental bodies, meanwhile, throw the primacy of sight into question. *Die Automate* (1814) and *Das Sanctus* (1816) challenge a set of German and Christian assumptions based on an oriental appearance. Joshua's study of *Klein Zaches, genannt Zinnober* reveals how the process of interpreting the external body as a reliable indicator of identity is undermined by 'the multi-layered meanings that are written onto the surface of bodies by others'.[19] This is also true of the Christian response to the Moorish Zulema and her suitor Hichem in *Das Sanctus*, and the German views regarding Hoffmann's mechanical Turk in *Die Automate.* In each case the oriental body refuses easy insertion into the categories ascribed to it by outside observers, retaining its ambiguity throughout the narrative. In the case of the Romantic characters, the difficulty in achieving a stable identity is related to the distance from the primordial state, and is symptomatic of the fragmented condition. In seeking to overcome this modern malady, characters are introduced unexpectedly into a mythologized world characterized by oriental elements. A new consideration of the significance of the Orient in Hoffmann's response to the mind/body problem sheds light on Romantic Orientalism as one possible means of countering 'Zerrissenheit' by providing an alternative to modern subjectivism and alienation from nature.

Das Märchen von der harten Nuß

The embedded tale in *Nußknacker und Mausekönig* (1816) is an allegorical treatment of the mind/body problem and its solution, which comes from the Orient. The separation of the cognitive faculties from intuitive senses, and the rationalist focus on the subjective mind, are symbolized in the affliction of Princess Pirlipat. As an infant, the princess survives a dangerous bite from the malevolent Frau Mauserinks, but the incident transforms her, leaving her with the deformity of an enormous head on a weak and tiny body. In the later work *Die Königsbraut* [*The King's Bride*]

(1821), a similar body is hailed by the foolish Dapsul von Zabelthau as the ideal, as it symbolizes the primacy of the head, and therefore mind. The extreme praise lavished on the misshapen body of Baron Porphyrio von Ockerodastes amounts to a comical parody of the Kantian model which specifies the human mind as the source of all possible knowledge:

> Alle Schönheit liegt in der Weisheit, alle Weisheit in dem Gedanken, und das physische Symbol des Gedankens ist der Kopf! — Je mehr Kopf, desto mehr Schönheit und Weisheit, und könnte der Mensch alle übrigen Glieder als schädliche Luxusartikel die vom Übel, wegwerfen, er stände da als höchstes Ideal! (IV, 1167)
>
> [All beauty lies in wisdom, all wisdom in thought, and the physical symbol of thought is the head! — The more head there is, the more beauty and wisdom, and if only man could cast away all remaining limbs, as damaging luxury items born of a malady, he would represent the highest ideal!]

In Princess Pirlipat's case, however, the deformity represents an imbalance which must be corrected, and Drosselmeyer is called to court and ordered to find a cure or be put to death. Rather than appealing to intellect or reason, Drosselmeyer employs a more intuitive approach: 'O heiliger Instinkt der Natur, ewig unerforschliche Sympathie aller Wesen', rief Christian Elias Droßelmeier aus, 'du zeigst mir die Pforte zum Geheimnis, ich will anklopfen, und sie wird sich öffnen!' ['O, holy and natural instinct, eternally mysterious affinity of all beings,' cried Christian Elias Drosselmeyer, 'you will show me the door to the secret, I will knock, and it will open!'] (IV, 273).[20] Using this approach, and with the co-operation of the court astronomer, whose method of gaining knowledge relies on natural phenomena, Drosselmeyer divines that the Princess will be cured by eating a special nut called Krakatuk. Accordingly, he sets out to look for the nut, travelling to the forests of Asia on his quest. Although he eventually finds the nut in Nuremberg, he was nevertheless right to look in Asia, for it is engraved with the name 'Krakatuk' in Chinese letters. During the years of Drosselmeyer's search, the Princess's deformity has become more pronounced, so that her tiny body is barely able to support her overgrown head. This extreme incompatibility of the head and body symbolizes the distancing of the intellect from the material world, and the manifestation of this problem as a debilitating condition represents its threat to Romantic harmony. Upon swallowing the Chinese nut, the Princess is instantly cured, and becomes a beautiful woman. This allegorical return to perfect balance comes about because of Drosselmeyer's instinctive reliance on an intuitive understanding of nature, and the seed (literally) of harmony is native to the Orient.

Solutions in Atlantis, Urdar, and Famagusta

Hoffmann's mythological stories *Der goldene Topf*, *Prinzessin Brambilla*, and *Meister Floh* provide a much more comprehensive treatment of both the separation of intellect from intuition, and the myth of the return to a harmonious state. Maria Tatar's dissertation examines the influence of Schubert's works on Hoffmann's writing, and points out in particular the very clear correlation between Hoffmann's Atlantis myth and Schubert's mythology in *Ansichten von der Nachtseite der Naturwissenschaft*.[21] Tatar notes the broad similarity between Schubert's view of 'the triadic progression of the history of mankind and/or the individual' and the interwoven narratives of Hoffmann's tale.[22] Her study neglects some of the details, however, and provides no comment on the oriental aspects of Atlantis, and their significance in the longed-for resolution of the modern crisis. Towards the end of Schubert's *Ansichten*, he retells in mythological form his theory of a future state of existence. His myth states that a beautiful youth will strive, with the help of a lily, to reach a temple from which he is separated by a stream. Once he has achieved his aim, the two conflicting worlds representing modern life and a natural state will come together in a lasting unity.[23] As Hoffmann transposes the myth of the youth and the lily onto modern Dresden in *Der goldene Topf*, the river Elbe comes into prominence as the body of water representing the separation of the two worlds, and indeed many of Anselmus's encounters with Serpentina and her sisters take place nearby or on the river. Furthermore, Lindhorst calls his daughters back across the river towards the end of the First Vigil, and Anselmus symbolically crosses the river when he throws himself into it before acceding to the higher plane represented by Atlantis. The central Atlantis myth also relates how the lily experienced an inner conflict, akin to the modern condition, as soon as she separated herself from her natural environment (II/i, 246). Significantly, this myth is instantly dismissed by the prosaic character Heerbrand as specifically oriental nonsense (II/i, 246). Moreover, the importance of the Orient in curing the Romantic condition within a northern or Germanic context is suggested by the emphasis on links between Nordic and oriental mythology. Lindhorst reports that his brother, who guards a valuable carbuncle, is closely watched by a jealous necromancer who lives in Lapland. This happens despite the fact that the carbuncle is in a grove near Tunis (II/i, 248). This symbolic synthesis of oriental and Nordic locations in myth is emphasized when Anselmus surmises that Lindhorst may either be awaiting news from the source of the Nile, or receiving a visiting magus from Lapland (II/i, 286). In keeping with Schubert's pronouncement on Atlantis as a lost world that existed for all cultures, Hoffmann's Atlantis is characterized by a fusion of mythologies that nevertheless draw on the Orient to present the third stage of Schubert's history of mankind: the restoration of harmony between the mind and nature.

Hoffmann's reworking of Schubert's myth is not simply imitative or derivative, but actively encourages critical engagement with the philosophy of new mythology. Sheila Dickson points out that the Romantic three-stage narrative on which the Atlantis myth is based was well known to Hoffmann's readers, a 'generation [who] would of course be familiar with Novalis, Schelling, Schubert et al., even if only at second, third, or even fourth hand'.[24] Hoffmann's use of mythology is therefore particularly reflective, as he picks up the narrative begun by earlier Romantics: the myth upon which he reflects is 'high Romantic myth' itself.[25] M. M. Raraty likewise notes that the Urdar myth in *Prinzessin Brambilla* references literary history, most notably the Romantic *Kunstmärchen* of Hoffmann's time.[26] In this way Hoffmann does not simply present a new mythology in the content of his stories, but undertakes to test claims that this new mythology provides a way of synthesizing primitive intuition and modern reflection. This is achieved, according to Dickson, because Hoffmann uses the form of the embedded story to retell the myths. While Hoffmann normally interweaves other fantastical elements, such as the supernatural, seamlessly into the fabric of his tales, the stories of Atlantis and Urdar are initially told in isolation from the main plots of *Der goldene Topf* and *Prinzessin Brambilla*. The reader is not at liberty simply to suspend disbelief or rationalize the myths as yet another example of the author's tendency to interrupt everyday life with supernatural elements. Instead, 'we are nudged into a different interpretative mode' and the myth provides us with an intellectual framework with which to consider the rest of the text.[27] This manoeuvre brings together the traditionally Romantic content of the myths — that is, their three-part patterns which by Hoffmann's time are well-rehearsed — with a formal innovation that demands the reader's intellectual engagement. An instantly recognizable myth, 'based on a common pool of ideas' becomes a new 'way of seeing'.[28] Schubert's mythical vision is brought to the modern Dresden familiar to contemporary readers of *Der goldene Topf*, but the initial isolation of Atlantis from Anselmus's story in the Third Vigil separates out the critical philosophical framework so that readers have the space to reflect on the role of myth in their own time.

In Hoffmann's mythological stories, the oriental characters are affected by the mind/body crisis because subjective observers from the modern world — the world of Hoffmann's readers — often fail to understand them. For this reason their appearance changes in accordance with the ebb and flow of the Romantic imagination, as they gain in splendour and visual impact when the Romantic spirit develops, but shrink or fade away when imaginative powers are not activated. Their mythical forms correspond to Schelling's claim that art should reveal a higher truth, portraying things 'not as they appeared in the empirical world, but according to their ideal form or "archetype"'.[29] In Hoffmann's stories this ideal truth becomes available only to those Romantic characters who let their senses and instincts guide them, but their new intuitive powers are shattered once they engage their critical faculties to the extent that the imagination is sidelined. The changing bodies of the mythological oriental figures represent both the transformative potential of the Romantic imagination, and the dangers inherent in severing mankind's connection to the natural world. This representative function is exemplified in the Sixth Vigil when Anselmus completes a successful day's work transcribing Lindhorst's oriental scripts, and Lindhorst accordingly grows in stature and takes on the majestic aspect fitting to his role as Geisterfürst [Prince of the Spirits]:

> Die ganze Gestalt war höher, würdevoller; der weite Schlafrock legte sich wie ein Königsmantel in breiten Falten um Brust und Schultern, und durch die weißen Löckchen, welche an der hohen offenen Stirne lagen, schlang sich ein schmaler goldner Reif.
>
> [His entire figure was taller and more dignified; the ample folds of his dressing-gown covered his shoulders and chest like a royal robe, and the white curls on his broad and lofty forehead were enclosed by a narrow circlet of gold.] (II/i, 275; *GP*, 41–42)

Anselmus's work is not yet complete, however, and so as he leaves in the evening

Lindhorst assumes his everyday form of an old man in a grey robe. Schubert likens the moment of Romantic fulfilment to the blooming of a plant, and in keeping with this analogy, Lindhorst awaits the moment when a cactus from his garden will blossom and produce a beautiful flower.[30] As noted in the previous chapter, Hoffmann connects the cactus to the Orient in an intertextual reference in *Meister Floh*, when Lindhorst is cited as an expert on the Indian thistle Zeherit, a cactus grandiflorus. This plant blooms only once a year before dying. This symbol of a Romantic *Liebestod* also represents fulfilment of the Romantic imagination in *Meister Floh*, as Pepusch and Dörtje Elverdink are finally transformed into a thistle and a tulip respectively, casting aside their bourgeois identities in order to become part of Famagusta's primordial wholeness.

The form taken by the oriental body is therefore an indicator of the health of the Romantic imagination, and observers' perceptions of these bodies not only reflect their own dispositions, but also act as markers in their poetic development. When Anselmus begins to approach poetic understanding, he gains the ability to see the oriental body in its most attractive form, and Serpentina transforms before his eyes from a snake into a beautiful, sensuous woman. The victory of Romantic imagination is depicted in a similar way in *Prinzessin Brambilla*. Princess Mystilis is reduced to a lifeless doll when court philosophers in Urdar try to understand her strange language by engaging their powers of intellect, but she instantly comes to life again and grows to a towering height as soon as Giglio and Giacinta burst into intuitive laughter:

> Und so wie das Paar lachte, da, o des herrlichen Wunders! stieg aus dem Kelch der Lotosblume ein göttlich Frauenbild empor und wurde höher und höher, bis das Haupt in das Himmelblau ragte, während man gewahrte, wie die Füße in der tiefsten Tiefe des Sees festwurzelten.
>
> [And no sooner did the couple laugh than — O wondrous miracle! — there arose from the lotus-flower's calyx a divine female figure which grew taller and taller until her head towered into the blue of the sky, while her feet were seen taking root in the furthest depths of the lake.] (III, 906; *GP*, 233)

Mystilis's connection to both the earth and the heavens represents the importance of the physical, natural world for the Romantic imagination, advocated in the text by Pistoja when he states the need for the wings of fantasy to be grounded by the body of humour (III, 910). The various physical forms taken on by oriental characters represent competing perspectives, but the unifying potential of the Romantic imagination allows them to be viewed in the form that most closely mirrors their spiritual reality, and so inner and outer life are unified.

In *Der goldene Topf* the possibility of a permanent resolution of the mind/body problem is, however, presented with ambivalence at best. Precisely because the solution lies in mythology, it is ultimately intangible and impossible to put into practice within the context of modern German life. As Tatar states,

> the optimism implicit in the fulfilment of the myth is undercut by the recognition that a permanent fulfilment is tenable only in terms of the myth — ephemeral in terms of reality, for it is limited to the creative visions of the artist.[31]

The Romantic turn towards a partly oriental 'neue Mythologie' is successful only in so far as it offers the artist fleeting moments of inspiration, but the modern crisis remains essentially unchanged. The estrangement of the intellect from the senses is best illustrated in a symbolic episode which sees Anselmus imprisoned in a crystal jar following his misguided attempt to interpret his encounters with Serpentina through the faculty of reason. His period of imprisonment, representing the modern burden of consciousness, is characterized by the conflict between rational thought and sensible intuition. While he cannot move his body, his thoughts seem to ricochet off the glassy surface and return to him 'im mißtönenden Klange' [with a discordant sound] (II/i, 303; *GP*, 67). Moreover, they drive him close to madness while drowning out '[die] Worte, die der Geist sonst aus dem Innern gesprochen' [the clear voice of his inner spirit] (II/i, 303; *GP*, 67). This brutal suppression of intuition and instinct is overcome when Anselmus renounces critical thought and subscribes instead to the doctrine of faith and love upon which Serpentina insists. The spell is broken and he is freed, but his union with Serpentina necessarily takes place in a context far removed from modern Dresden. Furthermore, while clues pointing to a future fulfilment abound, they serve to highlight the impossibility of resolving the Romantic crisis in the current world. This dilemma is in line with Schubert's belief that flashes of insight into the future harmonious state are damaging for the individual in the modern world, for they leave him bereft once they pass, and the pain of Romantic longing is exacerbated.[32] This theory finds expression when Anselmus becomes disconsolate after his first encounter with Serpentina and her sisters: 'Nur noch einmal blicket mich an, ihr holdseligen blauen Augen, nur noch einmal, ich muß ja sonst vergehen in Schmerz und heißer Sehnsucht!' [Give me one more look, you lovely blue eyes, just one more, or else I must die in agony and ardent yearning!] (II/i, 236; *GP*, 7). Anselmus's new ability to understand the language of nature arises when he activates his imagination and accepts his vision of the snakes from across the divide. By bridging the divide with his imagination, he loses his individual consciousness, becomes part of a wider existence in nature and consequently understands the essence of the elder trees, the evening wind and the rays of sun. When the vision passes, and the promise of unity offered by new mythology is withdrawn, Anselmus is more painfully aware than ever of the conflict which characterizes modern life.[33] The new mythology of *Der goldene Topf* is incapable of effecting anything other than a temporary change to modern life.

Furthermore, full initiation into the world of Romantic imagination and consciousness takes place only at the expense of the body. The mind/body problem is not resolved at the end of *Der goldene Topf*, but simply becomes irrelevant when Anselmus's earthly body is left behind. The boundary between new mythology and the redemptive Romantic death is blurred, as both are presented as closely related methods of escaping the dualistic condition.[34] Throughout the tale, the physical body is presented as a burden and a hindrance. As with many of Hoffmann's Romantic characters, Anselmus is out of step with his contemporaries, a problem which manifests itself in his inherent clumsiness as well as his ignorance of modern dress. The finite and flawed body places limits on the scope of existence, and reduces the power of imaginative thought. This is illustrated as Anselmus first attempts to enter Lindhorst's home, the gateway to Atlantis. His plan is foiled when the bell-pull transforms into a transparent white snake and attacks him. The attack leaves him senseless, his body broken and his thoughts lost:

> Die Klingelschnur senkte sich hinab und wurde zur weißen durchsichtigen Riesenschlange, die umwand und drückte ihn, fester und fester ihr Gewinde schnürend, zusammen, daß die mürben zermalmten Glieder knackend zerbröckelten [...] Die Schlange erhob ihr Haupt und legte die lange spitzige Zunge von glühendem Erz auf die Brust des Anselmus, da zerriß ein schneidender Schmerz jähling die Pulsader des Lebens, und es vergingen ihm die Gedanken.
>
> [The bell-pull sank to the ground and turned into a transparent white boa constrictor which coiled itself round him and squeezed him ever more tightly in its folds, until his limbs were crushed to pulp [...] The serpent raised its head and placed its long, pointed, red-hot metal tongue upon Anselmus's chest; a stabbing pain suddenly severed his vital artery, and he lost consciousness] (II/i, 244; *GP*, 14)

Dependence on the earthly body is presented negatively, as an attack on the body obliterates the powers of imagination and thought. Therefore, even as Anselmus is only beginning to approach poetic understanding, he starts to prepare to leave his body behind, abandoning himself to his imagination, 'wie losgelöst von Allem, was ihn an sein dürftiges Leben fesselte' [as though no longer tied to his impoverished life] (II/i, 252; *GP*, 21). The feeling of being shackled by the body is also experienced by the narrator in the final Vigil, when he dreams of Atlantis and bemoans the restrictive nature of everyday life. Any triumph over physical limitations, even that of the Romantic narrator who writes Anselmus's story, is transient as long as earthly life continues. Accession to another plane of existence demands the sacrifice of the body. This, however, sidelines the issue of dualism rather than resolving it.

Prinzessin Brambilla presents a fundamentally different, more hopeful conclusion than *Der goldene Topf*, despite Hoffmann's continued use of a mythological background tale based on Schubert's three-stage system of history. The protagonists, Giglio and Giacinta, overcome their estrangement from themselves and each other by taking inspiration from the Urdar myth, but unlike Anselmus they do not give up on physical existence. The dualistic condition, implicitly linked to Kantian thought and more explicitly to Fichtean philosophy within the narrative, is ultimately cured and the two actors go on to lead a happy life in their home city of Rome. At stake throughout the story is the self's relation to the self, and the related problem of the place of the self in the world. The latter issue is exacerbated by the fact that Giglio is not only a stage actor, but must find his place within the Roman carnival, as well as insert himself into the framework of the Urdar myth in order to overcome the dualism characterizing his responses to the world around him. The theatre setting is significant, as Giglio's challenge is to become a better actor, a task involving a progression from the highly declamatory style of over-worked tragedies, to a more intuitive improvisational style that comes from within. During the carnival, he tries out his new style but is beset by doubts and dizzying confusion as outer appearances constantly mask, or even distort, inner existence. Giglio's increasing sense of alienation from himself and the world culminates in Celionati's diagnosis of chronic dualism, succinctly summarized thus by the painter, Franz Reinhold:

> ich glaube, daß Ihr, Meister Celionati, mit Euerm chronischen Dualismus nichts anders meint, als jene seltsame Narrheit, in der das eigene Ich sich mit sich selbst entzweit, worüber denn die eigne Persönlichkeit sich nicht mehr festhalten kann.
>
> [I think, Signor Celionati, [...] that by your chronic dualism you mean simply that strange form of insanity in which the self is estranged from itself, so that the personality can no longer remain intact.] (III, 894; *GP*, 223)

This description calls to mind Kant's theory of appearances and things-in-themselves, in this instance applied to the ego, which even the self can never fully understand. The character Reinhold may also be a reference to the philosopher Carl Leonhard Reinhold, Fichte's predecessor at Jena.[35] Both Fichte and Reinhold were engaged in the search for a foundational principle of knowledge, i.e. a proposition of absolute knowledge which was truthful in itself without relying on any previous proposition as a condition for this truth.[36] Manfred Frank writes that the project 'seemed to reach completion in 1794 with Fichte's philosophy of the absolute ego'.[37] In August 1795, Fichte wrote to Reinhold on the issue, expressing the idea that one cannot exist as a being who determines other beings without also being determined oneself, so that ultimately the individual is in fact two individuals.[38] Reinhold has been described as 'the first *post*-Kantian', and Fichte was a champion of his search for a first principle of knowledge.[39] Their close cooperation as well as the paradox of a transcendental ego in which divisions take place informs Hoffmann's philosophical debate.

In *Prinzessin Brambilla* the theme of two selves is emphasized by the recurring motif of reflection. Both literal and mental reflection highlight the problems encountered in any attempt to understand the self. In the first chapter, as the crowds watch the wondrous coach enter the Pistoja Palace, they see their reflections in the coach windows, and mistakenly believe that they are in fact viewing themselves sitting inside the coach. This appearance of the material body in a reflection is substituted, in their minds, for the actual body, and so there is a breach between their understanding of their bodies and their physical location outside the coach. The issue is raised again in the concluding song from Celionati's story, which deals with mental rather than physical reflection: 'Der Genius mag aus dem Ich gebären | Das Nicht-Ich[...]' [The guardian spirit here can bring to birth | The not-self from the self [...]] (III, 904; *GP*, 232). This is a direct reference to Fichte's claim that a division takes place within the ego: 'das Nicht-Ich kann nur insofern gesetzt werden, inwiefern im Ich (in dem identischen Bewusstseyn) ein Ich gesetzt ist, dem es entgegengesetzt werden kann' [the not-self can be posited only on the condition that within the self (within the very same consciousness), a self is assumed, against which it can be opposed].[40] As Hilda Meldrum Brown notes, this application of Fichtean terms to Giglio's problem may be another of Hoffmann's parodies.[41] Thought, represented in *Prinzessin Brambilla* by genius, is damaging to inner and outer harmony as it leads to the splitting, within Fichte's ego, of the material self from the thinking self, and so the possibility of achieving transcendence is questioned. The story does not, however, call for a return to the golden age of immersion in nature, but looks forward to a new unity of thought and intuition, the counterpart to the third age in Schubert's philosophy of history. Helga Slessarev explains:

> according to [the Romantic philosophy of history] the harmony of the Golden Age of mankind has been disturbed by thought or reflection, and must be regained on a higher level which would combine Perception (the unreflective encounter with nature) and Reflection or Thought (of a higher sort than found in pure rationalism).[42]

This new mode of existence is offered by the symbolic narrative of the crystal from Atlantis that forms the Urdar Spring. From the prism of the crystal, intuition or perception will shine out as the 'Fötus des Gedankens' [the foetus of thought] (III, 821; *GP*, 163). In other words, a higher form of reflection can lead to a new sort of knowledge which unifies instinct and intellect, culminating in the self-knowledge experienced by Giglio and Giacinta when they look into the Well of Urdar.[43] In this case, Hoffmann's new mythology provides the inspiration for a different mode of existence, and Giglio and his beloved do not need to leave Rome behind because they find a way to overcome the Romantic condition on earth.[44]

As the vainest character, Giglio requires the most help to overcome the division between himself and the world around him, caused by his tragic posturing, which alienates his audience and makes him the object of ridicule. Raraty contextualizes this problem against Hoffmann's aversion to performances that privilege the person of the actor. In Hoffmann's view, the successful actor should 'deny his own existence in favour of an imagined one'.[45] Several agents, above all Celionati who exposes Giglio to the mode of thinking represented by new mythology, enable him to reform. Giglio's aesthetic education comes from a combination of the Urdar myth and his initiation, at Celionati's hands, into a different acting method. Ricarda Schmidt demonstrates that Italian *commedia dell'arte* and its reception, first of all by the Italian dramatist Carlo Gozzi (1720–1806) and later in German Romanticism, provide a crucial context for Giglio's transformation.[46] Hoffmann's inspiration for *Prinzessin Brambilla* came from eight drawings by Jacques Callot (1592–1635), taken from a series entitled *Balli di Sfessania* portraying *commedia dell'arte* figures.[47] Hoffmann lifts the characteristic features of these figures and imaginatively reworks them into Giglio's story of internal conflict. In the seventeenth-century tradition that Callot documented, the stock figures of *commedia dell'arte* have fixed identities: even if intrigues unfold when clothes are swapped, the characters' beliefs about who they are go unchallenged.[48] Gozzi reinterpreted the dramatic tradition, presenting characters whose inner spirit is the only true indicator of their identity. This inner truth must overcome confusion caused by external changes: this is the case in Gozzi's plays *Il re cervo* [*The Stag King*] and *Il monstro torchino* [*The Blue Monster*] to which *Prinzessin Brambilla* alludes.[49] The splitting of mind from body is Gozzi's addition to a theatrical tradition which did not typically see protagonists change their essential being, and Hoffmann adapts this innovation anew when he reimagines the externally antagonistic figures of *commedia dell'arte* as the internal divisions within Giglio. Schmidt writes:

> aus einem sozial und regional verankerten Unterschied der Typen in der *commedia dell'arte* und aus dem Kontrast extremer Körperbewegungen von zwei konkreten, miteinander agierenden Gestalten bei Callot [wird] bei Hoffmann ein intrapsychischer Konflikt. Eine solche Verschiebung des Konflikt-potentials vom Sozialen und Physischen ins Psychische signalisiert, daß Hoffmann Callots Stiche tatsächlich nicht einfach im Geiste seines Schöpfers literarisch umsetzt, sondern daß sie ihn zu einer Modernisierung anregen.[50]
>
> [the socially and regionally defined differences between the types in the *commedia dell'arte*, and Callot's contrast of the extreme bodily movements of two concrete figures acting together become a psychological conflict in Hoffmann's work. This removal of the conflict from the social and physical arena into the psychological realm indicates that Hoffmann does not simply present a literary reworking of Callot's engravings in the spirit of their creator, but that the engravings stimulate a modernization.]

For Giglio, this means a move away from the fixed identity embodied by *commedia dell'arte* figures. Changes of costume provoke genuine changes in personality and world-view. Giglio's internal divisions are externalized and worked through on the stage, for example when he symbolically slays his old self as he performs both the role of Giglio Fava and that of Capitan Pantalon [Captain Pantaloon]. He experiences '[eine] Identitätsfindung mit Hilfe der Kunst' [the discovery of identity with the help of art].[51] This leads to a more spontaneous style which enhances Giglio's skill as an actor because it is natural: Giglio literally embodies his roles as he takes on their identities. Lucia Ruprecht approaches the art of Giglio's performance from a similar viewpoint, arguing that the improvisational style of *commedia dell'arte* means that all fixed identities are avoided.[52] In particular, Ruprecht's analysis focuses on fluid movement: while the mechanical behaviour and obsessive return to the same role that we see in Nathanael (*Der Sandmann*) is pathologized as trauma, dancers in *Prinzessin Brambilla* can 'experiment with different roles' and thus 'avoid the lethal fixture of the subject to whom change is denied'.[53] Theorizing dance as 'a performed narrative of the subject', Ruprecht argues that Giglio's dances with himself, such as in the episode where he is slain by his double, both reflect the crisis of subjectivity and provide a potential remedy by offering an essential dynamism that is not to be feared, but embraced.[54] Ruprecht acknowledges that this healthy transformation may mask a darker confusion lurking beyond the context of the theatre: a 'delight in role-play is but the reverse of a pathological surrender to a schizophrenic sense of self'.[55] If Giglio is reformed as an actor, the post-Kantian dilemma persists nevertheless.

Complementing Giglio's new approach to his art, the universal backdrop of new mythology becomes necessary in order to make the change a permanent one. Urdar is instrumental to Giglio's progress and he creatively absorbs the message of the myth. Ross Chambers notes: 'The mythical world of Urdargarten, which is the locus of the *Märchen*, is a microcosmic mirror image of the fantastic, but real, world of the Roman carnival in which the events of the main story take place.'[56] The main story of an actor in the Roman carnival is taken up and reflected in the universally applicable myth of Urdar, and this act provides the key to a lasting change. To support this central point, Hoffmann inserts a debate in which Italian and German humour are compared, and perhaps unsurprisingly the latter is found to be superior. Franz Reinhold's description of the Italian form of humour as 'der reine Scherz' [the pure joke] (III, 813; *GP*, 157), pertaining only to surface appearances, is contrasted with his conception of German humour, which goes beyond the apparent and obvious meaning of a joke to indicate something deeper. In particular, Reinhold's claim, '[u]nser Scherz ist die Sprache jenes Urbildes selbst, die aus unserm Innern heraustönt' [our jokes are the very language of that primordial image, which speaks from deep within us] (III, 813; *GP*, 157), suggests that German humour both arises from the rich imagination of inner existence, and speaks to a universal and originary meaning. The Roman carnival, on the other hand, is found to be lacking in universality. Reinhold complains that the carnival masks represent individuals and specific facets of human nature, rather than portraying the essence of mankind in general ('mehr *die* Menschen, als *den* Menschen in Anspruch nehmen' [they concern *men* rather than *man*] (III, 814; *GP*, 158)). While the carnival succeeds in effecting certain changes, the crisis of the split self will remain where disproportionate importance is attached to surface appearances and costumes that do not necessarily lead to an inner change. Indeed, the merely superficial transformation of external appearances leads to crises and confusion for Giglio, and unhappiness for Giacinta, who knows that she cannot become a wealthy princess simply by wearing a dress befitting one. The carnival does engage the Romantic imagination, for Giglio is capable of meeting the elusive Princess Brambilla only when he casts aside his vanity and dresses in grotesque carnival clothing.[57] Nevertheless, in order to move away from the specificity of the carnival season and enact changes that will permanently enhance his experience of the world, Giglio must also partake of the remedy offered by the Urdar myth.

Urdar provides a context particularly apt for the new mythology project, which seeks to bring primordial harmony to a modern age. Critics such as Tatar and Monika Schmitz-Emans read Hoffmann's interpretation of the Schubert model as pessimistic or even nihilistic. Schmitz-Emans in particular is sceptical of the redemptive potential of Schubert's proposed third stage of history when transferred to Hoffmann's work, claiming that Hoffmann distorts the model so as to emphasize the sharp contrast between life in the present and a utopian future, rather than the continuity found in the *Ansichten*.[58] The world of Urdar, however, illustrates a more promising response to the challenge of new mythology. As an intermediary world between Atlantis and Rome, Urdar emerges as a setting more accessible and relevant to the modern artist than faraway Atlantis. Within this mythological world, there are problems typifying the modern condition, as the Magus Hermod becomes separated from Mother Nature, represented by the Queen of Atlantis, and must find a way to re-establish their former relationship. The similarities between the myth and Giglio's real life allow him to draw a meaning from it that he can relate to his own experience, and in this way Urdar provides effective answers to the problem of the split self. The myth is more than an idea, it is a way of thinking for Giglio, in line with Hoffmann's general approach to myth as a critical tool: 'Hoffmann encourages his readers to see the new myth as part of life (particularly of their lives) [...] Through myth Hoffmann wants to teach his readers to make sense of their world.'[59]

Typical of the nineteenth-century German quest for mythological origins, Urdar combines Nordic and oriental mythology to present a moral lesson with potentially universal consequences. When Reinhold hears the story of Ophioch and Liris for the first time, he remarks that it reminds him both of the Nordic Edda and Voluspa myths, and of Sanskrit.[60] The name Urdar is lifted directly from the Prose Eddas, in which Urdar is a spring underneath the ash tree Yggdrasil, the seat of the gods. Significantly Yggdrasil is a tree of the universe, with branches spreading across the whole world and over heaven, and as such Urdar is not only part of a mythical Nordic geography, but appeals to the universalism so admired in 'neue Mythologie'.[61] The magus Hermod also originates in the Eddas, as the son of Odin.[62] Oriental influences are also apparent, however, in Celionati's claim that Hermod is in fact the Indian magician Ruffiamonte. The alter ego of Mystilis is Princess Brambilla, an Ethiopian princess who has an African father and a Persian great-uncle.[63] Furthermore, within the story of Ophioch there is an enigmatic reference to a dolphin which suggests the Orient plays a role in the quest to overcome dualism. As he swims towards the East, the dolphin sprays a pure stream of crystal from his nostrils (III, 857). This is a reference to the crystal given to Hermod by the Queen of Atlantis as a sign of their reconciliation. Having travelled to Atlantis, Hermod keeps his promise to return to Urdar, where Ophioch has fallen into a deep melancholy caused by too much reflective thought. Upon Hermod's return, the healing Urdar Spring is formed from drops of the crystal's prism, and so crystal becomes representative of the potential to overcome self-estrangement. The dolphin's journey towards the Orient implies that the crystal stream, or Urdar, should be sought in the East, while Hermod/Ruffiamonte's connection to both Nordic and oriental myth exhibits the synthesis of Scandinavian and eastern mythologies in Hoffmann's story. Urdar is between North and East, and also provides a bridge between Rome and Atlantis when the Urdar Spring enters the main story of Giglio and Giacinta. Looking into the spring, they know themselves: thought and perception have combined to create genuine recognition. This leads to happiness on earth and improves the practice of their art. As actors, Giglio and Giacinta learn to improvise, performing intuitively without becoming estranged from themselves and each other, as had previously happened in the Roman theatre and during the carnival. Existential doubts are removed and Giglio no longer perceives his self as divided from his body. This new understanding is possible because the promised artistic utopia of Atlantis enters Giglio's world via the Nordic Orient, Urdar. The reflection of Giglio's daily life in the Urdar myth, however, means he does not need to leave Rome behind. Inspired by the myth, he overcomes his chronic dualism and continues his life as an Italian actor. Significantly, during this process, his inner and outer being merges so that Giglio's 'nichtssagendes Gesicht' [vacuous face] begins to take on a 'geistiger Ausdruck' [spiritual expression] (III, 891–92; *GP*, 221). Ultimately, the mythical Orient serves as an inspiration for present existence, rather than a possible future alternative to it, and in this way the mind/body divide is rectified on earth.

Die Automate

When the mythological context is not present, the urge to live in a harmonious state of existence causes problems for the Romantic character living in a modern era. Traditionally, later Romantic writing has been read as a cynical assessment of the chances for poetic fulfilment in the modern world.[64] These chances are particularly endangered when characters are confronted with the purely material products of a mechanistic age. The attempt to reject the mechanical in favour of a communion between the mind and body, and unity with the natural world, can lead to delusional behaviour and ultimately failure if the only inspiration for the poet is in fact lifeless. A famous example of this doomed mission is found in *Der Sandmann*, in which the poet Nathanael's love for his artistic muse Olimpia precipitates a fatal descent into madness upon his discovery that she is a mechanical doll. Nathanael's bid to unlock the Romantic potential of the feminine via a silent and mysterious figure who promises access to an inner world of love and spirituality breaks down when his muse is revealed to have no inner life whatsoever. In *Die Automate*, the lure of the feminine is replaced with another Romantic topos: oriental mystery. In this instance, observers of the fortune-telling Turk know from the start that he is a mechanical body, but his oriental features nevertheless ignite Romantic fancies in a similar manner to Olimpia's perfect female beauty. Attempts to cast the Turk as genuinely perceptive and gifted in the art of prophecy arise as a part of culturally conditioned stereotypes about the Orient, and are also symptomatic of the Romantic distaste for the mechanical. In this way, *Die Automate* is, like *Der Sandmann*, 'a cultural critique of [...] romantic imagination' that also points out the negative aspects of both an obsession with, and a refusal to acknowledge, developments in modern technology.[65] Confronted with the wholly mechanistic, the Romantic project falters as its disciples attempt to force a connection between a mechanical body and a non-existent mind that they must necessarily imagine.

The fortune-telling Turk exposes the weakness of subjectivity because distinct social and intellectual groups adhere stubbornly to their different perspectives, but none of these views are confirmed by the end of the tale. The reader is privy to the reactions of the general public, of scholars, of gifted mechanics, and finally the personal viewpoints of the two friends, Ludwig and Ferdinand. Members of the public are, quite willingly, taken in by the claim that the Turk can predict the future, and much of their confidence in his skill hinges upon his oriental appearance. In Hoffmann's writing, fortune-telling is generally a pursuit of the lower socio-economic classes, in a nod to its prolonged existence in religious and folk culture even in the modern age.[66] In *Der goldene Topf*, the fortune-telling alter ego of the Apfelweib is Liese, Veronika's former nursemaid, and in *Der Elementargeist* [*The Elemental Spirit*] (1821) another Liese, the aunt of a soldier's servant, foretells the future by reading coffee grounds. *Die Automate* sees the mass appeal of fortune-telling transferred to the modern marketplace, where the fortune-teller's mysterious quality is enhanced by his 'orientalische Grandezza' [oriental grandeur] (IV, 401). The attraction of the Orient for those seeking mystery is underscored by the opening line of the story, in which Turkishness, rather than the act of fortune-telling, is emphasized as a draw for the crowds: 'Der redende Türke machte allgemeines Aufsehen' [The speaking Turk caused a great sensation] (IV, 396).

This sensationalism mirrors a real-life and drawn-out episode of the late eighteenth century, when Wolfgang von Kempelen's mechanical chess-playing Turk astonished the masses and apparently defied all explanation.[67] Kempelen's mechanical Turk is also referenced in Hoffmann's novel *Lebensansichten des Katers Murr* [*The Life and Opinions of the Tomcat Murr*] (1819–21), this time to shed light on the situation of Chiara, the gypsy girl who, from a hidden location, provides the voice for Severino's 'invisible girl' trick. Just as Kempelen hid a man inside his machine so that the mystery of the Turk remained unsolved, Severino forces Chiara to hide in a small cabinet so that her pronouncements appear to be coming from the magical glass ball to which people are invited to direct their questions. Although Meister Abraham later reveals the rational explanation for the apparently disembodied voice, there is no answer as to how Chiara's visions of the future are so penetrating. Just like the fortune-telling Turk, she is believed to have a 'wahrhafte Weissagungsgabe' [a real gift for prophecy] (V, 186), a talent she practises from as young as the age of eight. The explanation partly offered for this uncanny ability is her oriental otherness: she is referred to as 'das liebe Mohrenkind' [the sweet Moor child] (V, 192), and it is not insignificant that Severino first finds her in the marketplace. Moving from the realm of low folk culture to the nineteenth-century marketplace populated by the masses, the act of fortune-telling is associated with the Orient to enhance its appeal, a trick which works because of the predominant stereotype of oriental mystery and magic as the counterpart to western reason.[68] Like the masses, the academics in Ludwig and Ferdinand's friendship group judge the Turk in terms of his mystery, avidly discussing his apparently miraculous answers to all questions pertaining to the future. The mechanics, meanwhile, are convinced that there is a rational explanation and investigate every facet of the Turk and his surroundings, but their 'Argusaugen' [Argus eyes] fail to uncover the secret (IV, 397). Popular, intellectual, and empirical responses are all characterized by a subjectivity that remains unanswered in the story's open ending, which sees Ludwig finally affirm the validity of the Turk's pronouncement just as Ferdinand rejects it.

Hoffmann's text reveals that the Romantic perspective is flawed, as attempts to subsume the Turk into a Romantic world-view fail. Birgit Röder shows how the rationalist investigation is trumped when the protagonists' inability to find an adequate explanation for the Turk's apparent power leaves them frustrated. Röder links this frustration to the western desire to rationalize, and thereby master, the oriental Other.[69] The Romantic view is equally challenged, however, and is likewise found to be lacking. Throughout the text, even as Ferdinand and Ludwig admit that the Turk is probably controlled by an outside force, they continue to assign cognitive and intuitive abilities to him. The pair move fluidly between rationalist and Romantic theories and cannot be fully satisfied by either. At first, Ferdinand adheres to the rationalist school, basing his deductions on empirical evidence. He agrees that the Turk's breath does come from his body, as experience proves this to be the case, but denies the existence of any proof linking this breath to words actually spoken by the Turk. Both also state that the Turk does not act of his own will, most overtly when Ludwig clarifies his own understanding of the automaton: 'der Türke, worunter ich natürlich jenes versteckte geistige Wesen verstehe' [the Turk, by which of course I mean that hidden, thinking being] (IV, 415). Nevertheless, they persist in attributing the qualities of a conscious mind to the Turk, and cannot bring themselves to separate the mind fully from the mechanical body. Ferdinand asserts that the Turk can be pleased or displeased by the questions asked of him, and when he receives a seemingly penetrating answer from the oracle, he tells Ludwig that the Turk has seized hold of his very inner being — a claim which recalls the notion of Romantic *Innerlichkeit* [inwardness]. As the tale reaches its ambiguous ending, the Turk's mysterious quality is impressed upon the reader in the final sentence: 'Der verhängnisvolle Spruch des Türken ist erfüllt' [The Turk's mysterious proclamation has been fulfilled] (IV, 427). The narrator also plays on the associations between the Orient and Romanticism, as the Turk and his pronouncements are described as 'voll Geist' [full of spirit] (IV, 398), 'weis' [wise] (IV, 399), and 'mirakulös' [miraculous] (IV, 399). In addition, the term 'geistreich' [full of spirit] appears frequently in relation to his answers.[70] Notably, Ludwig uses the same term when he describes Schubert in a discussion about nature philosophy and Romantic music, and shows how his ideas have been influenced by Schubert's *Ansichten*. Furthermore, Ludwig links his curiosity about the automaton to the Romantic project, expressing disappointment that Professor X, who carried out mechanical improvements on the Turk, does not initiate the friends into his secrets: 'wie sind wir doch so bitter getäuscht worden! wo sind die Aufschlüsse, nach denen wir trachteten, wie blieb es mit der lehrreichen Unterhaltung, in der uns der weise Professor erleuchten sollte, wie die Lehrlinge zu Sais?' [but we've been so cruelly deceived! Where are the insights for which we yearned, and what about the instructive conversation in which the wise professor was meant to enlighten us, just like the apprentices at Sais?] (IV, 418). This intertextual nod to Novalis references the Romantic idea of nature as a language of hieroglyphs, the decoding of which will reveal nature's secrets and restore primordial harmony. Significantly, Novalis's tale has an Egyptian setting and features the motif of the unveiling of Isis as a path to Romantic enlightenment and self-knowledge. Applying the theory of the hieroglyph to a mechanical body, however, is ultimately a flawed enterprise, as the purely material automaton is not a product of the natural world, and so cannot respond to a quest to achieve Romantic understanding.

For Ferdinand, the persistent attempt to reconcile the material and the spiritual leads to an implied onset of madness that illustrates the vanity of the mission. This is partially connected to the coexistence of the contradictory rational and Romantic views. Ludwig insists that the automaton is simply the vehicle for the voice of an outside force, but comes close to the heart of the matter when he notes that the form of the messenger — a Turkish body with a face apparently exhibiting wisdom — has been perfectly selected for this purpose (IV, 413). This particular body provokes the extreme reactions of the public and the two friends. The unsolved mystery hinges on the Turk's apparent penetration of Ferdinand's mind when he answers a question relating to the happiest moment of Ferdinand's life. This moment arose when

Ferdinand fell in love with a female singer, whom he had met in a dream before encountering her in real life. The Turk seems to exhibit an extraordinary power of perception when he appears to know about the singer despite Ferdinand's silence on the subject. When Ferdinand asks if he will ever again achieve such happiness, the Turk retorts that the singer will be lost to him forever at the precise moment when he sees her again. Although Ludwig suggests that Ferdinand has created the mystery himself, by projecting his own thoughts onto the Turk's words, Ferdinand rejects this claim. The prominence of the subject in Ferdinand's mind, however, suggests that Ludwig may be right, for Ferdinand is fixated on what he perceives to be the highest point of his life (IV, 407). His experience is, in fact, similar to the subjective experience of many others who have questioned the Turk: 'Oft überraschte ein mystischer Blick in die Zukunft, der aber nur von dem Standpunkt möglich war, wie ihn sich der Fragende selbst tief im Gemüt gestellt hatte' [The questioners were often surprised by mysterious insights into the future, which were, however, only possible within the context in which they had already imagined them deep in their own souls] (IV, 398). This explanation becomes complicated, though, when the oracle's prediction comes true. Ferdinand leaves town and does see the singer once more, on her wedding day. He reports that she is accompanied by Professor X, a mechanic obsessed with automata who may be the seemingly malevolent force behind the Turk's predictions. A complication follows as it is revealed that Professor X could not have been present at the wedding, because he had never left town during Ferdinand's absence. Ferdinand's implied delusional state is emphasized by his decision to withdraw both physically, by remaining away from the town for an unspecified length of time, and mentally, by living his life according to inner subjectivity rather than outer reality: 'Habe ich sie denn verloren? ist sie nicht im innern glühenden Leben ewig mein?' (IV, 427) [Have I really lost her? Isn't she mine forever, in the passion of my mind?].[71] In an unexpected twist, he also denies the Turk's power, even though his conviction that the Turk spoke the truth has haunted him throughout the tale. At the same time, Ludwig concedes that the Turk was right. The inability of the friends to be clear on the distinction between the Romantic and the mechanical is highlighted by Schmitz-Emans's observation that, despite their claim to cherish a natural sound above all else, they cannot distinguish between 'nature music' and its artificial reproduction by the automata in Professor X's garden.[72] As Schmitz-Emans rightly states, 'Ludwig und Ferdinand sind naïve Romantiker' [Ludwig and Ferdinand are naïve Romantics].[73] The attempt to romanticize a mechanical product ends in the breakdown of the self in madness, and Ludwig's knowledge of Schubert and Romantic harmony is not enough to remedy alienation in a mechanized world.

Das Sanctus

The inability of the subjective view to provide a comprehensive picture of the outside world does not only affect the individual. The close relation of subjectivism and desire becomes clear wherever efforts are made to stake a claim to an object — or a body — for a particular purpose, an act common in the execution of colonial ambition. *Das Sanctus* thematizes the attempted appropriation of a foreign body, in the form of a Muslim woman who is viewed in various ways by those who wish to exert control over her. The attempted control of the body by colonial, or more generally, western authority is one of Homi Bhabha's concerns in his discussion of mimicry. Mimicry, Bhabha claims, is 'one of the most elusive and effective strategies of colonial power and knowledge', representing the desire of the colonizer to transform the Other into a recognizable, familiar subject which nevertheless retains enough difference to guarantee the superiority of the western power.[74] The otherness which remains, however, means that the colonized body becomes what Bhabha terms a partial, or metonymic, presence. While a body may be appropriated or subjected to a certain essentializing gaze, its difference means that the colonial relation to it can never address the whole. Indeed, as Jacques Lacan argues, the gaze is consistently refused a complete picture of reality:

> In our relation to things, in so far as this relation is constituted by the way of vision, and ordered in the figures of representation, something slips, passes, is transmitted, from stage to stage, and is always to some degree eluded in it — that is what we call the gaze.[75]

Hence the splitting of the colonized body, in which the authoritarian power finds simply what it wishes to see. Furthermore, there is a slippage between the appropriated, naturalized body and the visible, irrefutable signs of otherness in this body. This slippage constitutes both an affirmation of and a threat to colonial power structures, underscoring the ambivalence of mimicry: 'The success of colonial appropriation depends on a proliferation of inappropriate objects that ensure its strategic failure, so that mimicry is at once resemblance and menace.'[76]

In *Das Sanctus*, repeated attempts are made by representatives of the Spanish camp to appropriate and assimilate a Moorish woman, Zulema, who comes to represent the religious and territorial conflict between the Spaniards and the Moors. Ownership of Zulema, and her physical position in the conflict, equates to possession of power for the competing camps. This becomes clear in the encounter between the Spanish Don Aguillar and Zulema's Muslim suitor, Hichem, when the men split the individual woman into two competing identities: the Moorish Zulema and the Catholic convert, renamed Julia. The Spanish endeavour to reform and convert Zulema reveals both the effects of western power, and its often wilful ignorance of signs of difference. For example, Zulema/Julia becomes a member of the Catholic choir, and her physical presence among the singers, as well as her participation, suggests to the prioress that she has abandoned her old culture and converted to Catholicism. Zulema/Julia, however, not only continues to wear her zither around her neck, but tunes the instrument so that she can play it in the choir. The prioress chooses to ignore the implications of this visible sign of cultural difference, and is therefore shocked when Zulema/Julia is drawn irresistibly towards the strains of zither music coming from outside the church.

Throughout the narrative, Zulema's identity is split under various gazes, as different viewers interpret her body in the manner which best corresponds to their ideal version of her. Joshua states: 'The gaze of the viewer is questioned constantly in Hoffmann's writing because the "imagined" conflicts with the "real" perception of a person — there is a recognized breach between them.'[77] Indeed, the question of Zulema's 'real' identity is overshadowed by the many images of her which are mediated through different viewers. Often, her name is ignored in favour of adjectival nouns which betray the viewer's essentialist and exclusive interpretation of her body. For Aguillar, whose interest in Zulema extends beyond the religious mission and takes on a thinly veiled sexual dimension, Zulema first appears as 'd[ie] Verschleiert[e]' [the veiled woman] (III, 150), a mysterious and therefore desirable woman. When he discovers her identity as the famed and admired singer of Granada, Aguillar wishes to set Zulema free, but this is deemed impossible by the priest, Agostino Sanchez. Cross in hand, Sanchez declares Zulema 'die Gefangene' [the captive] (III, 151), reducing her to a captive body, which no doubt corresponds to the captive soul Sanchez hopes to liberate in Catholic redemption, but also symbolizes a Spanish victory in the ongoing power struggle. Finally, the prioress prematurely believes her redemptive mission is complete when she sees Zulema's apparently submissive body, kneeling before an image of Mary, and she views Zulema/Julia as 'die Neubekehrte' [the recent convert] (III, 152). Each of these perceptions corresponds to Bhabha's description of the 'metonymy of presence',[78] as the images of Zulema produced represent only part of the truth, and crucially, it is the truth in the eye of the beholder which regulates the representations of her body. The narrator draws attention to the unreliable, subjective nature of these representations with a description of Aguillar's state of mind during a moment of reflection, 'Julia's Bild stand lebendig vor seines Geistes Augen' [The image of Julia was alive in his mind's eye] (III, 156). In fact, Zulema/Julia is only ever viewed by the mind's eye, as viewers superimpose their pre-conceived images onto her body.

These skewed versions of the body do not only work in the service of the appropriating power, however. Bhabha's reference to the 'menace' of mimicry points to the gap between truth and perception as a potential threat to western authority. This threat is illustrated in an episode in *Das Sanctus* in which the orientalist gaze is exploited by the Moor Hichem so that he can penetrate the Spanish camp and mount an attack. On their way to hear a mass, Aguillar and Queen Isabella encounter a destitute beggar wearing rags and raving incoherently outside the church. The Spanish guards, along with Aguillar and Isabella, experience an uncanny feeling when they hear the beggar play on his zither, but his presence is soon explained: 'es hieß: der Mensch sei ein gefangener wahnsinniger Mohr, der aber durch seine tollen Späße und durch sein verwunderliches Zitherspiel die Soldaten im Lager belustige' [they were told the man was a mad Moor who had been taken prisoner, and now entertained the soldiers in the camp with his wild performances and his strange zither music] (III, 153–54). The Moor is tolerated by the Spanish for his ability to keep their soldiers amused. Under the orientalist gaze, he remains other but has been appropriated into the Spanish camp and therefore has been mastered, the threat of his difference removed. It soon transpires, however, that the beggar is none other than Hichem, who, under this guise, infiltrates the Spanish camp and sets fire to the church. He declares himself after attacking Aguillar:

> Ja! wisse, verräterischer Christ, wisse, daß es Hichem der letzte des Stammes Alhamar ist, dem du Zulema raubtest! — Wisse, daß jener zerlumpte Bettler,

> der mit den Gebärden des Wahnsinns in eurem Lager umherschlich, Hichem war, wisse daß es mir gelang, das dunkle Gefängnis, in dem ihr Verruchte das Licht meiner Gedanken eingeschlossen, anzuzünden, und Zulema zu retten. (III, 156–57)[79]
>
> [Treacherous Christian! Know this: the man from whom you robbed Zulema was Hichem, the last living member of Alhamar's tribe! — Know this: that ragged beggar who crept around your camp behaving like a madman was Hichem! Know this: I succeeded in setting fire to that dark prison in which you wickedly shut up the light of my life, and I rescued Zulema.]

The reference to his family history, as well as the scornful repetition of 'wisse' [know this], reveal that Hichem is in fact a man proud of his heritage, in possession of strength and knowledge, qualities which necessarily bypass the orientalist gaze. Furthermore, he is able to exploit this gaze and use it against the Spanish to gain an advantage, knowing that they will believe in their own vision of a weakened, feminized, and raving oriental. Hichem's reference to the 'Gebärden des Wahnsinns' [behaviour of a madman] emphasizes the extent to which this perception depends upon the image of the body and its movement. Lacan's description of mimicry as camouflage, rather than adaptation, explains how the gaze tricks the eye. Hichem is initially an unnoticed threat as his body appears to show what the Spanish already see in their 'Geistes Augen' [mind's eye]. This is, however, an illusion, the effectiveness of which can be illuminated, once more, with reference to Lacan: 'Generally speaking, the relation between the gaze and what one wishes to see involves a lure. The subject is presented as other than he is.'[80]

Conclusion

Novalis's optimistic call in 1798, 'Die Welt muß romantisirt werden' [The world must be romanticized],[81] is characteristic of a movement seeking to come to terms with the effects of post-Kantian subjectivism and trying to find a new type of harmony, inspired by the primordial state but suitable for the modern world. This problem persists into later Romanticism. Kant's writing portrays the subjective but rational mind as the only tool available to individuals wishing to gain an understanding of the outside world. In Hoffmann's works, however, subjectivism exaggerates the rupture between the thinking self and its environment. The rationalist perspective is a limited one, and even the most careful empiricism does not provide a secure basis from which to form an absolute view of the world. The Romantic quest to unify the self and the world, the spiritual and the material, and the mind and the body develops into a theory of non-subjective universalism, and support for this theory is sought in the 'neue Mythologie' project. In Hoffmann's tales, Schubert and Schelling's mythological approach provides a possibility for bridging divisions. In the case of *Prinzessin Brambilla*, simply engaging with this mythology is enough to remedy the alienation of the self while remaining rooted in the modern world. The difficulty of overcoming subjectivism remains a prevalent theme, however. The act of allowing the mind to create the world leads to the formulation of one version of the truth to fit an agenda. In *Die Automate* this is a personal and aesthetic agenda, while in *Das Sanctus* a hegemonic view of a foreign body is formed in the service of national and religious ambitions. In each of the above examples, the Orient is a critical tool in Hoffmann's exploration of the problem. It provides the inspiration for the revitalizing myths of Atlantis, Famagusta, and Urdar, and oriental elements merge with ancient Nordic tales to form a truly universal, and unifying, mythology. Stereotypes about the Orient, however, expose the flaws of subjectivism. The otherness of the mechanical Turk, and of Zulema and Hichem, invites their viewers to form incomplete pictures of reality. As the case of the mechanical Turk reveals, even Romantic characters are not immune to the lure of subjective judgements, and the drive to romanticize the world backfires when the oriental inspiration is merely superficial. The Orient may offer a solution to the mind/body problem, but only when the self is prepared to become part of a greater whole and renounce the act of objectification. If this is not the case, disillusionment and madness beckon, and the mind/body problem remains unsolved.

Notes to Chapter 2

1. *Prinzessin Brambilla*, III, 868; *GP*, 202.
2. Eleoma Joshua, 'Misreading the Body: E.T.A. Hoffmann's *Klein Zaches, genannt Zinnober*', *EGY*, 4 (2010), 39–56 (p. 44).
3. 'Vermittelst der Sinnlichkeit also werden uns Gegenstände gegeben, und sie allein liefert uns Anschauungen; durch den Verstand aber werden sie *gedacht*, und von ihm entspringen Begriffe' [Objects are therefore given to us by means of sensibility, and it alone affords us intuitions; but they are thought through the understanding, and from it arise concepts], Immanuel Kant, *Kritik der reinen Vernunft*, ed. by Jens Timmermann (Hamburg: Felix Miner, 1998), p. 93; *Critique of Pure Reason*, trans. and ed. by Paul Guyer and Allen W. Wood (Cambridge: Cambridge University Press, 1998 ; repr. 2000), p. 172.
4. See Desmond Hogan, 'Kant's Copernican Turn and the Rationalist Tradition', in *The Cambridge Companion to Kant's* Critique of Pure Reason, ed. by Paul Guyer (New York: Cambridge University Press, 2010), pp. 21–40 (p. 26).
5. Brad Prager, *Aesthetic Vision and German Romanticism: Writing Images* (Rochester, NY: Camden House, 2007), p. 3. For background on Fichte, see also Rolf-Peter Horstmann, 'The Early Philosophy of Fichte and Schelling', in *The Cambridge Companion to German Idealism*, ed. by Karl Ameriks (Cambridge: Cambridge University Press, 2000), pp. 117–40, especially pp. 118–27.
6. Barbara Maria Stafford, *Body Criticism: Imaging the Unseen in Enlightenment Art and Medicine* (Cambridge, MA and London: MIT Press, 1991), p. 330.
7. F. W. J. Schelling, *Ideen zu einer Philosophie der Natur, als Einleitung in das Studium dieser Wissenschaft: Erster Theil* (Landshut: Philipp Krüll, 1803), p. 5.
8. Prager, p. 11.
9. Gotthilf Heinrich Schubert, *Ansichten von der Nachtseite der Naturwissenschaft* (Dresden: Arnold, 1808; repr. Darmstadt: Wissenschaftliche Buchgesellschaft, 1967), p. 4.
10. Ibid., p. 7 and p. 11.
11. See George S. Williamson, *The Longing for Myth in Germany: Religion and Aesthetic Culture from Romanticism to Nietzsche* (Chicago and London: The University of Chicago Press, 2004), p. 23.
12. Schubert, p. 3.
13. See Friedrich Schlegel, 'Gespräch über die Poesie', in *Kritische Friedrich-Schlegel-Ausgabe*, ed. by Ernst Behler, 35 vols (Munich: Ferdinand Schöningh/Zurich: Thomas, 1958-), II (1967), 284-351 (pp. 319-20). This type of characterization has led to post-colonial criticism of Schlegel for his orientalist viewpoint. See for example Edward W. Said, *Orientalism*, 3rd edn (London: Penguin, 2003), pp. 98–99.
14. Schlegel, II, 318.

15. Schubert, p. 5.
16. Ibid., p. 6.
17. Ibid., p. 11.
18. This belief was known as the 'Asen doctrine', which claimed that 'a wandering race of priests who called themselves the Asen had established their form of nature mythology in Asgard, in the cold reaches of the North', and the theory went alongside the eighteenth-century discoveries of links between Sanskrit and the German language. The doctrine was taken up in discussions of German mythology by Herder, Görres, and the Grimms. See Williamson, pp. 99–100. Within the Eddas, it is related that Odin came from Asia, in which 'the middle of the world' was to be found. Odin journeyed north from Turkey when he learned, via a gift of prophecy shared with his wife, that he would become renowned in the northern part of the world. Odin is specifically described as Asian: '[Odin] went northward to what is now called Sweden, where a king named Gylfi lived. When the king learned of the journey of these Asians, who were called Æsir, he went to meet them.' See Snorri Sturluson, *The Prose Edda*, trans. by Jesse L. Byock (London: Penguin, 2005), pp. 5–7 (p. 7). The *Edda* present a link between the development of human culture in Asia, and its relocation to Europe when Odin travels north: 'the people [in Asia] are most endowed with all the blessings: wisdom and strength, beauty, and every kind of skill' (Sturluson, p. 5). This fits in neatly with scholarly attempts to identify the Nordic people, including Germans, as the descendants of the first civilized races. See also Chapter 5, p. 121.
19. Joshua, p. 41.
20. The original text has 'Johann Elias Droßelmeier'. This is most likely a mistake on Hoffmann's part as the same character is referred to as 'Christian Elias Droßelmeier' throughout the rest of the story.
21. Maria M. Tatar, 'Romantic "Naturphilosophie" and Psychology: A Study of G. H. Schubert and the Impact of his Works on Heinrich von Kleist and E.T.A. Hoffmann' (unpublished doctoral thesis, Princeton University, 1971), particularly pp. 218–27. Similarly, Ernst Busch claims 'E.Th.A. Hoffmann ist ohne Schubert nicht zu denken' [Without Schubert, E.T.A. Hoffmann is unthinkable] in Busch, 'Die Stellung Gotthilf Heinrich Schuberts in der deutschen Naturmystik und in der Romantik', *DVjs*, 20 (1942), p. 30, cited in Monika Schmitz-Emans, 'Naturspekulation als "Vorwand" poetischer Gestaltung: Über das Verhältnis E.T.A. Hoffmanns zu den Lehren G. H. Schuberts', *MHG*, 34 (1988), 67–83 (p. 74).
22. Tatar, p. 218.
23. Schubert, pp. 324–25.
24. Sheila Dickson, 'E.T.A. Hoffmann: Mind, Mythology and Meaning', *FMLS*, 32:3 (1996), 251–63 (p. 256).
25. Ibid., p. 258.
26. M. M. Raraty, 'Introduction', in E.T.A. Hoffmann, *Prinzessin Brambilla*, ed. M. M. Raraty (Oxford: Blackwell, 1972), pp. ix–xlvi (p. xxxix).
27. Dickson, p. 258.
28. Ibid., p. 253 and p. 260.
29. Williamson, p. 61.
30. Schubert, pp. 317–18.
31. Tatar, p. 225.
32. See Schubert, pp. 317–18, and Tatar, p. 98.
33. After seeing Serpentina and her sisters, Anselmus cannot be sure whether to trust his rational deduction that the snakes were a figment of his imagination, or whether to listen to the voices telling him 'glaube — glaube — glaube an uns' [believe — believe — believe in us]. The result is 'ein toller Zwiespalt' [a wild conflict] (II/i, 239 and 238; *GP*, 9).
34. See also Tatar, pp. 208–09.
35. See Rolf-Peter Horstmann, 'The Early Philosophy of Fichte and Schelling', in *The Cambridge Companion to German Idealism*, ed. by Karl Ameriks (Cambridge: Cambridge University Press, 2000), pp. 117–40 (p. 118).
36. See Manfred Frank, 'Philosophy as "Infinite Approximation": Thoughts Arising out of the "Constellation" of Early German Romanticism', in *German Idealism: Contemporary Perspectives*, ed. by Espen Hammer (Abingdon and New York: Routledge, 2007), pp. 291–308 (p. 294).

37. Ibid., p. 294.
38. See J. M. Bernstein, 'Recognition and Embodiment (Fichte's Materialism)', in *German Idealism: Contemporary Perspectives*, ed. by Espen Hammer (Abingdon and New York: Routledge, 2007), pp. 183–205 (p. 184).
39. Paul Franks, 'All or Nothing: Systematicity and Nihilism in Jacobi, Reinhold, and Maimon', in *The Cambridge Companion to German Idealism*, ed. by Karl Ameriks (Cambridge: Cambridge University Press, 2000), pp. 95–116 (p. 102), and Horstmann, pp. 120–21.
40. Johann Gottlieb Fichte, 'Grundlage der gesammten Wissenschaftslehre, als Handschrift für seine Zuhörer', in *Johann Gottlieb Fichtes Sämmtliche Werke*, ed. by J. H. Fichte, 8 vols (Berlin: Veit und Comp., 1845–46), I (1845), pp. 83–328 (p. 106).
41. Hilda Meldrum Brown, *E.T.A. Hoffmann and the Serapiontic Principle: Critique and Creativity* (Rochester, NY: Camden House, 2006), p. 98.
42. Helga Slessarev, 'E.T.A. Hoffmann's "Prinzessin Brambilla": A Romanticist's Contribution to the Aesthetic Education of Man', *Studies in Romanticism*, 9:3 (1970), 147–60 (p. 156).
43. Romantic new mythology does not, after all, seek a return to primitive myth. The innovation comes from a desire to unite intuition and intellect. As Dickson explains, 'Through myth Hoffmann wants to teach his readers to make sense of their world individually, to recreate symbolically a sense of unity, by imposing an imaginative perspective upon experience, a process which, in the modern world, can only be conducted intellectually and indirectly.' See Dickson, p. 259.
44. Stephan Fischer claims the difference between *Der goldene Topf* and *Prinzessin Brambilla* lies in the prominence of dark enemy powers to be overcome in the former, compared to the battle with the self in the latter. As Giglio is not faced with any strange powers that must be overcome, the battle can be played out in a non-mythological setting as it is only with himself. See Fischer, 'E.T.A. Hoffmann's *Prinzessin Brambilla*: Auf der Suche nach der verlorenen Lust', *MHG*, 34 (1988), 11–34 (pp. 21–22). Essentially, the meta-narrative of the battle between good and evil requires a mythological setting, whereas the struggle to overcome self-estrangement is common to all and can take place in an everyday setting. Nevertheless, the secondary orientalized mythological setting is of central importance in bringing about Giglio's transformation on earth.
45. Raraty, p. xx.
46. Ricarda Schmidt, *Wenn mehrere Künste im Spiel sind: Intermedialität bei E.T.A. Hoffmann* (Göttingen: Vandenhoek & Ruprecht, 2006), pp. 141–94.
47. Ritchie Robertson, 'Introduction', in E.T.A. Hoffmann, *The Golden Pot and Other Tales*, trans. by Ritchie Robertson (Oxford: Oxford University Press, 1992), pp. vii–xxxii (p. xxiii).
48. Schmidt, p. 182.
49. Ibid., pp.182–83. Giglio acts in an adaptation of Gozzi's *Il monstro torchino*, and, as Schmidt points out, Celionati names a character from *Il re cervo*, the King of Serendippo, as Princess Brambilla's great-uncle. See Schmidt, p. 177.
50. Schmidt, p. 158.
51. Ibid., p. 181.
52. Lucia Ruprecht, *Dances of the Self in Heinrich von Kleist, E.T.A. Hoffmann and Heinrich Heine* (Aldershot and Burlington, VT: Ashgate, 2006), pp. 74–95.
53. Ibid., p. 74.
54. Ibid., p. xvi.
55. Ibid., p. 93.
56. Ross Chambers, 'Two Theatrical Microcosms: *Die Prinzessin Brambilla* and *Mademoiselle de Maupin*', *Comparative Literature*, 27:1 (1975), 34–46 (p. 38).
57. See ibid., p. 39.
58. Schmitz-Emans, p. 79.
59. Dickson, p. 259.
60. See also M. M. Raraty's notes in E.T.A. Hoffmann, *Prinzessin Brambilla*, ed. by M. M. Raraty (Oxford: Blackwell, 1972). Raraty explains: 'Sanskrit, the ancient literary language of India, was for a time regarded as the "Ursprache", the ancestor of all languages, and so uniquely appropriate as the language of the mythical Golden Age' (p. 127).

61. See Sturluson, *The Prose Edda*, pp. 24–26.
62. Ibid., p. 66.
63. Ricarda Schmidt explains Brambilla's literary genealogy: her great-uncle the King of Serendippo is the hero of Gozzi's *Il re cervo* [*The Stag King*] and her godmother is Tartagliona, an antagonist in Gozzi's *L'augellin belverde* [*The Green Bird*]. Pulcinella, a stock comedy character, is said to have taught her to play the lute. Schmidt argues that Celionati's introduction of Brambilla to a Roman public by way of listing her family heritage is in fact a means of making her recognizable to that public as an artistic literary figure who belongs above all to the *commedia dell'arte* tradition. See Schmidt, p. 177. This supports the view that *commedia dell'arte* is central to the characters' development: Giacinta fantasizes about being a princess and Brambilla is the lady of Giglio's dreams, so that they upbraid each other for seeking satisfaction outside their relationship. Only through the playful identity changes that come with acting can these dreams enter into the couple's reality and resolve the tensions between the lovers.
64. For a more nuanced picture, however, see Ricarda Schmidt, 'From Early to Late Romanticism', in *The Cambridge Companion to German Romanticism*, ed. by Nicholas Saul (Cambridge: Cambridge University Press, 2009), pp. 21–39.
65. Jürgen Barkhoff, 'Romantic Science and Psychology', in *The Cambridge Companion to German Romanticism*, ed. by Nicholas Saul (Cambridge: Cambridge University Press, 2009), pp. 209–25 (p. 223).
66. See also Chapter 5 (p. 133) for a discussion of the continued belief in witchcraft even in an enlightened age.
67. See Emily I. Dolan, 'E.T.A. Hoffmann and the Ethereal Technologies of "Nature Music"', *Eighteenth-Century Music*, 5 (2008), 7–26 (pp. 8–9) and Tom Standage, *The Mechanical Turk: The True Story of the Chess-Playing Machine that Fooled the World* (London: Penguin, 2002).
68. See Birgit Röder, '"Fort in die Welt! — nach Konstantinopel!": Das Orientbild im literarischen Werk E.T.A. Hoffmanns', *GLL*, 64:4 (2011), 501–20 (particularly pp. 506–11).
69. Ibid.
70. I suggest 'full of spirit' in this case as the more usual translation of 'geistreich' ('intelligent') does not quite capture the implications of the German, given the double meaning of 'Geist' in German (meaning either mind/intellect *or* spirit). It is the Turk's apparent spiritual power that holds his observers in thrall.
71. This is similar to the reaction of the painter Traugott in *Der Artushof* [*Artus Court*]. When his muse, Felizitas, marries a bourgeois official, Traugott exclaims, 'Nein, nein, Felizitas, nie habe ich dich verloren, du bleibst mein immerdar, denn du selbst bist ja die schaffende Kunst, die in mir lebt' [No, no, Felizitas, I never lost you, you will stay mine forever, because you are the creative power that lives within me] (IV, 206). The preference for an imagined muse rather than the real woman has been well documented in Romantic criticism, and in Ferdinand's case, as in Nathanael's, may well be a further symptom of the destructively subjective view.
72. Schmitz-Emans, pp. 81–82.
73. Ibid., p. 82.
74. Homi K. Bhabha, *The Location of Culture* (London and New York: Routledge, 1994), p. 85.
75. Jacques Lacan, *The Four Fundamental Concepts of Psycho-Analysis*, ed. by Jacques-Alain Miller, trans. by Alan Sheridan (London: The Hogarth Press and the Institute of Psycho-Analysis, 1977), p. 73.
76. Bhabha, p. 86.
77. Joshua, p. 43.
78. Bhabha, p. 89.
79. The original has 'mit den Gebehrden des Wahnsinns'. I have changed the spelling to the modern variant.
80. Lacan, p. 104.
81. Novalis, *Schriften: Die Werke Friedrich von Hardenbergs in vier Bänden und einem Begleitband*, ed. by Paul Kluckhohn and Richard Samuel, 5 vols (Stuttgart: Kohlhammer, 1960–88), II (1965), p. 545.

CHAPTER 3

Romantic Heroines: Oriental Women, Bourgeois Girls, and the Critique of the Feminine Ideal[1]

Was mir zu tadeln [...] ist, daß, außer der in der Tat erhaben grauenhaften Zigeunerin, [...] die Weiber flach und blaß gehalten sind

[*My criticism is that, apart from the sublimely horrifying gypsy woman, all the women remain flat and pale*].[2]

In the fourth volume of Hoffmann's *Serapionsbrüder* (1821), the literary friends of the frame narrative pause to reflect on the work of the Scottish novelist and poet Walter Scott. Ottmar and Vinzenz have read Scott's novel *Guy Mannering* (1815), and Vinzenz's discussion of the work reveals an admittedly ambiguous preference for the gypsy Meg Merrilies over the other female characters. The gypsy woman may arouse fear and uncertainty among the men, but she is, at least, free from that flaw exhibited by so many of Hoffmann's own German female protagonists: vapidity.[3] Gypsies had long been a focal point for illustrating European encounters with the Other, and recent studies by Deborah Epstein Nord and Nicholas Saul reveal how gypsies in literature were not only closely connected to, but often subsumed into, discourses on the oriental Other.[4] As an outsider, the gypsy woman is constructed in synonymous terms to the oriental woman, in opposition to the European ideal of femininity. As Epstein Nord comments, this difference is not always positively coded:

> Like the 'Oriental' or the colonized, racially marked subject, the Gypsy was associated with a rhetoric of primitive desires, lawlessness, mystery, cunning, sexual excess, godlessness, and savagery — with freedom from the repressions, both constraining and culture building, of Western civilization.[5]

The removal of gypsies and, more broadly, oriental characters to the borders of modern European life is achieved by their double exclusion, from the process of cultural advancement but also from social constraints. This latter point seems to be the main thrust of Vinzenz's argument. Her status as outsider means that the behavioural codes of nineteenth-century Scotland need not apply to the orientalized gypsy, and it is this factor that marks her out as more colourful than the other female characters and, it is implied, a more fruitful subject for the author keen to produce interesting fiction.

The idea of a strong oriental female character, with at least the suggestion of some independent agency, is particularly striking given the prevalent consensus that the oriental woman has traditionally been the object of sexual and political control. In recent decades, the fields of gender and post-colonial studies have converged in discussions on the fictionally constructed Orient, which represents a model of gendering that is not based on biological sex alone.[6] Sarah Colvin, for example, explores the implications for seventeenth- and eighteenth-century German theatre when traditionally female characteristics — sensuality, lack of reason, and moral weakness — are superimposed onto the oriental male character as a 'rhetorical device' to lessen the threat of the Islamic opponent at a time when the shadow of the Ottoman Empire continued to cast fear into the minds of German Christian audiences.[7] Colvin's linking of the feminine and the oriental revolves around the notion of twin threats to modern European male identity, with the feminine posing an interior threat, and the oriental an external one.[8] Therefore, both must be controlled and ordered so that the masculine remains dominant. Women are conceived of as weak and inferior, and the oriental male is reduced to the status of the feminine so as to minimize his power.[9] Deductive reasoning suggests that the oriental woman is doubly inferior, her image distorted by duplicate layers of stereotyping. Gayatri Spivak's oft-quoted 1988 essay, 'Can the Subaltern Speak?', explains the western, male attempt to describe and categorize as a means of achieving domination.[10] By claiming the right to construct knowledge based on a European male perspective, those who write history, and indeed fiction, participate in the extension of white male dominance by denying a voice to 'the subaltern' — for Spivak, the colonized Indian. The connection of knowledge and power becomes clear when even the ability to define oneself linguistically is taken away from the subaltern. Spivak makes a claim particular to the oriental female: 'If, in the context of colonial production, the subaltern has no history and cannot speak, the subaltern as female is even more deeply in shadow', a process Axel Dunker has aptly named the 'These von der doppelten Kolonialisierung' [thesis of double colonization].[11] Oriental females who assert their strength and independence, however, such as the gypsy discussed by the Serapion brethren, serve to undermine such constructions, and call for a rethinking of stable categories in which both the oriental and the feminine are explained, ordered, and controlled by the European male.

The Oriental Woman in German Romantic Fiction

It is nevertheless often the case that strong female characters conform to a different sort of stereotype, for in refusing to be mastered they enter the category of the dangerous Other, and German Romantic fiction provides many examples of this phenomenon.[12] Broadly speaking, the danger is a moral one, relating either to sexual temptation or to a denial of the Christian religion,[13] and in all cases it undermines the model of patriarchal dominance. Ulrike Stamm's study of nineteenth-century European travel writing argues that the oriental woman is presented as a personification of male sexual fantasies, which are projected onto the Orient so as to keep them at a safe distance.[14] The widespread translation in Europe of the *Arabian Nights* in the eighteenth century was a factor in igniting such fantasies, for as Lynne

Thornton claims, readers often ignored the spiritual aspects of the tales and focused instead on themes of sexuality, love, violence, and sometimes humour.[15] Thornton's study of nineteenth-century orientalist painting also notes the depiction on canvas of oriental women as 'träge, aufreizend, eitel, wollüstig oder affektiert' [idle, provocative, vain, lustful, or affected], and therefore the literary imagination and the visual arts collaborated to present a sexualized image.[16] This image is marked by ideas of splendour and excess, again drawn from the *Arabian Nights*, but widely used as a means of emphasizing the sensual side of the oriental female. This aspect is picked up in German Romantic fiction, in which the Orient is often both a place of mystery, 'die Heimat alles Wunderbaren' [the home of everything wondrous], and of opulence, with 'Perlen und Edelgesteine' [pearls and precious jewels] and fine clothes in abundance.[17]

Romantic writers responded to a particular set of ideas about oriental female beauty that bears out the notion of the East as a locus of sensuality and visual splendour, as well as addressing the tension between male sexual desire for the exotic, and fear that this desire may lead to a moral breakdown. The Muslim Zulima in Novalis's *Heinrich von Ofterdingen* (1802), for example, sings of her former life before she was captured by the crusading knights and brought to Germany, claiming that if only she were in her homeland, she would be wearing richly embroidered garments.[18] The eponymous Turkish heroine of Achim von Arnim's *Melück Maria Blainville, die Hausprophetin aus Arabien* [*Melück Maria Blainville, the House Prophet from Arabia*] (1812) also conforms to this image, welcoming her lover, Count Saintree, to a boudoir resplendent with golden roses. The result for the Frenchman is a dizzying loss of control as he is seduced in these exotic surroundings. His moment of weakness endangers his life: Melück makes use of the opportunity to cast a spell allowing her to take possession of his heart, literally, so that he is later unable to survive unless she is physically close by. Furthermore, Melück upsets the rational order of Enlightenment France by engaging in the act of prophecy, for which she is generally ridiculed by other characters. Although Arnim repeats aspects of the stereotype, most notably in Melück's passionate nature and by giving her magical powers, he also uses the character to criticize prevalent French social practices. For example, when Saintree first attempts to end his affair with Melück, he realizes she cannot be as easily dismissed as the other French girls with whom he has conducted love affairs, mainly because her emotional involvement is genuine. His peers implicitly approve of his efforts to separate respectable love from illicit passion, with Mathilde and Melück respectively, but the text presents this in a critical light as an act of cruelty: while Melück writes to him in despair, Saintree meets Mathilde and feels completely happy.[19] The unusual resolution of the love triangle, which sees Melück living together with Saintree and Mathilde and even acting as a second mother to their children, implies a move away from the binary categories of 'safe' and 'dangerous' women. Melück's marginalization in French society, however, illustrates that she is generally perceived as a danger, and few characters are ready to listen to her. Ironically, the downfall of the aristocracy stems from an extreme ideological adherence to the reason that they claim to prize, as Melück prophesizes: she foresees the death of the King, the nobility, and her beloved Saintree during the

French Revolution. Men ignore Melück at their peril and it is left to a woman — Mathilde — to vindicate her at the end of the story.

The threat posed to the European male by the oriental, non-Christian, sensual female is also explored in Ludwig Tieck's *Liebesgeschichte der schönen Magelone und des Grafen Peter von Provence* [*Love Story of the Fair Magelone and Count Peter of Provence*] (1797). Two faithful German lovers, the young knight Peter and the princess Magelone, are tested when they are accidentally separated and Peter almost drowns at sea. He is rescued by Arab sailors and brought to the court of a sultan, whose beautiful daughter Sulima — often referred to as the heathen Sulima — falls in love with him. A stereotypically sensuous and willing oriental woman, Sulima is soon overcome by her passion and invites Peter to run away with her.[20] Believing Magelone to be dead, he reluctantly agrees to the plan, but later repents his faithlessness and decides to abandon Sulima and leave the court alone. As he rows away, Sulima's song reaches him over the waves and awakens a telling mixture of desire and fear: 'Liebe wollte ihn rückwärts ziehn, Liebe trieb ihn vorwärts' [Love tried to pull him back, Love drove him onwards].[21] As sexualized beings whose physical attributes are often foregrounded, oriental women in Romantic fiction conform to one stereotype by serving as the object of male fantasy, but in fulfilling this function they also pose a threat to male control. A degree of narratorial sympathy for Zulima, Melück, and Sulima highlights their predicament all the more starkly: once they are viewed in terms of masculine desire, it is difficult for them to relate their stories on their own terms. Heinrich von Ofterdingen's change of heart as he develops from an enthusiastic admirer of the crusading knights to Zulima's sympathetic interlocutor is a pointed example of the potential advantage to be gained from a more cosmopolitan approach.[22]

Throughout German Romantic fiction, oriental women are inevitably contrasted with German, or at least European, counterparts, and rarely, if ever, appear as the only female characters in the text. Moreover, their differing relations to male protagonists are often central to the comparison. Heinrich von Ofterdingen encounters the young and beautiful Zulima before he meets the German Mathilde, and Tieck's Sulima, who is impatient to seduce Peter, is contrasted with the faithful Magelone, who spends years waiting for her lover to return. The similarly named Zulma in Tieck's epic tragedy, *Leben und Tod der heiligen Genoveva* [*The Life and Death of Saint Genevieve*] (1799), follows her lover to the battlefield while the saintly Genoveva, wife of the German knight Siegfried, waits at home for her husband. This play briefly deals with the victory of the Frankish ruler, Karl Martel, in stemming the Muslim European invasion at the Battle of Tours in the year 732. The Zulma episode is a short one, but is significant for this discussion as Zulma refuses to let herself be reduced to a sexual object. As she mourns the death of her lover in battle, a group of German Christian soldiers happen upon her and one instantly begins to admire her hair, lips, and breasts. When she hears the men discussing whether or not a union with a heathen woman would be immoral, she responds scornfully and reverses the standard model of control by silencing them with the words, 'O schweigt!' [O, be silent!].[23] Meanwhile, Arnim's prophetess, Melück, must compete with Saintree's French wife Mathilde for his love.

In Hoffmann's stories a similar pattern emerges. Like Novalis and Arnim, he critically appraises the male tendency to place European and oriental women in opposing categories. In *Der goldene Topf*, Serpentina functions as the opposite number to the German Veronika, and Anselmus's affections vacillate between the two throughout the text. *Klein Zaches genannt Zinnober*, meanwhile, portrays two women influencing the life of the protagonist Balthasar: the German Candida, with whom he falls in love, and the oriental fairy Rosabelverde, who hails from Dschinnistan, the land of the *Arabian Nights*. Finally, the double narrative *Die Irrungen* and *Die Geheimnisse* presents two potential matches for the Baron Theodor von S. from Berlin: an orientalized Greek princess and the Jewish-German Amalia Simson. The frequency of German–oriental female pairings demands a closer investigation into how femininity is constructed, and criticized, in texts that depict oriental women alongside their German counterparts. Traces of the popular Enlightenment tradition of using the oriental foreigner to reflect on European society, most famously exemplified in Montesquieu's *Lettres Persanes* [*Persian Letters*] (1721), seem to survive in German Romanticism. Furthermore, the oriental woman is often more lively than her German counter-image, as suggested by Vinzenz's observation on Walter Scott's novel, and so she provides a new perspective on Hoffmann's critical response to the early nineteenth-century discourse on femininity, and the expectations of how relations between the sexes should play out.

In studies of German literature and culture, a generation of post-Said critics have been keen to extend the discourse of Orientalism to the pre-colonial German states of the late eighteenth and early nineteenth centuries. They have, however, been slow to comment on Hoffmann's oriental women, with a few notable exceptions. James Hodkinson's brief study of Islam and gender in German Romanticism takes into account Hoffmann's tale *Das Sanctus* (1816).[24] Focusing on the central narrative of Zulema, a Moorish woman living in fifteenth-century Granada who is captured by the Catholic Spanish and undergoes conversion to Christianity, Hodkinson argues that the oriental woman becomes the object of a power struggle between the two religions. As a result, Zulema is weakened, dominated, and — inevitably, Hodkinson suggests — loses all traces of her Muslim identity. More recently, Birgit Röder has shown how the same narrative provides a critical analysis of western stereotypes relating to the oriental feminine.[25] In the tradition of Said and Spivak, Röder argues that the Spanish soldier Aguillar, who is captivated by Zulema's air of mystery, is motivated by a desire to understand and explain this mystery, and thereby to control Zulema. The fatal consequences that Zulema suffers suggest Hoffmann's criticism of the obsessive patriarchal desire to possess and dominate.[26] This aspect of colonial ambition is also examined in Axel Dunker's illuminating discussion of Hoffmann's little-known South Sea narrative, *Haimatochare* (1819).[27] Dunker references post-colonial discourses to reveal how Hoffmann's tale subverts, rather than reifies, the notion of western male dominance. *Haimatochare* tells the story of two British natural scientists, Menzies and Brougthon, who join an expedition to Hawaii. The text plays with the tradition of South Sea islanders as exotic, sexualized beings, as the two men, once fast friends, enter into a bitter dispute over which of them has the right to possess a beautiful islander named Haimatochare. Each of the men stakes his claim: Menzies because he saw her first, and Brougthon because he owns the rug on which Menzies found her sleeping. The islander is described in terms of her otherness: 'Farbe, Haltung, Aussehen, alles war sonst anders' [colour, posture, appearance, everything was different] (III, 672), and the attraction held by this exotic being drives the two men to a deadly duel. Only at the end of the tale is the twist revealed: Haimatochare is a type of insect, previously unknown to the scientific world, and each of the scientists has been keen to claim its discovery as his own. Although not a tale of an encounter with the Orient, *Haimatochare* employs the same stereotypes accorded to the oriental woman in Romanticism: before her true identity is unveiled, Haimatochare is characterized as the beautiful object of Eurocentric desire.[28] Furthermore, this desire proves dangerous, indeed deadly, for the western male under its thrall. According to Dunker, the fact that the beautiful islander turns out to be a louse not only confirms the western reduction of the exotic female to a voiceless and powerless being, but subverts this dominant view by ironizing the very cliché on which the story is based.

These three critics take the important step of drawing Hoffmann's writing into the post-colonial debates which have marked studies of German Romanticism in recent years, casting light on the relationship between gender and otherness. Dunker's work begins an important examination of Hoffmann's response to the power structures shaping the western male's quest to discover and possess the foreign woman, whose objectification renders her voiceless. Specifically, Dunker's identification of the implicit criticism at play in Hoffmann's tale is of significance for this discussion. This approach can be fruitfully widened to include texts in which the oriental woman is contrasted with a German counterpart. Hoffmann's work takes in the western response to the oriental woman and subjects it to ironic treatment, but the oriental woman herself also functions as a critical tool to undermine dominant discourses surrounding German femininity in the late eighteenth and early nineteenth centuries. The question of voicelessness and the related subaltern status, to cite Spivak's terms, must therefore be subjected to a more detailed examination. If Hoffmann satirizes male attempts to control an 'exotic' female presence, while presenting submissive, or at the least conformist, German female characters, the question of which characters are truly subaltern becomes less clear.

The Bourgeois Ideal

Hoffmann's critical gaze often turns towards the social conventions of his time, particularly with regard to the behavioural standards imposed upon women of the middle classes. The most common female type in his work is the young girl on the cusp of adulthood, whose thoughts have turned to marriage. To take just a handful of examples, Veronika of *Der goldene Topf*, Clara of *Der Sandmann*, Candida of *Klein Zaches, genannt Zinnober*, Ulla of *Die Bergwerke zu Falun*, Christina of *Der Artushof* [*Artus Court*] (1817), and Antonie of *Rat Krespel* (1817) all conform to this model. Hoffmann's sustained interest in depicting this type relates to a shift in the role of women which developed in the latter half of the eighteenth century and continued to influence domestic life during Hoffmann's most productive years. The late eighteenth-century growth of industry and the corresponding expansion of the bourgeois class meant that middle-class women were not called upon to provide financial support for their families. With women's productive value thus minimized, there developed a new emphasis on the value of learning how to make a good match in marriage, and so the concept of marriage for love was subordinated to parental demand that a daughter should find a husband based on practical considerations. Furthermore, a woman could hope to find power only in the domestic sphere. Thomas Klinkert and Weertje Willms describe this power as a reward for female integration into the normative roles ascribed by social convention and parental expectation: the power applied only to their relations with men, and was not a power of autonomy.[29] Literary depictions of the feminine ideal and magazines espousing moral values prepared young bourgeois women to accept their future roles, and documents such as J. H. Campe's 1789 *Väthterliche Rath für meine Tochter* [*Fatherly Advice for my Daughter*] demonstrate how this shift towards patriarchal dominance became embedded in the social conscience.[30] Obedient daughters make good candidates for wives and mothers. In Hoffmann's stories, young women are often presented as part of a father–daughter pairing, with the father cast as the suitor's judge. Veronika, Candida, and Christina acquiesce in varying degrees to parental wishes, and at the very least they are often accompanied by their fathers. A famous literary depiction of the domestic ideal can be found in Goethe's *Die Leiden des jungen Werthers* [*The Sorrows of Young Werther*] (1774), in which Werther first encounters Lotte as she looks after her young brothers and sisters and distributes bread among them. This scene is treated with irony in Hoffmann's *Meister Floh*, when Peregrinus is charmed by Röschen as she prepares a meal for her family: 'Den Peregrinus entzückte des holden Mädchens Beginnen, ohne daß ihm dabei Werthers Lotte und ihre Butterbrote in den Sinn kamen' [Peregrinus was delighted by everything the lovely girl did, without being reminded of Werther's Lotte and her bread and butter] (vi, 448; *GP*, 360).

The effect of parental control, patriarchy, and social expectation on young women is more often than not subjected to satirical treatment in Hoffmann's tales, and this satire reveals that subaltern status might more readily be named the fate of young German women than of oriental outsiders. Young aspiring wives develop into beautiful but robotic women incapable of independent thought as they enter into their ready-made roles. A classic example is Christina of *Der Artushof*. A one-dimensional character who aims only to be married, Christina has swallowed wholesale the didactic programme aimed at women of her age and class. She has little psychological depth and is incapable of engaging in any meaningful exchange with the man whom she apparently loves. Indeed, her enthusiasm for marriage is determined by her belief that it is the only way to give her life purpose. Accordingly, she does not wish to marry Traugott because she loves him, but rather loves him only because he wishes to marry her, 'denn was sollte sie wohl in aller Welt anfangen, wenn sie niemals Frau würde!' [for what in the world *could* she do, if she never became a wife!] (iv, 183). Hoffmann's characterization of the bourgeois wife as superficial and lacking in both spontaneity and intelligence becomes clear when Christina is asked to give comfort to her fiancé in a moment of distress, but is unable to step outside her assumed role:

> Christina begab sich auf ihr Zimmer, um sich nur ein wenig umzukleiden, die Wäsche herauszugeben, mit der Köchin das Nötige wegen des Sonntagbratens zu verabreden und sich nebenher einige Stadtneuigkeiten erzählen zu lassen, dann wollte sie gleich sehen, was dem Bräutigam denn eigentlich fehle.
>
> [Christina went to her room, just to change her clothes a bit, to organize the laundry, to agree on the necessary business of the Sunday roast with the cook and, while she was at it, to listen to a few bits of gossip from the town, after which she would go instantly to see what the matter was with her bridegroom] (IV, 197)

The social creation of such behaviour is also attacked in *Der Sandmann*, a tale that, among other things, draws attention to the reduction of women to silent and compliant beings.[31] Once Olimpia's secret is revealed, women in polite society are required to dance out of time and to yawn at tea parties simply in order to prove that they are not wooden dolls, the implication being that nothing in their conduct could otherwise differentiate them from Olimpia, whose conversational ability amounts to the occasional sigh of 'Ach! Ach!' [Oh! Oh!] (III, 43; *GP*, 112). Hoffmann's cynical view of relationships between the sexes is clear in the description of what happens when the women are encouraged, for once, to speak their minds:

> [Es] wurde von mehrern Liebhabern verlangt, daß die Geliebte [...] nicht bloß höre, sondern auch manchmal in *der* Art spreche, daß dies Sprechen wirklich ein Denken und Empfinden voraussetzte. Das Liebesbündnis vieler wurde fester und dabei anmutiger, andere dagegen gingen leise aus einander. 'Man kann wahrhaftig nicht dafür stehen', sagte dieser und jener.
>
> [[S]everal lovers demanded that their beloved should [...] [be] required not merely to listen, but also, from time to time, to speak in a manner that revealed genuine thought and feeling. The bonds between some lovers thus became firmer and pleasanter; others quietly dissolved. 'One really can't take the risk', said some.] (III, 46–47; *GP*, 115–16)

Insipid women are created by social convention, and men fashion for themselves wives with whom they cannot have meaningful communication. The motif of the automaton in *Der Sandmann* overtly draws attention to the behaviour already present in wider society, for as Klinkert and Willms note, parents (and later husbands) educate their daughters by 'blunting [their] feelings and making [them] behave like [automata] in society'.[32]

The Romantic Ideal

Alongside the interconnected models of the ideal daughter, wife, and mother runs a parallel discourse on femininity, which is chiefly the preserve of poets but is equally limiting to female independence. The Romantic veneration of the feminine as poetic inspiration is perhaps best encapsulated in Friedrich Schlegel's claim that women do not need as much education in poetry as men because woman's very essence *is* poetry.[33] Idolized women are therefore viewed not as developing poets, like many Romantic male protagonists, but as the embodiment of an already perfect and unattainable artistic ideal.[34] Such a position, however, has come under scrutiny from critics who see the adoration of an ideal woman, who serves as the artist's muse, as a means of entrenching the patriarchal order. Elizabeth Spelman's study of feminist thought claims that 'misogyny has always been compatible with having high regard for "exceptional" (and surely imaginary) women'.[35] Sally Winkle reads the adoration of the feminine in general as a denial of the individual woman's worth, while Margarete Kohlenbach uncovers how 'the real and bodily woman's role in this process of inspiration is to bring to life the latent and allegedly celestial image which already resides in the artist'.[36] The relationship between Romantic artist and muse, therefore, may be read not as one of mutual respect and engagement, but rather as driven by the needs of the male who wishes to achieve poetic development, and who creates an ideal muse to this end. An example is Heinrich von Ofterdingen's claim, shortly after he first meets his beloved Mathilde, that she embodies the true voice of poetry, which he can only hope to echo, a statement which cannot at this point be grounded in the pair's real interaction, as Mathilde barely speaks. Indeed, Todd Kontje draws a parallel between Mathilde and Hoffmann's lifeless doll Olimpia, in whom the would-be artist Nathanael sees the affirmation of all his creative efforts, despite her continued silence.[37] Both Heinrich and Nathanael correspond to Karen Swann's model of the Romantic male who creates an essentially empty muse: 'captivated by the mirror he constructs, he fails to realize it may simply reflect back his own enchantment'.[38]

Linked to this is the conceptualization of the muse as a spiritual being. As the personification of Romantic longing and eternal perfectibility, the muse is necessarily untouchable, a vision of the Romantic *Jenseits* on earth. Furthermore, she should not be sexualized, for as Klinkert and Willms note, the Romantic artist generally faces a choice between sex, a bodily act, and spiritual enlightenment.[39] Sexual desire compromises creativity, as does entrance into the bourgeois roles of husband and father, and so women held in esteem by Romantic artists must renounce their own sexuality in order to conform to the male-constructed ideal.[40] Ricarda Schmidt identifies a tendency in Romantic fiction to separate female characters into Venus and Madonna types, noting that, should the male protagonist choose the wrong type of woman, or should he love the Madonna figure in an earthly rather than a spiritual way, the consequences are unequivocally negative.[41] For this reason, idealized women often appear divorced from their physicality.

The demands regarding the silence of the muse are made clear in Hoffmann's tale *Der Kampf der Sänger* [*The Singers' Contest*] (1817). This notably draws on the earlier *Heinrich von Ofterdingen* to provide a portrait of a Mathilde who inspires Heinrich only when imagined and not when she is present. Novalis's Mathilde is linked to Heinrich's spiritual rather than sexual development: he sees her in a dream, underwater, and she later achieves a permanent state of non-corporeality when she dies but leaves behind her spirit to communicate with Heinrich via a tree. Hoffmann's Mathilde, a countess loved by Heinrich, remains equally distant. Heinrich's feeling of hopelessness regarding this love recedes when he is far away from Mathilde, as he imagines her lighting up songs in his heart, an image powerful enough to encourage him to restring his broken lute and play music. In this case, physical proximity to the muse is coded as damaging to the artistic mind, while a distant image of her engenders creativity. The prioritization of spiritual over earthly love is reinforced in the tale when Heinrich's friend Wolfframb von Eschinbach triumphs in a singing contest against an evil spirit. The spirit sings temptingly of the beautiful Helen, a figure associated with passionate love, but Wolfframb overcomes the challenge by singing of pure love, an action which drives the evil spirit away.

In Hoffmann's work, a rejection of the typical one-way relationship between the male artist and his muse becomes a satire on the unreflective Romantic poet who fails to recognize the limits of his ideals. According to Kohlenbach, Hoffmann's portrayal of such figures 'helps to reveal the shortcomings in the Early Romantic discourse on femininity'.[42] Schmidt rejects such a clear division between early and later Romanticism, stating that the later Romantics who showed a tendency to depict the obstacles in reaching the utopian ideal in fact responded to a discourse initiated by their predecessors. Hoffmann's cynical treatment of the relationship between artist and muse is proof of this ambivalent attitude towards the ultimate goal of Romantic longing.[43] Earlier Romantics including Karoline von Günderrode and Dorothea Schlegel anticipated this development by examining the limitations of idealized love, and Hoffmann carries on the trajectory by '[exploring] the gap between expectation and outcome'.[44] Hoffmann's parody is summed up succinctly in the tale *Klein Zaches, genannt Zinnober*, when the narrator describes the extreme demands of some poets for female perfection: 'Es gibt poetische Aszetiker, die noch weiter gehen und es aller weiblichen Zartheit entgegen finden, daß ein Mädchen lachen, essen und trinken und sich zierlich nach der Mode kleiden sollte' [There are poetic ascetics, who go even further and judge it to be against the very principle of feminine delicacy, if a girl should laugh, eat and drink, and dress herself charmingly in accordance with the fashions] (III, 566).

The negative consequences of this type of thought are outlined in *Die Jesuiterkirche in G*, in which the painter Berthold's constructed image of his perfect muse Angiola falls apart when he marries her. The situation worsens when she bears him a son: 'das vollendete mein Elend und der lange verhaltene Groll brach aus in hell aufflammenden Haß' [this completed my misery, and my long-suppressed resentment broke out as brightly burning hate] (III, 138). The text implicates Berthold in his wife's murder, and although this is never confirmed, it is clear that Berthold's disillusionment contributes to his madness and subsequent suicide. The problem is rooted in his earlier subscription to the impossible concept of embodied perfection: he is 'guilty of elevating a particular woman to the status of the Ideal, and the refusal to acknowledge this fundamental error leads to his destruction'.[45] Hoffmann's narratives therefore work to destabilize a construction of the ideal which fails to take into account the earthly setting in which art is created. Birgit Röder explains:

> On one hand, the artist longs for the Ideal and tries to capture and embody it in his work; on the other, he will never succeed in doing this. Although the artist may strive to catch a glimpse of the Ideal [...] he can only protect himself from the inevitable disappointment that ensues by maintaining a degree of critical detachment from his creation. It is this (ironic) distance that saves him from tragedy.[46]

Hoffmann's 'poetic ascetics', the disillusioned Berthold, and the unfortunate Nathanael are treated with varying degrees of parody or sympathy, but each illustrates that the search for a heavenly woman on earth is hopeless.

Der goldene Topf

In *Der goldene Topf*, the character Serpentina, who hails from the paradise Atlantis, fulfils the role of muse for the budding poet Anselmus. Their interaction, however, entails a departure from tradition in that Serpentina is neither required to renounce her sensuality, nor is she silenced. On the contrary, she expresses her own desires and guides Anselmus through his poetic initiation. The tale presents Anselmus's struggle to succeed in the competing spheres of bourgeois officialdom and poetic creation. The German Veronika, a young bourgeois girl, stands for his attraction to the former, while Serpentina, who morphs into a green-gold snake, embodies the realm of poetic imagination. Serpentina does not escape stereotyping: she is portrayed as extremely sensuous, and her ability to change her bodily form from that of a snake to a beautiful young woman draws heavily on the archetypal image of the seductive woman and the widely recognized motif of the serpent as a sign of temptation. In contrast, Veronika's purity is suggested by her white dress (II/i, 240).

The profound ambiguity of Hoffmann's story means, however, that such a distinct separation of the bourgeois Veronika and the oriental Serpentina somewhat simplifies the text. Indeed, the spheres inhabited by the two women are not always entirely detached from one another, and Veronika and Serpentina may even be read as two embodiments of the same woman. They share the same striking blue eyes, and Anselmus often cannot tell which of the two has been occupying his daydreams. Veronika has a vision of Anselmus in which he asks her why she pretends to be a snake, and although she appears not to understand the reference, she also experiences visions of Anselmus with Serpentina. Furthermore, like some of the other more prosaic characters in the tale, she approaches moments of artistic inspiration. While Veronika therefore resists absolute typification, it is, however, useful to note the difference in the degrees of independent thought expressed by the two women. Veronika occasionally steps outside the boundaries drawn for girls of her age and class, most notably when she engages in magic in an attempt to secure Anselmus as her husband. Ultimately, though, she reverts to more typically bourgeois behaviour, becomes passive, and relies on male admiration and a husband's status in order to complete her happiness. The distinctions made between Veronika and Serpentina therefore relate not so much to two entirely separate characters as to two types of female behaviour, passive and active, which correspond to Hoffmann's characterization of the unimaginative bourgeois woman and the Romantic oriental woman respectively.

Serpentina and Veronika may have the same romantic goal, but their motivation and methods are different. Martha B. Helfer contextualizes Serpentina in the tradition of the young girl subjected to paternal demand, claiming that she is conspicuously controlled by Lindhorst, who is the judge of whether or not Anselmus's work merits the prize of Serpentina's dowry, the golden pot.[47] This reading can be contested, however. Serpentina is neither passive nor relegated to the silence of the private sphere, demonstrating evidence of independent thought when she ultimately chooses to help Anselmus in his quest. His success is dependent upon her help, and it can be assumed that she offers this help only on her own terms, as other suitors fail in the task which Anselmus undertakes. While these men flounder in ignorance of their failure, Serpentina vocally urges Anselmus to have faith in her so that they can ultimately be together. Serpentina also claims that Lindhorst's story, which she narrates to Anselmus to help him in his task, is partly her own:

> [...] ich bin in diesem Augenblick nur da, um dir mein lieber Anselmus Alles und Jedes aus tiefem Gemüte, aus tiefer Seele haarklein zu erzählen, was dir zu wissen nötig, um meinen Vater ganz zu kennen und überhaupt recht deutlich einzusehen, was es mit ihm *und mit mir* für eine Bewandtnis hat.
>
> [I am here at this moment, my dear Anselmus, only to tell you, from the bottom of my heart, from the depths of my soul, everything you need to know, down to the smallest detail, in order to realize who my father is, and to understand quite distinctly how matters stand with him *and me.*] (II/i, 288; *GT*, 53, my emphasis)

In contrast, Veronika's love is transitory and based on her desire to become the fashionable wife of a Councillor. When Anselmus fails to attain this rank, Veronika agrees to marry the only other suitable bachelor in the tale, an official named Heerbrand, a change that does not in the least affect her vision of happiness, for 'she has wedded herself to a role and not to an individual human being'.[48] Unlike Serpentina, she does not exercise any real choice, and even her one transgressive act, when she practises magic in order to win Anselmus's love, is paradoxically motivated by a desire to conform. Hoffmann's satirical treatment of Veronika and Heerbrand's marriage of convenience is clear in his description of their prosaic engagement, which must be finalized before the soup gets cold. This contrasts with the Romantic vision of bliss contained in the image of Anselmus and Serpentina, united in Atlantis. While *Der goldene Topf* references the stereotypes of both wife and muse, Hoffmann nevertheless gives the oriental muse a degree of agency conspicuously lacking in her German mirror image.

Klein Zaches, genannt Zinnober

The narrative *Klein Zaches, genannt Zinnober* features three unmarried women: Candida, the daughter of a professor of Natural Science; the canoness Rosenschön; and the Indian princess Balsamine. Of these, Rosenschön is by far the most complex character as, masked beneath her respectable interior, she hides her true identity: a fairy named Rosabelverde from the mythical oriental world of Dschinnistan, land of the *Arabian Nights.* In keeping with Hoffmann's tendency to merge Germanic cultural influences with his fictional oriental creations, the name Dschinnistan was probably inspired by both Wieland and Novalis. Wieland published a collection of fairy tales named *Dschinnistan* (1786–89); furthermore, this collection included a tale named *Lulu oder die Zauberflöte* [*Lulu or The Magic Flute*], a 'pseudo-oriental genie-type of tale' that inspired the plot for Mozart's *Die Zauberflöte* (1791).[49]

Hoffmann directed performances of *Die Zauberflöte* in Dresden and his enthusiasm for Mozart is well known. Meanwhile, 'Klingsohrs Märchen' ['Klingsohr's Fairy Tale'], an embedded story in Novalis's *Heinrich von Ofterdingen*, includes a female character named Ginnistan. She is the nursemaid of both Eros and Fabel [Fable] and accordingly she introduces erotic pleasure and promotes creativity, notably when a writer in the story asks for her help. Dschinnistan/Ginnistan thus stands for the exotic, for feminized desire, and for poetry in the literary imagination.[50]

An ambivalent figure, Rosabelverde conforms to certain predominant stereotypes about oriental women, while simultaneously undermining both the bourgeois and the Romantic feminine ideals. Rosabelverde is in many ways a representative of the Orient as it is imagined by Romantic writers: she is beautiful and sensuous, and, most importantly, in touch with nature. The Romantic philosopher Gotthilf Heinrich Schubert, whose work Hoffmann admired, wrote in 1814 of a connection between oriental people and nature, stating that the language of flowers is 'in den Morgenländern zu Hause' [natural to Orientals].[51] This primordial connection to the natural world is observed in *Klein Zaches, genannt Zinnober* when Rosabelverde strolls through the forest listening to the language of the trees, bushes, and streams, and conversing with exotic birds. Moreover, her beauty is described as eternal and unchanging, suggesting a Romantic ideal unaffected by the everyday world, and her mysterious behaviour and suspected involvement in the dark arts mean that she is viewed as a potentially dangerous element in an otherwise carefully regulated society. Nevertheless, her determination to remain independent and her ability to control the ways in which men respond to her provide a striking contrast both to the German Candida, who is a bride twice before the story ends, and to the faraway princess Balsamine, who never appears in her own right and therefore has little bearing on the progression of events.

As a fairy from Dschinnistan, Rosabelverde is part of a group treated first with suspicion, and then aggression, by the authorities overseeing Prince Paphnutius's Enlightenment regime. Hoffmann's criticism of the Enlightenment in this text is aimed at utilitarianism and rationalistic thought, as Paphnutius is unimpressed by poetry and wishes to order and control his subjects, who had been allowed to develop freely in accordance with natural law during his father's reign. That cornerstone of Enlightenment thought so important from Lessing onwards — tolerance — is sadly lacking under the rule of Paphnutius and his reactionary adviser, Andres. One of Andres's first suggestions is that the fairies must be removed from the land and sent back to Dschinnistan, in order that the irrational arts they seem to encourage, such as magic and poetry, might be forgotten in the name of progress. His language when referring to the fairies and the *Arabian Nights* reflects a deep-seated fear of the oriental Other: he thrice claims that the fairies and their behaviour are dangerous, he declares them 'Feinde der Aufklärung' [enemies of the Enlightenment] (III, 545) and, by association, enemies of the state, and he emphasizes their threatening foreignness when he tells Paphnutius, 'daß sich verschiedene von diesen gefährlichen Personen in Ihrem eignen lieben Lande hier ganz in der Nähe Ihres Pallastes angesiedelt haben und allerlei Unfug treiben' [that several of these dangerous people have settled in your own beloved country, very close to your palace here, and are getting up to all sorts of mischief] (III, 544). The new patriarchal regime cannot tolerate dissidence, and as a female oriental, Rosabelverde is particularly troubling. Her neighbours accuse her of practising witchcraft and call for a trial, while the authorities plan to allow some of the fairies to remain behind, but only on the condition that they either marry or become usefully productive members of society. The new government, therefore, makes the same demands of the fairies that wider society makes of German women, attempting to control them and ascribe to them a functional value. Even when Rosabelverde assumes a disguise, changing her name to its Germanic variant, Rosengrünschön, she is asked to modify this name so that it might be better received in the new society. Accordingly, it is shortened to Rosenschön, 'denn in diesem Namen sei doch noch einiger Verstand und ein Ahnherr möglich' [for this name at least still had some sense, and carried the possibility of a forefather] (III, 540–41). Finally, influential men try to efface her altogether, by simply sidelining her existence with a claim that Dschinnistan is an imaginary realm. This statement is made despite the contradictory research of court advisers who have studied Dschinnistan and, predictably, provide proof that it is an inferior country, 'ohne Kultur, Aufklärung, Gelehrsamkeit' [without culture, Enlightenment, or erudition] (III, 547). Fear of Rosabelverde manifests itself in the patriarchal attempts to control her movements, to dictate her name, and finally to dominate her by understanding and undermining her origins, as exemplified by the Baron Prätextatus von Mondschein's frustrated efforts to research her family tree.

Rosabelverde emerges as an intelligent and independent individual, however, as she resists and even reverses attempts by powerful men to dictate her fate. While some of her actions are arguably misguided, they dominate the action and provide a critical insight into relations between the sexes and the attitudes shaping these. Rosabelverde refuses to capitulate to the demands of the new prince, who has outlawed magic. Instead, she uses her magical powers to persuade him to grant her immunity from his 'Aufklärungsedikt' [Enlightenment Edict], and she is so successful in this enterprise that he offers her a very favourable position overseeing the best diocese in the land. Far from a malevolent force, Rosabelverde not only uses her magic to help herself but is moved by piety and pity to improve the situation of the eponymous Zaches, a physically deformed boy who resembles a mandrake and has difficulty in walking and talking. Her magic spell does not alter his form or ability, but rather others' perceptions of him, so that he is given credit for the talents and achievements of other characters. While she ultimately admits that this is a flawed undertaking, because it fails to transform Zaches on the inside, Rosabelverde's spell becomes the central focus of the plot. The spell not only galvanizes the lovelorn poet Balthasar into action but, by distorting perspectives, it reveals certain gender-related prejudices in early nineteenth-century Germany. Candida, the object of Balthasar's love, is one of the characters duped by the spell and mistakenly praises Zaches for the writing and performance of a poem that is, in fact, created by Balthasar. As a result, she falls in love with Zaches, now known as Zinnober, and they are engaged to be married. As high-ranking officials also come under the effect of the spell, Zinnober is given a prestigious position and is eventually knighted. As a result, Candida's father, Mosch Terpin, who is only partly affected by the spell and is aware of Zaches's physical shortcomings, encourages the marriage as it may in turn lead to professional gains for him: 'Er ist des Fürsten Liebling, wird immer höher steigen — höher hinauf, und ist mein Schwiegersohn!' [He's the Prince's favourite, he's coming up in the world and keeps climbing higher, and he'll be my son-in-law!] (III, 598). Terpin views his daughter's upcoming marriage in terms of its professional and social currency, with little regard for her personal happiness. Rosabelverde's spell, then, traditionally viewed by critics as an unfortunate mistake,[52] is also a means by which Hoffmann exposes and satirizes the parental ambition that turns daughters into pawns.

When compared to both Candida and the absent Balsamine, Rosabelverde's character functions as a critical response to the treatment of German women, as well as to the generic Romantic view of the East as a faraway land of poetic inspiration. Not only does this text criticize the roles ascribed to bourgeois women by Hoffmann's contemporaries, but it also questions the value of the untouchable muse for poetic innovation. Rosabelverde occupies the middle ground between the submissive wife/daughter and the intangible, timeless muse represented by Candida and Balsamine respectively. Candida is an ambivalent character, for although she is for the most part silent, and plays a secondary role to the male characters Mosch Terpin, Balthasar, and Zaches, she is not entirely unsympathetic or one-dimensional. She certainly conforms to the model of the unthreatening fiancée with a limited intellectual capacity: she has forgotten what she has learned from her rudimentary reading of German literature, and her creative skills amount to writing the laundry list in a clear and legible hand. Nevertheless, she is no Christina (*Der Artushof*), she does not affect false sensibilities by sighing for effect, and although she lacks a poetic disposition, she does possess 'ein tiefes inniges Gefühl' [a deep and heartfelt sensibility] (III, 566) and a sense of humour. The chief target of Hoffmann's criticism is not so much Candida herself as the male reaction to her. Balthasar, as his friend Fabian rightly points out, ignores Candida's rather prosaic yet pleasant nature and instead places her into the category of poetic muse. Typically of the aspiring poet, Balthasar does not base his response on the (minimal) interaction he has with Candida, but rather internalizes an inaccurate image of her to aid his own poetic development. Like Nathanael, he imagines that his beloved has understood his very essence, and even when he cannot bring himself to meet her eyes, he feels her gaze burning in *his* heart. His response to her is in fact a response to his own artistic ambitions, as is clear from his exclamation: 'fühlte ich nicht an dem Druck ihrer Hand meine Seligkeit?' [didn't I feel my own salvation at the touch of her hand?] (III, 576). While Fabian is sensitive to the process shaping Balthasar's relationship to Candida, his own response is even more reductive, as he describes her in diminutive terms as 'des Professors niedliches Töchterlein' [the Professor's sweet little daughter] (III, 556).

Rosabelverde, on the other hand, is presented neither as a prospective wife, nor as a daughter; she does not serve to flatter any male romantic or poetic ambition, and in her interaction with men she emerges as either the superior party or, at the least, as an equal. In her confrontation with the wise magus Prosper Alpanus, who works to break her spell, Rosabelverde is neither silenced nor forced to resort to seduction to win his respect. Moreover, she rejects his claim to dominance. When he tells her that in entering his home, she has come entirely under his power, her response is spirited: 'in Ihrer Gewalt, Herr Doktor? — Törichte Einbildung!' [in your power, Doctor? — What a foolish notion!] (III, 607). A battle of wits and magic follows, in which the pair ultimately recognize each other as worthy opponents, and even though Rosabelverde admits in the end that her spell was misguided, she does not lose Alpanus's respect. This respect also arises in part from Alpanus's admiration of Rosabelverde's education thus far. The link between the oriental woman and the natural world is reflected in Rosabelverde's formative years, spent in Dschinnistan where she could develop spiritually and intellectually in accordance with her own will, unrestricted by the social guidelines set out for her European counterparts. This is a stereotypical portrayal of an unfettered existence that is positively coded in Romantic constructions of the Orient to illustrate the apparent artistic freedom to be found in the East.[53] Nevertheless, it is also important in an analysis of Rosabelverde's role in highlighting gender relations in Hoffmann's Germany. Her lack of familial and sexual relationships with men allows her to retain her own voice and to remain independent of male influence, and in this way she provides a critical counterpart to Candida, who eventually marries Balthasar.

In terms of Hoffmann's response to the Romantic muse, a comparison between Rosabelverde and Balsamine is useful in indicating his ambivalence. Prosper Alpanus first mentions Balsamine in conversation with Balthasar, explaining that he fell in love with her two thousand years prior to the events of the narrative. In the parable of *Klein Zaches, genannt Zinnober*, Balsamine represents the oriental ideal that might transform western poetry. The rejuvenation of European poetry sought in the East is based on an ancient, eternal India, unchanged by time, and this ideal is personified in Balsamine, who has been asleep for two thousand years. Furthermore, her image inspires a magician living in Germany, and the symbolic use of magic to represent poetry as a means of defeating empiricism is at the heart of this text. In this sense, Balsamine represents the Romantic model later criticized by Edward Said when he writes:

> Friedrich Schlegel and Novalis, for example, urged upon their countrymen, and upon Europeans in general, a detailed study of India because, they said, it was Indian culture and religion that could defeat the materialism and mechanism (and republicanism) of Occidental culture. And from this defeat would arise a new, revitalized Europe [...] But what mattered was not so much Asia as Asia's *use to* modern Europe.[54]

Alpanus's claim that poetry was the foundation of their love seems to bear out this viewpoint. Furthermore, Balsamine fits Spivak's model of the subaltern: she remains unseen throughout the narrative, and even when Alpanus hears from her it is through a male intermediary, the magician Lothos. Despite Alpanus's claim to love Balsamine, it is Lothos's voice that calls him back to India. His disappearance over a flaming rainbow at the conclusion of the story further suggests Hoffmann's scepticism towards a wholesale acceptance of the Indic ideal, as he self-consciously draws attention to the fictitious nature of the happy ending.[55] An investment in the intangible oriental muse as a means of creative inspiration is at best an uncertain method, and Alpanus's complete disappearance from the German setting serves to highlight this point. Rosabelverde, however, remains in Germany, where she consistently resists attempts to efface magic, and transforms her appearance in order to survive the new regime. In this way, she undermines the stereotype of the eastern woman as distant and eternally unchanging. Hoffmann therefore not only presents an independent oriental woman as a critical lens through which to view attitudes to young German girls, but uses Rosabelverde as a way of questioning the value of the distant muse, who can be associated with oriental mystery in German Romanticism. These aspects of the text work in parallel with the much-discussed critical reaction to the Enlightenment for which *Klein Zaches* is already famed.

Die Irrungen/Die Geheimnisse

Like *Klein Zaches*, the double narrative *Die Irrungen/Die Geheimnisse* centres on mistaken identity, with an oriental woman at the heart of the confusion.[56] A Greek princess travels to Berlin to find Teodoros Capitanaki, the Greek prince destined to be her husband. Once in Germany, she mistakes the hapless Baron Theodor von S. for the prince, who, she hopes, will lead the 1820s Greek revolution and free her people from Ottoman rule. The Baron falls in love with her without, however, managing to glimpse her face or find out her name, and so he becomes equally confused about her identity. The resulting chaotic narrative provides a comical yet critical insight into the assumptions made when the male gaze fixes on the seemingly mysterious oriental female. Moreover, this gaze is reversed as the princess expresses her own views about the Baron and Berlin, in a rare example of a direct female voice in Hoffmann's work.

The Baron's attraction to the princess is largely based on male-constructed stereotypes which she promptly rejects. A major source of the comedy in these tales is the Baron's tendency to become entangled in his own daydreams and draw the most fantastical conclusions from the events of his everyday life. This behaviour characterizes his response to the princess, as he is attracted to her mysterious nature, coded as both Greek and oriental in the tale, and he nurtures a belief that they are linked by fate despite never having spoken to her. His first, indirect, encounter with her comes when he discovers a bundle of letters she has written and stored in a blue purse. Along with the letters is a yellow ribbon with Chinese-style characters written on it, and a bottle of rose oil. These exotic items serve to increase the Baron's curiosity. When he reads her letters and discovers her involvement in magic, he is further drawn in, and his enchantment is, typically, described as both a wonderful and a dangerous feeling: 'diese Spannung [mußte] bis zum halben Wahnsinn steigen, als er sich selbst in den Zauberkreisen gefangen sah, die das Blättlein, oder vielmehr jenes unbekannte Wesen, der es angehörte, um ihn gezogen' [Now this tension climbed to fever pitch as he saw himself caught in the magic circle that the pages, or rather that unknown being to whom they belonged, had drawn around him] (v, 472). Throughout the stories, the Baron treats the princess much like a Romantic muse, thinking of her as his 'Engelsbild' [angel] (v, 462), even though he cannot see her face beneath her veil. She is 'der Gegenstand seines Sehnens und

Hoffens' [the object of his yearning and his hopes] (v, 497), and he ascribes to her characteristics that he has imagined, based only partly on what he knows of her. His idealized Greek, a 'Himmelskind aus dem fernen Götterlande' [heavenly child from the faraway home of the gods] (v, 473) in fact has a 'Turandotsblick' [gaze of Turandot] (v, 495), but the Baron is not deterred by details as he constructs an image based on his own sensibilities. Following this, he attempts to woo the princess using time-honoured traditions, which end in comical failure as he misjudges the situation on each occasion. His piano-playing in the Fuchs Konditorladen does not, as he hopes, stir up passionate feeling in the princess, and when he rides past her home in order to display his superior horsemanship, to his chagrin he is thrown from his saddle. Each of these incidents serves to prove, however, that his infatuation with the princess is in fact an infatuation with himself, as he feels compelled to display imagined talents that hold no relevance for her.

Through the male protagonists, Hoffmann creates the most striking parody of the relationship between artist and muse in his entire oeuvre. The real-life Hoffmann and the Baron are linked by their shared name, Theodor, and *Die Geheimnisse* pushes this self-reflexive style to new heights, featuring Hoffmann as a character (whose name is shortened to Hff), trying to track down his protagonists so that he can conclude his tale. In the process, he also falls in love with the Greek princess. Hff's infatuation begins when he reads a poem written by the Greek princess. In this way, like a more extreme Nathanael, the author falls in love with his own creation twice over, admiring not only his own character but also the poem which, he is careful to remind us, in fact comes from his own pen. In describing this incident, Hoffmann the author claims that Hff the character's emotional reaction follows a set pattern, common to all male artists searching for inspiration. The love arises from a lack of passion in real life, but the female character is soon forgotten once her essence has been captured in words: 'Eine Frau mag es aber wohl gleichgültig ansehen, wie ein geistiges weibliches Wesen nach dem andern, in das der schriftstellerische Gemahl verliebt gewesen, geschrieben, gedruckt und dann mit behaglicher Beruhigung gestellt wird in den Bücherschrank' [A wife may well look on with indifference as one angelic female being after the other, with whom the husband, an author, has been in love, is written down, printed and then with comfortable ease is filed away in the bookshelf] (v, 525). This blunt statement summarizes the muse's purpose in serving the writer's need. The mystery surrounding the princess, however, means that it is not so easy for Hff to write about her, and his fascination increases as he strives in vain to communicate in written words the beauty that he senses in his heart (v, 524–25). Röder's observation that the European male is excited by the elusive quality of the oriental woman is pertinent to this text, which perfectly illustrates the motivation for the male interest: 'das erotische Rätsel "Weib" und gar erst "orientalisches Weib" zu lüften' [uncovering the erotic mystery of 'woman' and, moreover, of 'the oriental woman'].[57]

The Greek princess, however, forms her own opinions about Berlin and the Baron, and rather than passively accepting his advances, she refuses to compromise her ambition of finding a man capable of leading the Greek army. A significant portion of the story is expressed in her voice, through the letters she has written to a friend named Chariton. This narrative device has its roots in what Srinivas Aravamudan terms 'Enlightenment Orientalism', a literary movement which, among other things, aimed to '[interrogate] settled assumptions' about European culture.[58] One way of achieving this aim is the employment of an outsider's perspective to criticize the established norms of western society, and the eighteenth-century form of the epistolary novel proved a popular means. Mme de Graffigny's *Lettres d'une Péruvienne* [*Letters from a Peruvian Woman*] (1747) provides a striking example of a female outsider commenting on French society, and Hoffmann's princess falls into this tradition for, like Graffigny's protagonist Zilia, she will not relinquish her attachment to a lover from her homeland in order to remain with a western man whom she cannot love. The princess's letters reveal her thoughts on modern Berlin, and these are unequivocally negative. The city appears to her as cold, deserted and lifeless, and the fashion of the time does not fare any better. It is 'häßlich' [ugly] and 'abscheulich' [horrible], overcoats are cut in an odd fashion, and strangest of all are the top hats: 'die Kopfbedeckung, die aus einer cylinderförmigen Mütze aus steifem Filz mit einem Rande besteht und die man "Hut" nennt' [they cover their heads with a cylindrical cap made of stiff felt with a brim, and they call it a 'hat'] (v, 469–70). Overall, Berlin emerges as a superficial and alienating place, where outer appearances are accorded more value than human relationships.

When dealing with the Baron, the princess emerges as a much more spirited character than her German counterparts. This effect is increased by the juxtaposition of her thoughts and actions with those of the fashionable women of high society. Directly following a letter in which the princess expresses her doubts about the Baron's identity, suggesting that he may not be the hero she had desired, the reader is treated to the views of Frau von G., an elegant tea party hostess. Her thoughts on the Baron are much more complimentary, and are largely based on his social credentials: 'Es ist ein herrlicher Jüngling, voller Verstand, hinreißender Bildung und dabei von einer Fantasie und einem seltnen Geschmack im Anzuge, daß ich ihn schmerzlich vermisse in meinem Zirkel' [He is a marvellous young man, with much sense, striking accomplishment, and, as well as all that, possessed of imagination and an exceptional taste in dress, so that I miss him greatly in my circle] (v, 530). The Jewish-German Amalia Simson is a more obvious counterpart to the mysterious Greek, as suggested when the Baron momentarily mistakes her for the princess. Amalia's intentions regarding the Baron, however, are quite different from those of the princess: she hopes to find a husband, and although the Baron had previously courted and rejected her, she renews her advances, behaviour partly explained by the fact that she is now ageing and therefore her search for a husband is becoming more urgent. Amalia engages in hypocritical behaviour to attain her goal. Having publicly scorned the Baron for his failed attempt to travel to Greece, she later asks him to tell her about the trip, affecting amazement when he does so. This strategy does not fail to flatter his vanity, and his admiration for Amalia begins to return. In contrast, when he finally meets the princess, she silences him when he attempts a clichéd romantic address, and barely listens when he redoubles his efforts. Rather, she informs him of her requirements: a brave man to lead the masses to victory. As it becomes clear that the Baron is not this man, the princess returns to Greece without him. Her refusal to engage in hackneyed courting rituals and to compromise her ambitions for the sake of making a respectable match imply Hoffmann's criticism of the Berlin ladies keen to increase their social standing by association with a man whose only obvious attribute is his aristocratic title.

Conclusion

Many of the key stereotypes traditionally associated with the Orient in the years leading up to, and during, the Romantic era are notably reduced in Hoffmann's portrayal of the oriental woman. Hoffmann follows the work of writers such as Novalis and Arnim whose presentation of oriental otherness is tempered by the suggestion that at least some of the differences might be viewed positively, or that they might afford new opportunities for revising long-held opinions. On the whole, the characterization of Serpentina, Rosabelverde, and the Greek princess does not propagate stereotypes designed to entrench European superiority. On the contrary, Hoffmann's female oriental characters provoke reflections on the situation of German women and their treatment at the hands of their fathers, their prospective husbands, and male artists. They react against convention and resist domination, and in doing so they cast light on the arguably inferior situation of their German equivalents. Furthermore, in describing fraught relations between the sexes, Hoffmann often makes German men the target of his humour, for example when Mosch Terpin and the Baron Theodor von S. are shown to be motivated by self-interest and vanity respectively. While Hoffmann's German women conform to social expectation, he does not, generally speaking, depict them as the feminine ideal, and the conventions surrounding the construction of the muse are undermined. The investment in an unattainable woman can lead to delusion and poor judgement, and is often exposed as a manifestation of the male ego. Hoffmann does not simply conflate the imaginative construction of the muse and that of the Orient in order to inspire a creative engagement with the East that essentially reduces the Orient to an empty cipher. Instead, he brings oriental females into a German setting in order to 'rethink the Self through the other', removing their inferior status and thereby bringing nineteenth-century gender relations and the flaws of artistic practice into sharp relief.[59]

Notes to Chapter 3

1. This chapter is a longer and substantially revised version of my previously published book chapter, 'Who is the Subaltern? A Consideration of the "Oriental Woman" in the Work of E.T.A. Hoffmann', in *Bonds and Borders: Identity, Imagination and Transformation in Literature*, ed. by Rebecca DeWald and Dorette Sobolewski (Newcastle: Cambridge Scholars Publishing, 2011), pp. 19–28. Published with the permission of Cambridge Scholars Publishing.
2. Hoffmann, *Die Serapionsbrüder*, IV, 1114.
3. For a differently focused discussion of this episode, see Jürgen Barkhoff, 'Female Vampires, Victimhood, and Vengeance', in *Women and Death: Representations of Female Victims and Perpetrators in German Culture 1500–2000*, ed. by Helen Fronius and Anna Linton (Rochester, NY: Camden House, 2008), pp. 128–43 (pp. 133–41). Barkhoff reads the comment as an important frame for Hoffmann's narrative about a female vampire figure, 'Vampirismus' (the name later

attributed by critics), which follows the friends' discussion. According to Barkhoff, this tale also 'destabilizes the dominant gender discourses of [the] time' (p. 141) by revealing a vampiric woman to be a victim of a male order, rather than a monster with diabolical agency.

4. See Deborah Epstein Nord, *Gypsies and the British Imagination, 1807–1930* (New York: Columbia University Press, 2006) and Nicholas Saul, *Gypsies and Orientalism in German Literature and Anthropology of the Long Nineteenth Century* (London: Legenda, 2007).
5. Epstein Nord, p. 3.
6. See Sarah Colvin, *The Rhetorical Feminine: Gender and Orient on the German Stage, 1647–1742* (Oxford: Clarendon Press, 1999).
7. Ibid., p. 29.
8. Ibid., p. 283.
9. Richard King similarly notes: 'Just as the myth of India has been constructed as the "other" (i.e. as "not-West") to the West's own self-image, women have been defined as "not-male" or other in relation to normative patriarchal paradigms.' See King, 'Orientalism, Hinduism and Feminism', in *Orientalism: A Reader*, ed. by A. L. Macfie (Edinburgh: Edinburgh University Press, 2000), pp. 336–42 (p. 338).
10. Gayatri Chakravorty Spivak, 'Can the Subaltern Speak?', in *Marxism and the Interpretation of Culture*, ed. by Cary Nelson and Lawrence Grossberg (London: Macmillan, 1988), pp. 271–313.
11. Ibid., p. 287, and Axel Dunker, 'Die schöne Insulanerin: Kolonialismus in E.T.A. Hoffmanns Südsee-Erzählung *Haimatochare*', *DVjs*, 76 (2002), 386–402 (p. 401).
12. This is a long tradition, and Colvin notes its existence in the early modern German states: 'women, blacks and Turks are rhetorically related groups for early modern writers: inconstancy, devilishness, and the triumph of passion over reason are ideas associated with all three' (Colvin, p. 285).
13. Meg Merrilies's magical prophesying could fall under the latter category.
14. Ulrike Stamm, 'Die hässliche Orientalin: Zu einem Stereotyp in Reiseberichten des 19. Jahrhunderts', in *Orientdiskurse in der deutschen Literatur*, ed. by Klaus-Michael Bogdal (Bielefeld: Aisthesis, 2007), pp. 141–62.
15. Lynne Thornton, *Women as Portrayed in Orientalist Painting* (Paris: ACR, 1994), p. 4.
16. Lynne Thornton, 'Frauenbilder: Zur Malerei der "Orientalisten"', in *Europa und der Orient 800–1900*, ed. by Gereon Sievernich and Heinrich Budde (Berlin: Bertelsmann Lexikon, 1989), pp. 342–55 (p. 342).
17. Wilhelm Heinrich Wackenroder, *Ein wunderbares morgenländisches Märchen von einem nackten Heiligen*, in *Werke und Briefe*, ed. by Gerda Heinrich (Berlin: Union Verlag, 1984), pp. 304–08 (p. 304), and Heinrich von Kleist, *Das Käthchen von Heilbronn*, in *Werke und Briefe*, ed. by Siegfried Streller, 4 vols (Berlin: Aufbau, 1978), II, 122–237 (p. 128).
18. 'Könnt ich dir die Myrthen zeigen | Und der Zeder dunkles Haar! | Führen dich zum frohen Reigen | Der geschwisterlichen Schaar! | Sähst du im gestickten Kleide | Stolz im köstlichen Geschmeide | Deine Freundinn, wie sie war' [If I could show you the myrtles | And the cedars of dark tresses | If I could lead you to the happy throng | Of dancing brothers and sisters | You would see in embroidered dress | Proud in precious jewels | Your friend, as she once was], Novalis, *Schriften: Die Werke Friedrich von Hardenbergs*, ed. by Paul Kluckhohn and Richard Samuel, 4 vols (Stuttgart: Kohlhammer, 1960–1977), I, 234.
19. Achim von Arnim, *Sämtliche Romane und Erzählungen*, ed. by Walther Migge, 3 vols (Munich: Hanser, 1962), II, 568.
20. Stamm notes that the fantasy of the sensual oriental woman is closely bound up with the representation of a patriarchal system that is implicitly approved by male authors. Stamm, p. 142.
21. Ludwig Tieck, *Werke*, ed. by Marianne Thalmann, 4 vols (Munich: Winkler, 1963), II, 152–53.
22. James Hodkinson writes:

> From his encounter with Zulima Heinrich not only hears another song, different from those he has heard hitherto, but learns again that poets in general must listen to and allow space for others' voices: in leaving the castle, withdrawing from the crusaders' songs, Heinrich offers Zulima the space to use hers [...] Heinrich

is embracing more passionately a belief in allowing others the space for self-representation.

(James Hodkinson, 'Moving Beyond the Binary? Christian–Islamic Encounters and Gender in the Thought and Literature of German Romanticism', in *Encounters with Islam in German Literature and Culture*, ed. by James Hodkinson and Jeffrey Morrison (Rochester, NY: Camden House, 2009), pp. 108–27 (p. 118))

23. Tieck, *Werke*, II, 360–551 (p. 404).
24. James Hodkinson, 'Moving Beyond the Binary? Christian–Islamic Encounters and Gender in the Thought and Literature of German Romanticism', in *Encounters with Islam in German Literature and Culture*, ed. by James Hodkinson and Jeffrey Morrison (Rochester, NY: Camden House, 2009), pp. 108–27.
25. Birgit Röder, '"Fort in die Welt! — nach Konstantinopel!" Das Orientbild im literarischen Werk E.T.A. Hoffmanns', *GLL*, 64:4 (2011), 501–20.
26. Ibid., p. 514. See above, pp. 63–66, for a discussion of the colonial gaze and its relation to the oriental body.
27. Axel Dunker, 'Die schöne Insulanerin: Kolonialismus in E.T.A. Hoffmanns Südsee-Erzählung *Haimatochare*', *DVjs*, 76 (2002), 386–402. Hoffmann's story is at least partly based on real-life voyages of discovery, and when writing the tale he appealed to his friend, the botanist and writer Adalbert von Chamisso, for factual details relating to the ship name and the insect among other things. Chamisso was appointed botanist on board the *Rurik* during a Russian expedition to the Pacific in 1821. See Anneliese W. Moore, 'Hawaii in a Nutshell: E.T.A. Hoffmann's *Haimatochare*', *Hawaiian Journal of History*, 12 (1978), 13–27, for detailed background information.
28. Dunker, p. 401.
29. Thomas Klinkert and Weertje Willms, 'Romantic Gender and Sexuality', in *Romantic Prose Fiction*, ed. by Gerald Gillespie, Manfred Engel, and Bernard Dieterle (Amsterdam and Philadelphia: John Benjamins Publishing Company, 2008), pp. 226–48 (p. 236).
30. Sally A. Winkle, *Woman as Bourgeois Ideal: A Study of Sophie von La Roche's Geschichte des Fräuleins von Sternheim and Goethe's Werther* (New York: Peter Lang, 1988), p. 42.
31. An exception, of course, is the articulate Clara, but she does not escape being called a lifeless automaton by her fiancé, in an ironic episode.
32. Klinkert and Willms, p. 231.
33. *Kritische Friedrich-Schlegel-Ausgabe*, ed. by Ernst Behler, 35 vols (Munich: Ferdinand Schöningh/ Zurich: Thomas, 1958-), II (1967), 269.
34. See also Martha B. Helfer, 'The Male Muses of Romanticism: The Poetics of Gender in Novalis, E.T.A. Hoffmann and Eichendorff', *GQ*, 78:3 (2005), 299–319.
35. Elizabeth V. Spelman, *Inessential Woman: Problems of Exclusion in Feminist Thought* (London: The Woman's Press, 1990), p. 30.
36. Winkle, p. ix, and Margarete Kohlenbach, 'Women and Artists: E.T.A. Hoffmann's Implicit Critique of Early Romanticism', *MLR*, 89 (1994), 659–73 (p. 659).
37. Todd Kontje, *German Orientalisms* (Ann Arbor: The University of Michigan Press, 2004), p. 95.
38. Karen Swann, 'Harassing the Muse', in *Romanticism and Feminism*, ed. by Anne K. Mellor (Bloomington and Indianapolis: Indiana University Press, 1988), pp. 81–92 (p. 88). For a more nuanced picture of Novalis's treatment of women, see James Hodkinson, *Women and Writing in the Works of Novalis: Transformation beyond Measure?* (Rochester, NY: Camden House, 2007).
39. Klinkert and Willms, pp. 239–45.
40. See also Kohlenbach, p. 660.
41. Ricarda Schmidt, 'From Early to Late Romanticism', in *The Cambridge Companion to German Romanticism*, ed. by Nicholas Saul (Cambridge: Cambridge University Press, 2009), pp. 21–39 (p. 31).
42. Kohlenbach, p. 673.
43. Schmidt, pp. 31–37.
44. Ibid., p. 31.
45. Birgit Röder, *A Study of the Major Novellas of E.T.A. Hoffmann* (Rochester, NY: Camden House, 2003), p. 87.

46. Ibid.
47. Helfer, pp. 309–11.
48. John Reddick, 'E.T.A. Hoffmann's "Der Goldne Topf" and its "Durchgehaltene Ironie"', *MLR*, 71:3 (1976), 577–94 (p. 584).
49. Burton D. Fisher, *Mozart's 'The Magic Flute'* (Boca Raton, FL: Opera Journeys Publishing, 2001), p. 14.
50. 'Klingsohrs Märchen' appears in the ninth chapter of *Heinrich von Ofterdingen*. Novalis, *Schriften*, I, 290–315. Friedrich A. Kittler foregrounds Ginnistan as an agent of desire: 'Ginnistan plays the part of all female imagoes' (Friedrich A. Kittler, *The Truth of the Technological World: Essays on the Genealogy of Presence*. trans. by Erik Butler (Stanford: Stanford University Press, 2013), p. 4).
51. Gotthilf Heinrich Schubert, *Die Symbolik des Traumes* (Bamberg: C. J. Kunz, 1814; repr. Heidelberg: Lambert Schneider, 1968), p. 27.
52. See Horst S. Daemmrich, *The Shattered Self: E.T.A. Hoffmann's Tragic Vision* (Detroit: Wayne State University Press, 1973), pp. 64–66.
53. See also, for example, Karoline von Günderrode's *Geschichte eines Brahminen* [*Tale of a Brahmin*] (1805). This concludes with a very positive description of a young Indian girl's education as blissfully unconstrained.
54. Edward W. Said, *Orientalism*, 3rd edn (London: Penguin Classics, 2003), p. 115.
55. As Daemmrich writes, 'The imaginative-magic sphere clearly functions as a foil which draws attention to man's plight and folly' (*The Shattered Self*, p. 64).
56. The Greek princess is orientalized by way of her fondness for Constantinople's bazaars, her gaze, which is compared to that of Isis, and her 'Turandotsblick' [gaze of Turandot] (V, 495).
57. Röder, '"Fort in die Welt!" [...]', p. 514.
58. Srinivas Aravamudan, *Enlightenment Orientalism: Resisting the Rise of the Novel* (Chicago: University of Chicago Press, 2012), p. 4.
59. Dorothy M. Figueira, *The Exotic: A Decadent Quest* (Albany: State University of New York Press, 1994), p. 3. Cited in Chen Tzoref-Ashkenazi, 'India and the Identity of Europe: The Case of Friedrich Schlegel', *Journal of the History of Ideas*, 67 (2006), 713–34 (p. 717).

PART II

Cultural Production

CHAPTER 4

Staging the Orient: *Alla Turca* and Indian-Style Music

Heute sah ich im Theater Mozarts Entführung aus dem Serail zum zwanzigsten mal mit demselben Entzücken
[*Today I saw Mozart's* Abduction from the Seraglio *for the twentieth time, with as much delight as ever*].[1]

When Hoffmann's Peregrinus Tyss records in his diary his impressions of Mozart's popular opera, he becomes part of a cultural development that had been growing in Germany immediately prior to and during the Romantic period: the enthusiasm for oriental-style music. This responded first and foremost to political developments in the German-speaking states, where the division between the Christian West and the Islamic East, represented by the Ottoman Empire, remained entrenched in the cultural imagination long after the seventeenth-century threat of Islamic military expansion into Europe had receded. Before the defeat of the Ottomans at the 1683 Siege of Vienna, the long history of Christian–Muslim encounters on the battlefield in the medieval and pre-modern eras had already been punctuated by a series of flashpoints, from the eighth-century Battle of Tours to the culmination of the Reconquista in Granada in 1492. The tenacity of this religious conflict in the public memory long after Vienna is hardly surprising given its duration, and the role of the Austrian capital in deciding the outcome of the conflict lent a special significance to the literary and cultural focus on the Orient in the German-speaking states. As fear of the Turkish armies declined throughout the eighteenth century, the cultural impact of the Ottoman expansion into Europe took hold: the fashion for *turquerie* increased as a result of new access to Turkish culture and music.[2] Todd Kontje traces the development of this trend from its initial influence on fashion to its later effects on music, while Nasser Al-Taee asserts that the eighteenth century saw a 'Western musical infatuation with the Turkish seraglio and the *alla turca* style'.[3] Particularly influential for German portrayals of the old Islamic foe were the popular comic operas of composers who resided in the Habsburg court, such as Christoph Willibald Gluck's 1764 *La Rencontre imprévue* and Joseph Haydn's 1775 *l'incontro improvviso*, both of which portrayed intrigue and abduction in a harem setting.[4] Most famous and successful within this genre, however, was Mozart's *Die Entführung aus dem Serail* of 1782, which Mozart had initially hoped to premiere during the centenary commemoration of the 1683 Austrian victory.[5]

In addition to Turkish influences, German composers and opera-goers were not immune to the attraction of Indian-style music. Gerry Farrell's study of the western reception of Indian music shows that it was closely linked to Romantic artistic ambitions.[6] In attempting to rediscover 'a pristine Hindu past', composers of Indian-style music might further the Romantic aim of searching for a lost paradise.[7] In keeping with Edward Said's theory of Orientalism, Farrell claims that since the eighteenth-century discovery of India as a cultural as well as geographical entity, Indian music has served to inspire romantic exoticism in the West.[8] In general, this brand of one-sided cultural influence took the form of attempts to arrange Indian songs for western musical instruments, and so a westernized version of the Indian style developed, rather than a direct engagement with Indian music itself.[9] As with the study of Sanskrit texts, this trend arrived in Germany via the English-speaking world. Perhaps the most famous example of the Anglophone influence on the German reception of Indian-style music was inspired by the work of the Irish poet Thomas Moore. Under the supervision of Graf Karl von Brühl, director of the Berlin Theatre, Moore's 1817 'Oriental Romance' *Lalla Rûkh* was transformed into a festival production of theatre and song which premiered in Berlin on 27 January 1821. This marked the occasion of a visit by the Grand Duke Nicholas of Russia, who took a lead role in the production alongside his wife, Princess Charlotte of Prussia.[10] The play was accompanied by the music of the Italian Gaspare Spontini, who resided in Berlin and was admired by Hoffmann as a master composer.[11] Two weeks after the premiere the success of the production was marked by a repeat performance, which Hoffmann attended, having tried and failed to procure a ticket for the first showing. Alongside the royal performers, a number of Hoffmann's acquaintances appeared onstage, including Friedrich de la Motte Fouqué in the role of a gentleman from Kashmir and von Brühl as an Arab.[12]

Hoffmann's diaries and personal letters reveal that he was a keen follower and critic of both *alla turca* and Indian-style music. Although this interest continued throughout Hoffmann's creative life, it has gone largely ignored by both literary and music critics.[13] On 25 November 1795 he wrote to his friend Theodor Gottlieb von Hippel, telling of his attendance at a performance of Salieri's *Axur, re d'Ormus* (1788). This *opera buffa* adaptation of Salieri's earlier opera *Tarare* (1787) included such oriental elements as a harem setting, Brahmin priests, and an unrelenting tyrant, and the production moved Hoffmann so much that he expressed a fervent wish to compose such a work himself (I, 41).[14] He was less impressed, however, by Wenzel Müller and Karl Friedrich Hensler's Singspiel *Das Sonnenfest der Braminen* [*The Sun Festival of the Brahmins*], which he saw in December 1795 and judged 'bis zum Überdruß alltäglich' [unrelentingly banal] (I, 45). Gluck's opera *Armide* (1777), featuring the eponymous sorceress from Damascus and her love for the Christian knight Rinaldo, had a more lasting influence, with composer and opera becoming the subject of Hoffmann's first published work of fiction, *Ritter Gluck*, in 1809. In the same year Hoffmann wrote a review of Friedrich Witt's Symphony Number 6 in A Minor, also known as the *Sinfonie turque*, for the *Allgemeine musikalische Zeitung*.[15] Moreover, in his role as theatre director in Dresden and Leipzig, Hoffmann oversaw productions of oriental operas, including André-Ernest-Modeste Grétry's *Zémire et Azor*, an adaptation of the *Beauty and the Beast* tale with Persian characters, in

September 1813. Furthermore, he directed no fewer than six performances of Mozart's *Die Zauberflöte* [*The Magic Flute*] during the Dresden years, and prior to this had even participated in a Bamberg production of the same opera, playing the glockenspiel in a performance in February 1809.[16]

Hoffmann the Composer and the Orient

As a composer and librettist, Hoffmann's work was influenced both thematically and musically by the growing popularity of the Orient on stage. In 1804, the same year as he changed his third forename to Amadeus in homage to Mozart, he began work on a seldom-discussed libretto entitled *Der Renegat* [*The Renegade*], which was, however, never finished. The plot was heavily influenced by *Die Entführung aus dem Serail*, with the only significant change being its setting in Algiers rather than Mozart's Turkey.[17] *Der Renegat* is the story of a Frenchman, St Cyr, whose wife Elisa has been kidnapped by an Algerian crew and is being kept against her will in the harem of the Regent of Algiers. With the help of his pragmatic friend Joseph and the renegade Ebn Ali, a Christian Frenchman by birth who has converted to Islam, St Cyr takes part in a dramatic *Singspiel*, performed to the Regent with the aim of tricking him into giving up Elisa so she can return to the husband she loves. This is as far as the libretto goes in its unfinished state, but similarities to Mozart's opera are clear. Elisa's grief at the separation from her husband, and her refusal to capitulate to the Regent's passions, echo Konstanze's faithful devotion to Belmonte and her rejection of the Pasha Selim. Both works also commence with an aria sung by the European male expressing his desire for a reunion with his beloved, and the theme of using deception to win back the beloved runs through both. The renegade character is another common feature, as is the revelation of kinship between characters that inhabit different cultural milieux. Although Hoffmann's libretto is unfinished, there are suggestions that this revelation is to come when Ebn Ali reveals in an aside his previous name, Bertrand, and hints at a known relationship, possibly familial, with St Cyr. Finally, the passion of the oriental despot for the virtuous European woman is also foregrounded, with a particular peculiarity: the sadness of the female captive makes her all the more desirable to her captor. In Hoffmann's libretto, this theme is exaggerated and the Regent's desires may be read as a parody of those of Mozart's Pasha Selim.[18]

In 1809 an opportunity to set an oriental story to music arose when the Bamberg theatre director Julius von Soden asked Hoffmann to write the music for his 'indisches Melodram' [Indian melodrama], *Dirna*. This composition has been noted as one of Hoffmann's most successful musical works before the opera *Undine* (1814).[19] Following its premiere in Bamberg in October 1809, *Dirna* was played twice more in the city and was later performed in Salzburg in March and July of 1811, and in Donauwörth in autumn 1812.[20] Like *Lalla Rûkh*, the inspiration came from a source in English.[21] Soden was influenced by the travel writing of the Englishman John Henry Grose, who had sailed to Bombay in 1750 in the service of the East India Company.[22] His book, *A Voyage to the East Indies* (1757), was translated into French a year after its first publication, and then into German by Georg Friedrich

Casimir Schad in 1775. Soden used an extract of Schad's translation for his libretto, which he claimed was based on a real incident. It is the story of an Indian woman, Dirna, who is kidnapped and raped by the nabob Zami, and subsequently bears him two children. Having been thus dishonoured, she is seen as unfit to return to her husband, unless she sacrifices her children according to the orders of the High Priest. The possibilities for creative oriental colouring are many: the first act is set in an Indian garden and contains an *intermezzo* with dancing girls, and Dirna and her husband visit the temple of the High Priest where a choir of Brahmins sing. Furthermore, in Soden's version Dirna and her children are saved by the arrival of the Great Mogul, who has Zami put in jail and allows Dirna to return to her husband. Between June and September 1809, Hoffmann was preoccupied with writing the music for *Dirna*, and on 11 October 1809 he noted the success of the premiere, at which he was called to the stage to receive his applause.[23]

The *Alla Turca* Style

In order to understand how theatre and opera with oriental themes shaped Hoffmann's musical aesthetics, it is necessary to examine briefly the form the Orient takes in European music. The *alla turca* style popularized by the operas of Gluck and Mozart arose from the challenge of presenting Turkish-style music in the absence of actual Turkish instruments to an audience familiar only with the classical western tradition. The result was a set of oriental signifiers, employed by composers who wished to represent, within the context of traditional European orchestras, the music of the Ottoman military Janissary bands.[24] These signifiers included the use of specific instruments to approximate to the sounds of the Janissaries. Matthew Head's study of Orientalism in Mozart's work has demonstrated how *alla turca* music aimed to represent Ottoman military music without departing from western musical tradition.[25] In the words of A. L. Ringer, 'Western harmonic law prevails', so that 'in Viennese circles exoticism remained an extrinsic rather than an intrinsic phenomenon'.[26] This admittedly orientalist trick of representing the East via a European medium was necessary in order to communicate the composer's intention to his European audience. In general, Turkish music came to be signified by certain instruments, including the bass drum, borrowed directly from the Janissary tradition, the triangle, intended to approximate to the bells of the Turkish crescent, and the piccolo, used to imitate the high-pitched Janissary zurna.[27] Furthermore, this style was characterized by a high volume of sound, indicating on the whole aggression and violence.[28] For example, the overture to *Die Entführung aus dem Serail* introduced the Turkish style in the sections to be played *forte*, in contrast to the more classically traditional, and quieter, style used when European characters appeared onstage.[29] Gerhard Allroggen explains how Hoffmann used the same device in his music for *Dirna*, describing the instrumentation as 'janitscharenmäßig' [like the Janissary bands], for example when the character Zami marches onstage for the first time to a range of instruments including triangles and kettle drums.[30] Over time, these signifiers came to represent not only the Janissary bands, but also Turkey and even more generally, the Orient, as Head notes:

> For some members of a late eighteenth-century Viennese operatic audience, the *alla turca* style of Gluck, Haydn and Mozart was the only source of knowledge about Turkish music. Thus despite its often comic character it possessed a subliminal authority and persuasive power as a representation.[31]

As a result, the style evoked for its audiences the whole, rather than a part of the Ottoman Empire, becoming the 'musikalische Chiffre für den Orient' [musical signifier of the Orient].[32] The sheer prevalence of this style meant that the use of high-pitched pipes, kettle drums, triangles or cymbals became a kind of shorthand for composers wishing to communicate an image of the East. Moving away from its originally intended aim of specifically representing Ottoman military music, the mere sound of the kettle drum, piccolo, triangle, or similar instruments was enough to prompt an imaginative journey to the Orient for eighteenth- and early nineteenth-century audiences.

The literary response to oriental-style music in the Age of Goethe has received little attention in the field of German Orientalism thus far. Commentators have focused on the singing voice of such oriental female characters as Novalis's Zulima and Hoffmann's Zulema, in *Heinrich von Ofterdingen* and *Das Sanctus* respectively, and have noted the general exoticism of oriental singing or music when it appears in literature.[33] In a different way, W. Daniel Wilson reveals how the themes of the above-mentioned *Singspiele* were taken up and adapted in literature towards the end of the eighteenth century.[34] However, the mechanics of how the oriental sound was produced by European musicians, and how writers responded to this trend, have been largely overlooked in literary criticism on Hoffmann until very recently. A noteworthy exception is Irmgard Egger's analysis of the instruments mentioned in the text to reveal the influence of *alla turca* music on both the frame and the embedded narratives of *Das Sanctus*.[35] Egger does not, however, provide details of Hoffmann's extensive interest in the *alla turca* style outside this text.

In Hoffmann's fictional work, the tradition of oriental music established in Vienna is frequently cited. In a few instances, it retains its original meaning of representing the Janissary bands, although these are rarely mentioned directly. As Marie enters the Puppenreich in *Nußknacker und Mausekönig* (1816), she observes a group of apes in military clothing playing Janissary music (IV, 291–92) and the battle she witnesses between the Great Mogul's retinue and the Turkish Janissaries is characterized by the combination of tumultuousness and high-pitched, shrill sounds that European audiences had come to expect from Ottoman military music.[36] By the late eighteenth century, European regimental bands had appropriated Janissary music for their own purposes, and generally included a Turkish percussion section.[37] Furthermore, this style was now also performed for popular entertainment, a development which Hoffmann references in *Die Automate* (1814) and *Die Brautwahl* [*The Choosing of a Bride*] (1819). In the former, Ludwig recalls having attended as a boy a performance by automata portraying the Danzig Arsenal by playing on drums and pipes, while in *Die Brautwahl* Tusmann claims to have seen his beloved Albertine celebrating her marriage by dancing to Janissary drums. Much more common in Hoffmann's stories, however, are references to instruments that are deemed oriental, which in musical terms serve little more than a decorative purpose, but which immediately notify the listener of an oriental theme. These instruments often accompany parades which are not always of a military nature but do signify the presence of oriental characters, in very broad terms. For example, Carota in *Die Königsbraut*, who turns out to be associated with oriental magic, welcomes his guests to his underground palace to the sounds of pipes, drums, and cymbals.[38] *Prinzessin Brambilla* contains a parade of twelve Moors and mysteriously veiled women on unicorns moving to the same type of music, and also refers to the use of the *alla turca* style on stage, when during a *commedia dell'arte* performance, drums, cymbals, and pipes are played as Arlecchino is carried to his throne by Moors.[39] The opening of *Die Bergwerke zu Falun* [*The Mines at Falun*] (1819) situates this music even further east. Members of the East India Company celebrate their return home by playing a sort of hybrid music; an amalgamation of European sounds and a style, one assumes, they have learned in India: violins and oboes mix with pipes and drums. Finally, in *Die Doppeltgänger* [*The Doppelgänger*] (1821), an old gypsy woman plays the triangle, and as her people move about the strains of oriental-style music can be heard. In terms of their responses to these sounds, Hoffmann's characters are representative of the audiences of the time, for they recognize in the instrumental ciphers an invitation to embark upon an imagined voyage to the Orient. This automatic equating of entire heterogeneous cultures to a symbolic few bars of music is observed in Hoffmann's *Das steinerne Herz*, when Willibald hears piping and drumming and makes the correct assumption that the Turkish Ambassador is approaching (III, 326).

Hoffmann's Reviews of Oriental Music

As a musician and critic, Hoffmann was not entirely immune to the sort of effect that the oriental cipher has on his own fictional characters. An enthusiastic response to the type of music intended to evoke images of oriental exoticism appeared in his review of the *Lalla Rûkh* festival pageant, which was published in August Kuhn's journal *Zeitung für Theater und Musik zur Unterhaltung gebildeter, unbefangener Leser* in 1821.[40] This extremely flattering review reveals Hoffmann's susceptibility to the oriental style as a means of transporting the listener to distant lands. He begins with high praise for the production as a whole, claiming that the combination of tableau theatre and poetry was an inspired idea that encourages the artistic imagination in a manner reminiscent of his own Serapiontic principle: 'Die Wirkung glich einem mächtigen Zauber, der den ganzen Sinn befängt und sich, aus unsrem innersten Wesen heraus, wie ein schöner Traum gestaltet, den wir, dem schimmernden Feenreich entrückt, noch lange fortträumen' [The effect was like a powerful magic which captures all the senses and takes its form from our innermost being, like a beautiful dream that we carry on dreaming long after we have been torn away from the shimmering fairy kingdom] (V, 609). As part of a musical culture in which composers attempted to signal the Orient by employing specific instruments, Hoffmann, like his contemporaries, readily obliges on this occasion by imagining a Romantic paradise as soon as he hears what he understands to be Indian music. Upon hearing the section accompanying the 'Fest der Rosen' [The Festival of the Roses], Hoffmann reports, he felt as if he perceived a beautiful cloudless spring day, with gentle winds breezing through the meadows and woods, and the scent of flowers rising into the air in a symbolic representation of the sighs of Romantic longing (v, 610).[41] Furthermore, he picks out specific passages in which the music evokes the Persian and Indian settings. As Lalla Rûkh sets off on her journey to meet her betrothed, Hoffmann notes the playing of 'etwas seltsame indische Musik' [strange Indian music], comprised of flutes, oboes, kettle drums, bells, and even trombones (v, 610). Even instruments firmly within the classical tradition are open to appropriation for an oriental effect, for Hoffmann judges a passage in which strings are played *vibrato* the most appropriate means possible of announcing the character of the Prophet Mohanna (v, 610). Finally, he makes special mention of an *andante* passage in which three sopranos and a tenor sing a melody without words, and his praise of their voices recalls the effect of Serpentina's crystal-like tone: 'Dies Andante, von glockenrein intonierenden Krystalstimmen vorgetragen [...] ist von der erstaunlichsten, wunderbarsten Wirkung' [This *andante,* sung with crystal voices as clear as a bell [...] has the most astounding and wonderful effect] (v, 611).

Hoffmann makes his readers aware at the start of the review that Spontini was obliged to make use of previously composed material in order to finish the whole composition in time for the production. This makes Hoffmann's readiness to fall under the spell of the orientalizing effects particularly interesting, for he was well aware, for example, that the march which opened the pageant had come from an older opera of Spontini's which was not well known in Berlin and was not, therefore, specific to the setting of *Lalla Rûkh.* Nevertheless, he speculates that, had Spontini been given sufficient time to compose a new march especially for the occasion, it would have awoken a wonderfully exotic vision in the minds of the audience (v, 610). This high praise may be partly attributed to attempted flattery of Spontini, who had recently been appointed general music director of the Berlin State Opera. Furthermore, although Hoffmann had welcomed Spontini to Berlin by publishing a *Gruss an Spontini* [*A Greeting for Spontini*] in the 1820 *Vossische Zeitung*, his reviews of the composer's earlier work had been much less complimentary, and he may have wished to emphasize his growing admiration in a favourable review.[42] Nevertheless, this review provides evidence that Hoffmann's response to oriental-style music included an automatic association of India with particular instruments, as well as a leap of the imagination which instantly connected an Indian style to Romantic longing. The music was admittedly enhanced by the spectacle of the pageant, which Hoffmann deemed 'der herrlichste Schmuck eines wahrhaft königlichen Festes' [The most exquisite jewel of a truly majestic festival] (v, 609). However, Hoffmann's willingness to identify the exotic East in music which was not even originally connected to the *Lalla Rûkh* pageant (at least not in its entirety) reveals the power of the oriental cipher for the Romantic imagination. The suggestion of India might arise from an empty cipher, but this is sufficient to provide a way in to the imagined Orient for contemporary audiences.

Despite his ringing praise for Spontini's Indian-style music, Hoffmann was not always so readily persuaded of the merits of employing specific oriental-style instruments to create a particular effect. His 1809 review of Friedrich Witt's *Sinfonie turque* is strongly critical of composers who bring the Turkish percussion section to the concert hall, noting that in this setting, the sound becomes overwhelming rather than impressive (I, 518). Hoffmann frames his discussion within the history of the *alla turca* style and its fortunes in Europe as it became increasingly frequent in theatre productions before finally exploding into the concert hall as a striking feature of a growing number of symphonies. The Witt review reveals Hoffmann's two major objections to this development in instrumental music. First of all, he argues, the concert hall is simply not big enough to accommodate the noise of the bass drums, described here as deafening. Faced with the task of performing purely instrumental pieces, the rest of the orchestra is also likely to be drowned out by the Turkish percussion, a danger which is overcome in the theatre as it is large enough for the bass drum to be played from the furthest corner of the orchestra, and to resonate through a large space. More importantly for an understanding of Hoffmann's musical aesthetics, he sees Turkish music as unsuited to the symphony and, the reader infers, to all instrumental music by extension. Emily Dolan sees Hoffmann's criticism arise from a turbulent period in the history of orchestral music.[43] At the turn of the nineteenth century, new instruments were becoming part of traditional orchestras, orchestras were growing in size, and composers were keener than ever to produce striking effects in their work, sometimes to the detriment of musicality. Consequently music critics tended to focus increasingly on the topic of musical effect. Dolan explains this concept as primarily shaped by instrumentation. In other words, composers aimed to produce musical effect by exploiting the various tones and contrasts of different instruments.[44] One method commonly employed by composers who wished to stir their audiences was an incorporation of the *alla turca* style, which often designated a battle scene in opera because of its military and violent associations.[45] This representative aspect was lost, however, when the same effect moved from the theatre into the instrumental music of the concert halls. Although such effects originated in dramatic musical genres, the influence of opera was such that 'the development of instrumental genres mimicked that of the theater'.[46] The result was a striking effect which was nevertheless detached from its original meaning:

> Like the grandiose plots of French opera, both the military and the Turkish themes excused, indeed necessitated, the use of outlandish orchestration. Trumpet calls, exotic percussion, and even imitation gun fire and cannon roar to conjure distant lands, the horror of war, and the glory of victory. In time, these effects were taken up by composers whose symphonies had no overt military, or indeed, 'programmatic' themes of any sort.[47]

It is this development which seems to cause Hoffmann's main objection to Witt's *Sinfonie turque* and similar compositions. Although he admits that so-called Turkish music is in fact inauthentic, he nevertheless accords it a place in the theatre, where it is played in overtures in order to indicate the character of the piece to come. In this sense it is suited to opera, where it supports the action on stage. In contrast, it is a sign which loses its significance in the concert hall, because it no longer alludes to Turkey, but is intended simply to enhance the enjoyment of the music as a whole.[48] Hoffmann is highly sceptical of this approach, which appeals to audiences who, in his view, have no ear for truly great music: 'Indessen, Hr. W. hat nun auch einmal eine Sinfonie turque mit der großen Trommel und allem Zubehör geschrieben und dadurch dem Geschmack derer gefrönt, die auf diese Weise musikalisch, oder vielmehr unmusikalisch, erschüttert werden wollen' [And now Mr Witt has also composed a Turkish symphony with the kettle drum and all its accoutrements, thereby indulging the taste of all those who wish to have their senses stirred by something musical — or rather, something unmusical.] (I, 519). The effect on the audience is therefore a superficial one, for they are moved by music which has neither a contextual basis nor any genuine feeling, and which aims primarily to entertain. This privileging of the sensual over the spiritual has a detrimental effect on musicality.[49] Egger provides further insight into the reasons for such objections: in addition to the shrillness of the instruments, the *alla turca* style was characterized by frequent changes from the major to the minor key, a method which produced dissonant music with, at least for the audiences of the time, a strangely threatening tone.[50] Essentially, the Orient came to be representative of dissonance in music, and the West with harmony.[51] While relevant for contemporary portrayals of Islam, this was also of significance in the debate about musical effect. Hoffmann's solution to this problem is hinted at in the concluding part of the review, where he praises the *adagio* section in which Witt elects to use instruments for their melodious qualities rather than their popular associations. The result is a pleasant and truly musical passage, of which Hoffmann cannot resist noting, 'selbst der erklärteste Freund der großen Trommel wird es gern geschehen lassen, daß sie diesmal ganz schweigt' [even the most self-proclaimed friend of the kettle drum will be happy to let it remain quiet on this occasion] (I, 520).

Oriental Music and the Romantic Absolute

To understand Hoffmann's position on the separation of content and form as unmusical, an examination of the principles of Romantic art becomes necessary. Birgit Röder succinctly summarizes the goal of Romantic artists thus: 'the central aim of the Romantic project is to capture the Ideal more fully and thereby bring the individual into closer contact with the Absolute'.[52] Artistic representation of the Absolute forms the subject matter of Georg Wilhelm Friedrich Hegel's *Vorlesungen über die Ästhetik* [*Aesthetics: Lectures on Fine Art*] (published 1835), in which he makes a pronouncement on how the Ideal must be achieved.[53] According to Hegel, the Ideal takes the form of a sensuous representation of the Absolute. In Romantic terminology, the Absolute refers to the absolute spirit, or the one Being in which all particulars are subsumed into a greater unity: 'Damit [...] der Geist zu seiner Unendlichkeit gelange, muß er sich ebensosehr aus der bloß formellen und *endlichen* Persönlichkeit zum *Absoluten* erheben' [to attain its infinity the spirit must all the same lift itself out of purely formal and *finite* personality into the *Absolute*].[54] Hegel makes a clear distinction between what he terms *das Absolute* or *die Idee als solche* [*the absolute idea* or the *idea in existence*] and *das Ideal* or *die Idee als das Kunstschöne* [*The Beauty of Art or the Ideal*].[55] As art is by necessity a sensuous mode of representation, thus the artistically produced Ideal cannot actually be the absolute Idea, as this is purely spiritual. The Ideal is the presentation, in reality, of the Idea, and the two must be closely connected: 'das Ideal ist die mit ihrer *Realität* identifizierte Idee' [the Ideal is the Idea identified with its *reality*].[56]

Therefore, because the only means accessible to mankind of perceiving reality are the senses, the sensuous realm cannot be overlooked even in the quest for a greater spiritual unity with the Absolute. This apparent dichotomy is expressed in Hegel as the relationship between form and content. In a true work of art, content is the absolute Idea, and form is its sensuous representation (i.e. in painting, sculpture, music etc.). The Ideal can temporarily overcome the division of the sensuous and the spiritual, thereby pointing to an absolute unity, but in order to do so, there must be a close correspondence between form and content. When these are adequately connected, the Ideal is produced, but the artist must take pains to purify his work of all elements that do not correspond with the absolute Idea. This important task is alluded to in *Lebensansichten des Katers Murr*, when the composer Kreisler shares with the abbot his ideas about art, in particular his view of excessive detail in portraits as tasteless. To illustrate his point, he gives the hypothetical example of religious paintings of the Holy Family dressed in modern style. Such speculation provokes his rhetorical question: 'Würde Euch das nicht als eine unwürdige ja abscheuliche Profanation des Erhabensten erscheinen?' [Would it not seem to you an unworthy, indeed a terrible profanity against the most sublime?] (v, 368). Ultimately, a work of art is a means of revealing the spirit only when it is stripped of superficial, purely sensuous, additions.

Examining the relationship between music and the Absolute, one gets to the core of the Romantic project. It has been widely documented that the Romantics, with Hoffmann at the forefront, championed music as the most Romantic form of art.[57] By deduction, they therefore judged music the best possible artistic means of accessing the Absolute. Hegel places music at the centre of the Romantic arts, while perhaps the most programmatic statement on Romantic music is to be found in Wilhelm Heinrich Wackenroder and Ludwig Tieck's 1797 biography of the fictional musician Joseph Berglinger.[58] While works of art are highly regarded among the Romantics, the Ideal is essentially a means to an end.[59] In Hegel's view, this is what distinguishes Romantic art from Classical art. The latter achieves a perfect representation of the Ideal in its most beautiful form, but for the Romantics, the spiritual quest for the Absolute is privileged over any external object. With this in mind, Hegel makes his famous statement that the principle behind all truly Romantic art is 'absolute Innerlichkeit' [absolute inwardness], in other words, the knowledge that immersion in the physical world is not the path to spiritual truth.[60] In common with the Romantics, Hegel claims that this principle of subjective interiority is central to music.[61] The reason for this is that unlike painters or sculptors, musicians cannot fix their productions into an externally lasting form. Music is not open to lengthy contemplation, but is retained only in the subjective memory, and furthermore, as it is not directly representative of any object, its subject matter must arise within the composer's imagination. For this reason, music is the art most suited to Romantic interiority, as Hoffmann's fictional musicians are apt to comment:

> Unser Reich ist nicht von dieser Welt, sagen die Musiker, denn wo finden wir in der Natur, so wie der Maler und der Plastiker, den Prototypus unsrer Kunst? Der Ton wohnt überall, aber die Töne, das heißt, die Melodien, welche die höhere Sprache des Geisterreichs reden, nur in der Brust des Menschen. (II/ii, 443)[62]

> [Our kingdom is not of this world, the musicians say, because where would we find in nature, as the painters and sculptors do, the prototype of our art? Sound is everywhere, but the musical notes, that is, the melodies, which speak the higher language of the spirit realm, are only in our souls.]

The interior quality of music means it has the potential to lift listeners temporarily above external concerns, as Joseph Berglinger finds when he listens to church music and the present moment seems to fall away.[63] Finally, Hegel's theoretical conceptualization of absolute truth as a final resolution of the conflicts one encounters in the finite realm, and the role of music in this process, finds its literary expression in the following passage from Wackenroder:

> Ein andermal wieder wirkten die Töne eine wunderbare Mischung von Fröhlichkeit und Traurigkeit in seinem Herzen, so daß Lächeln und Weinen ihm gleich nahe war; eine Empfindung, die uns auf unserem Wege durch das Leben so oft begegnet und die keine Kunst geschickter ist auszudrücken als die Musik.[64]

> [Another time, the sounds produced a wondrous mixture of joy and sadness in his heart, so that he wanted both to smile and to cry; a feeling that we often encounter on our journey through life, and which no art can express so well as music.]

Romantic dualism is temporarily conquered, and absolute unity comes within reach as music resonates in the breast of the listener.

Hoffmann's position on the role of music in fulfilling Romantic ambitions becomes clear in his 1810 review of Beethoven's Fifth Symphony. The most famous of Hoffmann's reviews, this has been widely acknowledged as not only an outstanding piece of musical criticism but as a statement on Romanticism itself.[65] Hoffmann begins by claiming a privileged position for music, specifically instrumental music, as a purely Romantic art with the power to open up an unknown world which words cannot describe.[66] Praising Haydn, Mozart, and Beethoven as masters of instrumental music, he adds that their genius lies in a deep understanding of the peculiar character of music, rather than simply the ability to showcase virtuoso talent (I, 533). Reading between the lines, it is evident that Beethoven's Fifth succeeds for Hoffmann as an expression of the Absolute, if one bears in mind that this entails the subordination of the particular to the whole:

> Beethoven hat die gewöhnliche Folge der Sätze in der Symphonie beibehalten; sie scheinen phantastisch an einander gereiht zu sein, und das Ganze rauscht manchem vorüber, wie eine geniale Rhapsodie: aber das Gemüt jedes sinnigen Zuhörers wird gewiß von *einem* fortdauernden Gefühl, das eben jene unnennbare, ahnungsvolle Sehnsucht ist, tief und innig ergriffen und bis zum Schluß-Akkord darin erhalten. (I, 550)

> [Beethoven has adhered to the usual arrangement of movements in a symphony;

> they are presented with imagination one after the other, and the entire piece rushes past many of us, like a brilliant rhapsody, but the learned listener will feel his soul tightly gripped by *one* lasting feeling of indescribable, prophetic longing, a feeling that will hold him until the final chord.]

This effect, whereby the audience is moved by the piece in its entirety rather than by certain passages of brilliance, is still held up as a model more than a decade after the Beethoven review, in Hoffmann's 'Nachträgliche Bemerkungen über Spontinis Oper Olympia' [Retrospective Remarks on Spontini's Opera *Olympia*] (1821) (v, 613–57). Once more, the claim is made that music achieves its highest expression when the listeners become so absorbed in the whole that they can no longer think of its parts (v, 615). The inference is that decorative trills and moments of virtuosity in fact detract from the general impression, and are an obstacle on the path towards achieving the Ideal. In his essay 'Brief über Tonkunst in Berlin' [A Letter about Music in Berlin] (1815), Hoffmann's strong criticism of Spontini focuses on the composer's attempts to create striking effects by constantly exploiting the breadth of instruments and range of volume available to him. This approach negates the possibility of any emotional climax to the music, because listeners are so relentlessly bombarded with the sound of loud instruments that their effect is rendered minimal, and the compositions are soulless. A similarly soulless effect is created by singers in *Der Renegat*: as the women of the harem sing to impress the Regent, they imitate Elisa's genuine sadness so that the Regent can listen to the sorrowful song he so enjoys. Their actions lead to a moment of Romantic insight from the otherwise comical despot figure, as he cannot enjoy music when it is based on false emotion, no matter how technically skilful. Speaking to Elisa, the Regent claims:

> du sollst die erste sein und bleiben, Liebchen — das nenn' ich doch den Dey zu amüsieren wissen — nicht so wie die andern Salzsäulen — die schluchzen nur *a Tempo* — du verstehst das besser, 's geht dir so von der Hand! (I, 888)
>
> [you are and will remain superior, my sweet — that's what I call entertaining the Regent — not like those other pillars of salt — they just sob to the beat — you have a better feeling for it, it comes naturally to you!]

Hoffmann's conclusion that music can be lacking in inner truth is supported by ironic oxymoronic descriptions. As musicians attempt to carry the audience away on a wave of impressive effect using superficial means, they succeed only in creating a sense of 'trunkne Nüchternheit' [drunken sobriety], 'kalte Glut' [a cold glow] and 'klangloser Lärm' [toneless noise] (II/ii, 403–04).

Given the significance of the Orient as a Romantic symbol, Hoffmann's ambivalence towards music with an oriental theme is perhaps surprising. Yet his strikingly different reviews of Spontini's *Lalla Rûkh* and Witt's *Sinfonie turque* provide clues as to his view on the role of oriental music in the journey to the Absolute. To return briefly to *Lalla Rûkh*, it is worth emphasizing, again, the effect the piece had on Hoffmann: he reports that all his senses were captured and he felt as if transported to another world. Crucially, this new world comes through synaesthesia. Hoffmann hears the music and imagines seeing a beautiful spring day and smelling the scent of flowers. This combination of sound with inner vision and imagined scent results in an overwhelming impression of Romantic longing (v, 610). The sensuous impression made by the music approaches the spiritual, or, in Hegelian terms, the form has come as close as possible to the content and the Ideal is achieved. Peculiar to this Romantic music is its power to transport the listener to an orientalized paradise via a union of the senses which promotes an inner vision.[67] Hoffmann links synaesthesia to a romanticized Orient in which absolute unity can be achieved. The search for a lost paradise that characterizes Romantic longing can end only when man has become aware of his loss, overcome the resultant tragic dualism and found a new paradise in which the prelapsarian state may be combined with a new poetic understanding. This problem and its resolution are treated in the story of Chrysostomus, narrated in a letter to the composer Johannes Kreisler.[68] As an innocent child, Chrysostomus intuitively connects to the natural music of birdsong he hears in the woods, but when he grows up to become a technically accomplished musician, this natural connection is lost to him.[69] Upon realizing this loss, he overcomes it by returning to his father's garden where a mysterious stone had inspired him as a child, and achieves a new understanding of music as an art which is experienced through all the senses:

> Ich sah den Stein — seine roten Adern gingen auf wie dunkle Nelken, deren Düfte sichtbarlich in hellen tönenden Strahlen emporfuhren. In den langen anschwellenden Tönen der Nachtigall verdichteten sich die Strahlen zur Gestalt eines wundervollen Weibes, aber die Gestalt war wieder himmlische herrliche Musik! (II/i, 452–53)
>
> [I saw the stone — its red veins rose like dark carnations, whose scent moved upwards in visible, brightly ringing rays. In the slowly rising notes of the nightingale the rays grew into a beautiful female figure, but this figure was once again heavenly, glorious music!]

The moral of the tale for Kreisler is that a true musician experiences colours, scent, and light through music, and that for the musician true sight is 'ein Hören von innen' [a listening from within] (II/i, 453). Music is likened to a language of nature, but also to a hieroglyph whose mystery is revealed by the Romantic musician. Once more, the role of music and that of the Orient in accessing the Absolute are brought together as Kreisler's task, as a composer, of creating the musical hieroglyph is likened to the act of sitting by the entrance to the Temple of Isis and beginning a new study (II/i, 454).

The significance of the Orient for truly Romantic music is therefore related to its role in representing the paradise which the Romantics strive to regain. This world becomes a 'Reich der Töne' [kingdom of music] which speaks to the listener's inner being, temporarily resolving conflicts and hinting at the Absolute through its ability to unite the senses. Oriental-themed music can achieve this only if it has a transformative potential like that experienced by Hoffmann at the *Lalla Rûkh* pageant; should this be the case, then music and the Orient come together on the path to the Absolute.

Ritter Gluck

In Hoffmann's earliest published tale, *Ritter Gluck*, the narrator is treated to two performances of Gluck's oriental opera *Armide*, but only one of these performances succeeds in lifting him above the everyday onto a spiritual plane. The first performance takes place in a traditional theatre setting with a full orchestra; the second is given by a mysterious musician who preoccupies the narrator throughout the tale and ultimately claims to be Gluck himself, a rational impossibility as the composer has been dead for over twenty years at the time of the tale's narration. Although the musician has only a piano and his own voice at his disposal, his performance has a much more striking and emotional impact on the narrator than that of the orchestra in the theatre.

There has been much critical debate over the 'true' identity of the strange musician in *Ritter Gluck*.[70] In one popular reading, he is the first in a series of Hoffmann characters who suffer from madness and delusion. James McGlathery describes the figure as 'blissfully and simply mad', Allen Thiher similarly calls him 'a mad musician', and for Diana Stone Peters he is an '*artiste manqué*' because he experiences an ecstatic absorption in his art that approaches delusion and leaves no room for communication with an audience.[71] Other scholars assess the character in light of his artistic ability. Hugo G. Walter claims that he represents artistic genius and Victoria Dutchman-Smith points to the merits of the character's 'authentic artistry'.[72] Yvonne Hörman argues that the public mistakes his isolation for a sign of insanity when he has in fact consciously withdrawn from a society which cannot appreciate his genuine talent.[73]

Whether one views the Gluck figure as delusional, as a revenant, or as a figment of the narrator's imagination, his views on music should at the least be taken as partly representative of the qualities admired by Hoffmann in the historical Gluck. Abigail Chantler summarizes these thus: 'For Hoffmann the basic tenets of Gluck's operatic aesthetic were wholly concordant with his own vision of a poetic idea with metaphysical dimensions.'[74] Like Hoffmann after him, the historical Gluck was a champion of a plain style unblemished by 'pointless decoration' and characterized by 'truth, clarity and simplicity'.[75] It is this simplicity which Hoffmann so admired in Gluck's *Armide*. The plot of this opera leaves open the possibility for much oriental colouring: set during the Crusades, it tells of how the eponymous Damascene seductress keeps the Christian Knight Rinaldo under her spell in an enchanted garden, only to be abandoned by him when he ultimately decides to return to a virtuous way of life. Both Armide's furious desire for revenge when Rinaldo rescues the Christian soldiers she has imprisoned, and her inability to kill Rinaldo because of her passionate love for him, fit the eighteenth-century stereotype of the irrational oriental. Nevertheless, Gluck is to be praised, according to Hoffmann, for a restrained style which contains notes of the exotic but does not descend into ostentation. The integrity of the piece remains intact as its tragic soul is not compromised by meaningless frills.[76] Furthermore, for Gluck dramatic expression takes precedence over conventions of musical syntax. In *Ritter Gluck* the composer character is sympathetic to this philosophy, and teaches the narrator to listen in a similar spirit. As the story begins, the narrator is disturbed by an orchestra playing music that flouts accepted rules of musical composition. His cry, 'Welche rasende Musik! Die abscheulichen Oktaven!' [Such wild music! Those dreadful octaves!] (II/i, 20) refers to the rule whereby the progression of two voices in parallel octaves was deemed aesthetically offensive. The mysterious musician criticizes this insistence on technical correctness above all else. His interjection, 'Verwünschtes Schicksal! Schon wieder ein Oktavenjäger!' [Confounded fate! Another octave hunter!] (II/i, 20) is an attack on critics who listen only for technical imperfections, rather than embracing music's spiritual richness. The Gluck figure sympathizes with true artists who, like Gluck himself, reject virtuosity and are prepared to 'sacrifice the rules, if this would enhance the emotional impact and the effect on the listener.'[77]

Although both performances of *Armide* in the text are based on Gluck's composition, the styles in which they are performed make different impressions on the listener. The narrator becomes aware that Gluck's opera is being staged when he passes the theatre and hears loud music and the beating of kettle drums. His immediate realization that this is a performance of *Armide* suggests again the common association of specific instruments with an oriental theme. The composer character is also present, and provides a semi-comical commentary on the music and action onstage, noting with despair that the beating of the kettle drums continues relentlessly as it accompanies a march and so must be repeated until all characters are onstage. The overall effect is a negative one, leading the composer to exclaim 'Welcher böse Geist hat mich hier festgebannt?' [What malevolent spirit has kept me bound here?] (II/i, 28). Upon learning the narrator's wish to hear *Armide*, the composer responds 'Sie sollen *jetzt* Armida hören!' [*Now* you'll hear Armide!] (II/i, 29), and leads him from the theatre. This action suggests that the theatre production is lacking the true spirit of Gluck's piece, and that the over-zealous beating of the kettle drums fails to enhance the exotic theme.

The alternative performance takes place in the musician's home, in an old-fashioned music room. Before making the final declaration that he is none other than Gluck himself, the musician performs the overture and the final scene from *Armide* on the piano, occasionally singing the notes as well. In keeping with Hoffmann's aesthetic preferences and indeed those of the historical Gluck, the musician performs with innovation but never falls prey to the temptation to dazzle his audience: 'Vorzüglich waren seine Modulationen frappant, ohne grell zu werden' [His modulations were particularly striking, without ever becoming shrill] (II/i, 30). The oriental element is retained when he manages to replicate the sound of the kettle drums with his singing voice (II/i, 30), but there is nothing unnecessarily decorative about this version. By keeping his style simple even where innovative, the musician approaches the Absolute, as suggested by his claim that he composed this particular work after returning from the 'Reich der Träume' [Kingdom of Dreams]. This is the realm of poetic imagination, into which few are able to enter. Even fewer succeed in passing through and leaving this realm behind, in order to achieve the realization of the visions they had while in a state of creative imagination. The artistic reward for doing so is contact with the eternal and inexpressible, or absolute truth. Its expression as the Ideal begins within the soul of the artist, a point succinctly made when the narrator realizes that the music score from which his unusual companion plays is completely blank.[78] This is an obvious metaphor for Romantic *Innerlichkeit*, and the observation that the musician has achieved the Absolute is supported by his experience in the Kingdom of Dreams. In this Romantic realm, the senses are unified in music as light and sound become one: 'Da fuhren Lichtstrahlen durch die Nacht, und die Lichtstrahlen waren Töne, welche mich umfingen mit lieblicher Klarheit' [Rays of light came through the night, and the rays were musical notes, embracing me with sweet clarity] (II/i, 25).

Furthermore, the narrator has now become a Romantically receptive listener. The narrator feels the music resounding inside him as he listens, and he seems to leave the present behind as he enters into a moment in which all emotions come together in a great unity.[79] This absolute unity is achieved, not by the orchestra's 'oriental' effects, nor by obsessive adherence to technical rules, but by an individual who accesses the Romantic realm inspired by Gluck's piece.[80] *Armide* is shown to be most effective then, not when players try to indicate the oriental theme with specific instruments, but when the individual is inspired to reach out from within towards the Romantic paradise suggested by the magical oriental setting. Indeed, Hoffmann seems to have followed his own advice in this respect when composing the music for *Dirna*. Despite the occasional *alla turca* sounds in the overture and intermezzo, and the oriental-style instrumentation noted by Allroggen,[81] the piece is not generally characterized by attempts at exotic tones. Werner Keil notes:

> Hoffmanns Musik zur *Dirna* ist dabei an keiner Stelle 'indisch' oder um ein indisches Klangbild bemüht, wenn man von den (sparsam) in der Overtüre und dem Tanzintermezzo eingesetzten Triangeln und Schellen absieht. Im Gegenteil singen am Ende die indischen Priester im meist vierstimmigen Männerchorsatz in weltlichem Kantatenstil, undramatisch, melodisch wenig bewegt, dafür weihevoll und auf Klangwirkung bedacht.[82]
>
> [Hoffmann's music for *Dirna* is at no point 'Indian', or concerned with producing an Indian sound, if we disregard the triangles and bells that are (sparingly) included in the overture and the dance intermezzo. On the contrary, the Indian priests at the end sing mostly as men's choruses of four voices in the style of secular cantatas, simply and with little change in melody, and for this reason, solemnly, with great emphasis on the impact of the sound.]

In both his literary and musical work, Hoffmann rejects as non-Romantic any effort to replicate the Orient formally through external means.

Das Sanctus

The Kapellmeister in *Das Sanctus* is another example of a composer figure wishing to create an oriental-themed opera. The Kapellmeister has a vested interest both in Bettina, his musical protégée, and in Zulema, the central figure in the story told by the travelling enthusiast. Both women lose their ability to sing, and in each case this loss is viewed as a punishment for a transgression deemed blasphemous: the German Bettina and the Moorish Zulema (ostensibly a Catholic convert) both leave the church during the singing of the Sanctus. Bettina does so because she has been engaged to sing at a tea party, while Zulema is tempted outside by the sounds of zither music representing her native culture. Although the travelling enthusiast tells the story in order to provide a cure for Bettina's affliction, the Kapellmeister sees it primarily as an opportunity to find material for a new opera. Recently, Röder has sought to rehabilitate the Kapellmeister as a key figure in *Das Sanctus*, arguing that he is much more than simply the recipient of the enthusiast's story.[83] While noting the parodic elements in his character, such as his tendency towards exaggeration and selfishness, Röder claims that the Kapellmeister is the character most open to imaginative influence as he has an ability to lose himself completely in a fictional story. Furthermore, his wish to compose an opera based on Zulema's tale reveals his capacity to draw musical inspiration from a variety of art forms.[84]

While Röder is correct in identifying the Kapellmeister as a key character, she does not comment on the type of opera he dreams of composing, and this element is central in an examination of his musical credentials. Initially, he shows the potential to be open to the Absolute. Even his wildly exaggerated desire that Bettina should die rather than live without her singing voice is rooted in Romantic sensibilities: he claims he will miss 'die herrlichen Canzonette — die wunderbaren Bollero's und Seguidilla's, die wie klingender Blumenhauch von ihren Lippen strömten' [the magnificent canzonettas — the wonderful boleros and seguidillas, that flowed from her lips like the ringing breath of a flower] (III, 141). As noted above, this synaesthetic relationship between music and flowers is replicated elsewhere in Hoffmann to denote a Romantic immersion of the senses in the Absolute. Bettina's lost voice means the loss of the Ideal, as she realizes for herself when she explains her condition to the doctor as akin to being a dream in which she knows she has the ability to fly, and yet reaches in vain for the skies. There has been a break between the sensuous and the spiritual, and so she is no longer able to express in musical form the Romantic realm of song. Zulema is afflicted with the same problem, and Röder explains the tragedy of her story as a misunderstanding by the men who fight over her for ideological as well as personal reasons: they try to label her, and she is destroyed in the process, for as a singer of 'pure music' and an embodiment of 'art in its most universal sense', she is no longer available for categorization as Christian or heathen.[85] At first, the Kapellmeister also seems interested in the potential of music to capture the Absolute. When the enthusiast begins his story, he responds eagerly: 'Wer weiß, welches Samenkorn die erwünschte Erzählung in mein Gemüt wirft und was für Riesenlilien daraus entsprießen' [Who knows what seed this welcome story will plant in my mind, and what magnificent lilies will spring forth from it] (III, 148). Sensing the potential for creative inspiration offered by the oriental setting of Moorish Granada, he immediately begins to wonder how the story could transfer to the stage. Furthermore, he appears to follow the process that is essential for the production of the Ideal. According to Hegel, although *Innerlichkeit* is key, art is necessarily derived in the first instance from the sensuous sphere, and here the Kapellmeister responds to the external stimulus of the enthusiast's story.[86] He hopes, however, that this will penetrate his soul, so that great music might be born — again symbolized by the Romantic image of the lily. This process corresponds to Hegel's insistence on the spiritualization of the sensuous.[87]

The Kapellmeister's artistic project soon descends into the superficial, however, as his enthusiasm for the oriental theme is expressed in terms of the instruments used to represent it. The opening line of the story, which simply situates it historically in the fifteenth century and geographically in Granada, is enough to provoke his colourful description of the type of opera he might produce from this material: 'Es wird eine Geschichte aus den Kriegen der Mauren mit den Spaniern, wie ich merke, so was hätt' ich längst gar zu gern komponiert. — Gefechte — Tumult — Romanzen — Aufzüge — Cymbeln — Choräle — Trommeln und Pauken — ach Pauken!' [I see it's going to be a story from the wars between the Moors and the Spaniards. I really should have composed something like this a long time ago. — Battles — commotion — romances — parades — cymbals — chorales — drums and kettle drums — oh! kettle drums!] (III, 148). The mere thought of the Moors is enough to stimulate an imaginative leap from medieval Spain to the music of the Ottoman Empire. From his later praise of Mozart, the reader might reasonably infer that the Kapellmeister is familiar with *Die Entführung aus dem Serail* and therefore with the *alla turca* style.[88] He is determined to match this style of music to a story which he has not even heard yet, simply because he perceives an oriental theme. Furthermore, he proves more responsive to the external oriental elements of the tale than to its central message about the supremacy of the individual Romantic voice. As the enthusiast tells of the strange zither music which penetrates the choir music from outside the church, he describes the unusual tones as 'beinahe wie das gellende Gepfeife der kleinen mohrischen Flöten' [almost like the shrill piping of the little Moorish flute] (III, 153). Egger reads this description of shrill music as Hoffmann's response to the so-called 'Krieg der Töne' [War over Sound] which erupted around 1800. The oriental instruments are mentioned in a negative context in order to illustrate the problematic nature of dissonance in modern music, a phenomenon Hoffmann viewed as anti-Romantic.[89] This links to the enthusiast's motivation in telling the story: he knows Bettina is listening, and wants her to understand the nature of her transgression in interrupting the singing of the Sanctus.[90] The Kapellmeister misses the point, however, and thinks instead about the only oriental-style music of which he has any knowledge: 'Flauti piccoli — Oktavflötchen' [piccolos — octave flutes] (III, 153). Even when he realizes he will not be able to compose an opera from the story, he remains interested in the parts of the plot which would be best illustrated with the traditional Turkish-style military music: 'das Gefecht zwischen dem Mohren Hichem im Schuppenharnisch und dem Feldherrn Aguillar ging mir auf in Musik' [the battle between the Moor Hichem in his scale armour and the general Aguillar appeared to me in musical form] (III, 158). Moreover, the Kapellmeister's final judgement is that the story does not provide sufficient material for an opera, but that it does offer the musician 'einige sonderbar klingende Akkorde' [some peculiar-sounding chords] (III, 160). This focus on the particular means that the Kapellmeister misses the universal aspect of the tale represented by Zulema's voice. His ambitions to create an opera are limited by his enthusiasm for the musical effects which represented the Orient to a nineteenth-century audience but which have no bearing on the content of the story. These empty ciphers do not allow for the union of form and content, and so the Kapellmeister fails in his mission, despite the promising remarks which suggest that he could have an ear for Romantic music.

Conclusion

In recent years, music critics have begun to take issue with the stereotypes inherent in oriental-style music created by western composers. The increasing acknowledgement of the fact that these composers operated within a social and political context means that their music is shown to respond to the predominant bias of their time. *Die Entführung aus dem Serail*, for example, is partially 'a reflection of eighteenth-century Viennese moral and musical conflicts with the Turkish Empire'.[91] Likewise, critics have widely demonstrated how the German Romantic literary response to the Islamic Other is a product of the widespread curiosity in eighteenth- and nineteenth-century Germany about the perceived violence and sensuality of the East. Literary critics have been slow, however, to identify the link between music and literature in this respect as providing a critical commentary on the process of cultural production. An examination of Hoffmann's musical tales reveals that within German Romantic writing, there are pockets of resistance to the hegemonic representation of the Orient in western music. Hoffmann rejects the unthinking use of oriental instrumentalization as superficial, inauthentic, and, worst of all, unmusical. Using oriental props in the context of operatic or instrumental compositions does not lead to truly Romantic music and, in Hoffmann's fiction, is unmasked as an absurd practice. The oriental theme, however, may provide the inspiration to create pure Romantic music, unblemished by decorative trills. Hoffmann's *Dirna*, with its restrained use of the *alla turca* style, has received critical approval for this very approach. Admittedly, *Der Renegat* shows an early admiration for the *alla turca* theme, and Hoffmann continued to admire Mozart and Gluck throughout his life. The latter in particular is, however, an example of a musician who understood the all-important fusion of form and content, and in this practice, the significance of the Orient for Hoffmann's musical aesthetics is revealed. As a symbolic Romantic paradise, the Orient may only be accessed through *absolute Innerlichkeit*, a state of reflection which the most powerful music can bring about. By eschewing the superficial formal aspects of popular oriental music, Hoffmann accords a much greater importance to the Orient as an inspiration for pure music.[92]

Notes to Chapter 4

1. Hoffmann, *Meister Floh* (VI, 393; *GP*, 313).
2. See Nasser Al-Taee, *Representations of the Orient in Western Music: Violence and Sensuality* (Surrey and Burlington, VT: Ashgate, 2010), p. xii.
3. Todd Kontje, *German Orientalisms* (Ann Arbor: The University of Michigan Press, 2004), p. 61, and Al-Taee, p. 3.
4. Al-Taee, p. 21 and p. 79.
5. Ibid., p. 127. See also W. Daniel Wilson, *Humanität und Kreuzzugsideologie um 1780: Die 'Türkenoper' im 18. Jahrhundert und das Rettungsmotiv in Wielands 'Oberon', Lessings 'Nathan' und Goethes 'Iphigenie'* (New York: Peter Lang, 1984). Wilson argues that each of the three major works mentioned in his title take the motif of abduction and rescue from the popular *Singspiele* and rework it in the name of classical humanism.
6. Gerry Farrell, *Indian Music and the West* (Oxford: Clarendon Press, 2007).

7. Ibid., p. 1.
8. Ibid., p. 3. Farrell notes that while India had been familiar to Europeans as a geographical location since the early seventeenth century via the East India Company, it was only in the late eighteenth century that a western interest in Indian culture began to develop (p. 1 and p. 16).
9. Ibid., p. 20.
10. See John Henning, 'Goethe and "Lalla Rookh"', *MLR*, 48:4 (1953), 445–50 (p. 446), and Hartmut Steinecke and Gerhard Allroggen's commentary, 'Gesänge zu dem Festspiele "Lalla Rukh"', in Hoffmann, *SW* v, 1108–12.
11. See Abigail Chantler, *E.T.A. Hoffmann's Musical Aesthetics* (Aldershot and Burlington, VT: Ashgate, 2006), pp. 149–53.
12. Steinecke and Allroggen in Hoffmann, v, 1109. Fouqué also translated Moore's work into German: *Lalla Rukh, oder die mongolische Prinzessin: Romantische Dichtung aus dem Englischen in den Sylbenmassen des Originals* (Berlin: Schlesinger, 1822).
13. Gerhard Allroggen, Rudolf Herd, Friedrich Schnapp, and Werner Keil also look at this topic, although their discussions are limited to examinations of Hoffmann's music for Julius von Soden's 'Indian melodrama', *Dirna* (see later in this chapter).
14. On Salieri, see John A. Rice, 'Axur, re d'Ormus' and 'Tarare', in *The New Grove Dictionary of Opera* <www.oxfordmusiconline.com> [accessed 13 June 2012].
15. Hoffmann, 'Sinfonie turque pour 2 Violons, Alto, Basse, 2 Flûtes, 2 Hautbois, 2 Clarinettes, 2 Bassons, 4 Cors, 2 Trompettes, Timbales, grand Tambour, Triangle etc. composée par Witt. No. 6. à Offenbach, chez Jean André. (Pr. 5 Fl.)', *SW*, I, 518–21.
16. See the commentary in *SW*, II/ii, 657.
17. Hoffmann, *Der Renegat: Ein Singspiel in zwei Aufzügen*, *SW*, II, 875–91. The work was first published in 1903/4 by Hans von Müller. See also the commentary in *SW*, I, 1344–46. It may also have been influenced by Karl Theodor Breithaupt's 1759 *bürgerliches Trauerspiel* [domestic tragedy], *Der Renegat*, in which an English son leaves his father, and his religion, behind when he runs away to Turkey and assumes the Turkish name 'Zapor'. Another possible source is Emanuel Schikaneder's 1792 Singspiel, *Der Renegat, oder Anton in der Türkei* [*The Renegade, or Anton in Turkey*], one of five follow-ups to Schikaneder's more successful Singspiel, *Der dumme Gärtner aus dem Gebirge, oder die zween Anton* [*The Foolish Gardener from the Mountains, or, the Two Antons*] (1789). See Robert R. Heitner, *German Tragedy in the Age of Enlightenment* (Berkeley and Los Angeles: University of California Press, 1963), pp. 198–202, and Peter Branscombe and David J. Buch, 'Dumme Gärtner aus dem Gebirge, Der [*Der dumme Gärtner aus dem Gebirge, oder Die zween Anton* ('The Dumb Gardener from the Mountains, or The Two Antons')]', in *The New Grove Dictionary of Opera*, <www.oxfordmusiconline.com> [accessed 8 February 2013].
18. This comparison is also suggested by Georg Ellinger, who emphasizes the difference between the noble-minded Pasha and Hoffmann's comical Regent. See Ellinger, *E.T.A. Hoffmann: Sein Leben und seine Werke* (Hamburg and Leipzig: Verlag von Leopold Voß, 1894), p. 29.
19. See Werner Keil, 'E.T.A. Hoffmann als Komponist', in *E.T.A. Hoffmann — Leben — Werk — Wirkung*, ed. by Detlef Kremer (Berlin and New York: Walter de Gruyter, 2009), pp. 425–48 (p. 442) and Rudolf Herd, 'Hoffmanns "Dirna" wieder aufgetaucht!', *MHG*, 15 (1969), 2–3 (p. 3).
20. See Herd, p. 3.
21. See Friedrich Schnapp, 'Die Quellen von Sodens Melodram *Dirna*', *MHG*, 15 (1969), 4–6.
22. Werner Keil, 'E.T.A. Hoffmann, Dirna: Ein indisches Melodrama', essay in inlay booklet of E.T.A. Hoffmann, *Dirna*, Martin Herrmann, Werner Klockow and Angelika Krautzberger, Deutscher Kammerakademie Neuss, cond. by Johannes Goritzki (Classic Produktion Osnabrück, 999 607–2, 2001), pp. 5–8 (p. 7).
23. See also Herd.
24. For a brief history of Turkish-style music and its fortunes in Europe in the period leading up to German Romanticism, see Edmund A. Bowles, 'The Impact of Turkish Military Bands on European Court Festivals in the 17th and 18th Centuries', *Early Music*, 34:4 (2006), 533–60.
25. Matthew Head, *Orientalism, Masquerade and Mozart's Turkish Music* (London: Royal Musical Association, 2000), p. 27.
26. A. L. Ringer, 'On the Question of "Exoticism" in 19th Century Music', *Studia Musicologica Academiae Scientiarum Hungaricae*, 7 (1965), 115–23 (p. 120).

27. Head, p. 60.
28. Al-Taee notes that '[t]he *alla turca* used piccolo and Turkish percussion instruments to emulate the shrieking sounds of the Ottoman army' and, furthermore, that 'the *alla turca* [...] was meant to denote Ottoman cruelty and savagery' (p. 93).
29. See Al Taee, pp. 129–30.
30. Gerhard Allroggen, 'E.T.A. Hoffmanns Musik zur Dirna', *MHG*, 15 (1969), 31–39 (p. 36).
31. Head, p. 20.
32. Allroggen, p. 34.
33. James Hodkinson notes that Hoffmann characterizes the Moorish music in *Das Sanctus* in terms of 'its discordance with the Christian musical context', and Birgit Röder describes the reaction of the Christians to the music of the Moorish camp as a mixture of fascination and fear. For Martha B. Helfer, Novalis's Zulima is 'the embodiment of exotic, oriental poetry'. See James Hodkinson, 'Moving Beyond the Binary? Christian–Islamic Encounters and Gender in the Thought and Literature of German Romanticism', in *Encounters with Islam in German Literature and Culture*, ed. by James Hodkinson and Jeffrey Morrison (Rochester, NY: Camden House, 2009), pp. 108–27 (p. 120); Birgit Röder, *A Study of the Major Novellas of E.T.A. Hoffmann* (Rochester, NY: Camden House, 2003), pp. 144–45; and Martha B. Helfer, 'The Male Muses of Romanticism: The Poetics of Gender in Novalis, E.T.A. Hoffmann, and Eichendorff', *GQ*, 78:3 (2005), 299–319 (p. 304).
34. Wilson, *Humanität und Kreuzzugsideologie um 1780*.
35. Irmgard Egger, 'Krieg der Töne — Konkurrenz der Diskurse: Dissonanz und Konsonanz bei E.T.A. Hoffmann', *HJb*, 16 (2008), 98–108 (p. 102).
36. 'Das war ein Drängen und Stoßen und Treiben und Gequieke!' [There was crowding and pushing and rushing and squeaking!] (IV, 298).
37. Head, p. 58.
38. Hoffmann clearly considered cymbals to be a part of the oriental percussion group, as evidenced in *Nachricht von einem gebildeten jungen Mann* [*A Report of an Educated Young Man*], in *Kreisleriana* by the mention of 'türkischen Trommel und Becken' [Turkish drums and cymbals] (II/i, 425).
39. The theatrical oriental parades in *Prinzessin Brambilla* may have been partly inspired by an incident which took place in 1813. On 5 June 1813, the director Joseph Seconda was forced to close the theatre where Hoffmann was employed as musical director. However, Seconda secured permission for his company to perform at the Dresden Hoftheater, and the actors made a journey to this theatre which Hoffmann described as '[e]ine lächerliche Reise — die mir Stoff zu der humoristischten Erzählung geben würde' [a ridiculous journey — which would give me material for the funniest tale]. The entire company paraded to the court in costumes taken from the theatre, some of which were oriental in style. Even pets were decked in flowers so as to resemble animals brought from distant lands. These 'exotic' animals were presented to the King by actors dressed in the costumes of the Moorish slaves from the opera *Axur*. See Hoffmann's letter to Friedrich Speyer dated 13 July 1813 (I, 284–92).
40. E.T.A. Hoffmann, 'Gesange zu dem Festspiel "Lalla Rûkh", in Musik gesetzt von G. Spontini' (V, 609–11).
41. This recalls the oriental paradise at the end of *Der goldene Topf*, particularly the flowers whose scent seems to call out 'Wandle, wandle unter uns, Geliebter der du uns verstehst — unser Duft ist die Sehnsucht der Liebe' [Walk among us, beloved, who understands us — our fragrance is the yearning of love] (II/i, 319; *GP*, 81).
42. Hoffmann, 'Gruss an Spontini', *SW*, III, 714. On Hoffmann's critical view of Spontini's earlier work, see Hoffmann, 'Briefe über Tonkunst in Berlin' in II/ii, 394–405 (401–04). For an explanation of Hoffmann's changing and ambiguous attitude toward Spontini, see David Charlton (ed.), *E.T.A. Hoffmann's Musical Writings: Kreisleriana, The Poet and the Composer, Music Criticism*, trans. by Martyn Clarke (Cambridge: Cambridge University Press, 1989), p. 72 and pp. 178–79.
43. Emily Dolan, 'The Idea of Timbre in the Age of Haydn' (unpublished doctoral thesis, Cornell University, 2006), particularly ch. 4, '"Effect! Effect!": Immediacy and Early 19th Century Musical Practice', pp. 178–238.
44. Ibid., p. 181.

45. Ibid., p. 189.
46. Ibid., p. 182.
47. Ibid., p. 191.
48. Abigail Chantler notes: 'The terms in which Hoffmann described Witt's music [...] betray his view of the work as primarily entertaining rather than spiritually elevating' (p. 87).
49. See also Dolan, p. 232.
50. Egger, p. 102.
51. Ibid., p. 103.
52. Röder, *A Study of the Major Novellas of E.T.A. Hoffmann*, p. 10.
53. Georg Wilhelm Friedrich Hegel, 'Vorlesungen über die Ästhetik', in Hegel, *Werke*, ed. by Eva Moldenhauer and Karl Markus Michel, 20 vols (Frankfurt: Suhrkamp, 1970), XIII–XV.
54. Ibid., XIV, 129; translation from G. W. F. Hegel, *Aesthetics: Lectures on Fine Art*, trans. by T. M. Knox, 2 vols (Oxford: Oxford University Press, 1975), I, 518 [hereafter referred to as Knox].
55. Ibid., XIII, 104–05; Knox, I, 92, 110, 153.
56. Ibid., XIII, 316; Knox, I, 244.
57. See for example Klaus-Dieter Dobat, *Musik als romantische Illusion: Eine Untersuchung zur Bedeutung der Musikvorstellung E.T.A. Hoffmanns für sein literarisches Werk* (Tübingen: Max Niemeyer, 1984) and R. Murray Schafer, *E.T.A. Hoffmann and Music* (Toronto: University of Toronto Press, 1975). The latter claims that in the relationship between music and literature, for Hoffmann 'it is the music which penetrates the literature and not the other way around' (p. 28).
58. Wilhelm Heinrich Wackenroder and Ludwig Tieck, *Herzensergießungen eines kunstliebenden Klosterbruders* [*Heartfelt Outpourings of an Art-loving Friar*], in Wackenroder, *Werke und Briefe*, ed. by Gerda Heinrich (Berlin: Union Verlag, 1984), pp. 139–247. Hoffmann was familiar with this text and used a variation of the name Berglinger in *Der Artushof* (1817), which introduces the fictional German painter Berklinger.
59. See also Röder, *Major Novellas*, p. 10.
60. Hegel, XIV, 129; Knox, I, 519.
61. See Herbert Schnädelbach, 'Hegel', in *Music in German Philosophy: An Introduction*, ed. by Stefan Lorenz Sorgner and Oliver Fürbeth, trans. by Susan H. Gillespie (Chicago and London: The University of Chicago Press, 2010), pp. 69–93 (p. 79).
62. Hoffmann, *Ahnungen aus dem Reiche der Töne*, II/ii, 439–46. This story was initially meant for the *Morgenblatt für gebildete Stände* and was published in this journal in 1816. As publication took so long, however, Hoffmann also worked the story into *Johannes Kreislers Lehrbrief* [*Johannes Kreisler's Correspondence Lesson*] (1815, see later in this chapter). The sentiment is also echoed by Joseph von Eichendorff, whose famous Taugenichts from 1826 picks up a violin with the joyful exclamation, 'Unser Reich ist nicht von dieser Welt!' [Our kingdom is not of this world!]. See Joseph von Eichendorff, *Aus dem Leben eines Taugenichts* [*From the Life of a Good-for-Nothing*], in Eichendorff, *Werke*, ed. by Ansgar Hillach, 3 vols (Munich: Winkler, 1970), II, 565–647 (p. 583).
63.

> Die Gegenwart versank vor ihm; sein Inneres war von allen irdischen Kleinigkeiten, welche der wahre Staub auf dem Glanze der Seele sind, gereinigt; die Musik durchdrang seine Nerven mit leisen Schauern und ließ, so wie sie wechselte, mannigfache Bilder vor ihm aufsteigen.
>
> [The present moment disappeared before his eyes, his inner being was purified of all those trivial earthly cares, of the dust that truly masks the shining of the soul; the music penetrated to his nerves with a quiet shudder, and as it changed, it caused many images to rise up before him.] (Wackenroder and Tieck, p. 231)

64. Ibid., p. 233.
65. See Chantler, p. viii.
66. 'Die Musik schließt dem Menschen ein unbekanntes Reich auf; eine Welt, die nichts gemein hat mit der äußern Sinnenwelt, die ihn umgibt, und in der er alle durch Begriffe bestimmbaren Gefühle zurückläßt, um sich dem Unaussprechlichen hinzugeben' [Music opens up an unknown world for us; a world that has nothing in common with the external world of the senses that

surrounds us, a world where we leave behind all feelings that can be defined in words, in order to give ourselves over to the undefinable] (I, 532).

67. This transformative power is also linked in Hoffmann to the Orient itself. In Hoffmann's *Briefe aus den Bergen* [*Letters from the Mountains*] (1820), the narrator sees a beautiful woman and instantly feels connected to an inner magic which he states he can otherwise only access through Dschinnistan. See *Briefe aus den Bergen*, *SW*, III, 688–713 (691).
68. *Johannes Kreislers Lehrbrief*, II/i, 447–55. This is a version of the tale *Ahnungen aus dem Reiche der Töne* (see n. 62, above).
69. Technical training is shown to spoil musical appreciation in *Kater Murr*. Meister Abraham's father, an organ builder, is obsessed with exact detail and technical accomplishment. The organs he makes, however, do not produce a pleasant tone, a failing Meister Abraham attributes to his father's personal lack of a musical ear. Trained in his father's ways, Abraham grows to detest music until later in life, when he hears organ music that seems to awaken a sort of inner magic.
70. For an overview of the various identities that have been assigned to the character, see Ricarda Schmidt, *Wenn mehrere Künste im Spiel sind: Intermedialität bei E.T.A. Hoffmann* (Göttingen: Vandenhoek & Ruprecht, 2006), pp. 23 and 40–43.
71. James McGlathery, 'Madness in German Romanticism', in *Thematics Reconsidered: Essays in Honor of Horst S. Daemmrich*, ed. by Frank Trommler (Atlanta: Rodopi, 1995), pp. 187–99 (p. 191); Allen Thiher, *Revels in Madness: Insanity in Medicine and Literature* (Ann Arbor: The University of Michigan Press, 1999), p. 190; Diana Stone Peters, 'E.T.A. Hoffmann: The Conciliatory Satirist', *Monatshefte*, 66:1 (1974), 55–73 (p. 60).
72. Hugo G. Walter, *Sanctuaries of Light in Nineteenth-Century European Literature* (New York: Peter Lang, 2010), p. 87; Victoria Dutchman-Smith, *E.T.A. Hoffmann and Alcohol: Biography, Reception and Art* (London: Maney Publishing for the Modern Humanities Research Association, 2010), p. 30.
73. Yvonne Hörmann, *Die Musikerfiguren E.T.A. Hoffmanns: Ein mosaikartiges Konglomerat des romantischen Künstlerideals* (Würzburg: Königshausen & Neumann, 2008), pp. 89–103.
74. Chantler, p. 133.
75. Stefan Lorenz Sorgner and Oliver Fürbeth, 'Introduction', in *Music in German Philosophy*, pp. 3–25 (p. 9).
76.

> Gluck ist melodiös, wie es nur irgendein tragischer Komponist sein kann, ja seine Melodieen haben da, wo es durch das Drama bedingt wird, einen süßen südlichen Hauch, wie z. B. bei Rinaldo's Eintritt in Armida's Zaubergarten. Aber der tragische Ernst, die tiefe Bedeutung, die in Glucks Melodieen herrscht, läßt nicht zu, daß sich eine einzige Floskel, die nur dasteht, um, außer dem Zusammenhange mit dem Ganzen, das Ohr augenblicklich zu kitzeln, einschleiche.
>
> [Gluck is melodic in the way that only a tragic composer can be; at the parts where the plot requires it, his melodies even have a sweet, southern breath, for example as Rinaldo enters Armida's magical garden. But the tragic seriousness, the deep meaning that characterizes Gluck's melodies, does not allow for a single phrase to creep in if it is there only momentarily to tickle our ear, independently of the piece as a whole.] (V, 621)

77. Francien Markx, *E.T.A. Hoffmann, Cosmopolitanism, and the Struggle for German Opera* (Leiden: Brill, 2016), p. 79. I am indebted to Markx's overview of contemporary responses to Gluck's perceived technical flaws, and Hoffmann's answer to such criticism. See particularly Chapter One, 'Ritter Gluck: On the Art of Judging Opera' (pp. 71-118).
78. Twelve years after publishing the story Hoffmann was to remark, 'Es ist nämlich bekannt, daß Gluck, als er starb, eine ganze Oper im Kopf ausgearbeitet hatte, ohne eine einzige Note aufzuschreiben' [Indeed it is well known that when Gluck died, he had worked out an entire opera in his head, without writing down a single note] (V, 618).
79. 'Alles, was Haß, Liebe, Verzweiflung, Raserei, in den stärksten Zügen ausdrücken kann, faßte er gewaltig in Töne zusammen' [Into his music, he powerfully concentrated everything that, in the strongest terms, expresses hate, love, despair, and fury] (II/i, 31).
80. Unfortunately, the musician is at best a semi-success as he fails to fulfil the artist's task of

mediating between divine inspiration and modern society. Diana Stone Peters states: 'The audience should not consist of a single sympathetic "Du" [...] or of a small intellectual elite [...] but of ordinary human beings among whom some common bond must be sought if art is to endure' (Peters, p. 55). This failure to find a broad audience does not, however, discount the musician's genuine ability to recreate the true spirit of Gluck's music. See Hörmann, p. 100 and Schmidt, *Wenn mehrere Künste im Spiel sind*, p. 41.

81. See above, p. 99.
82. Keil, 'E.T.A. Hoffmann als Komponist', p. 443.
83. Birgit Röder, 'Das Sanctus', in *A Study of the Major Novellas of E.T.A. Hoffmann*, pp. 142–52.
84. Ibid., p. 149.
85. Ibid., p. 146.
86. See Hegel, 'Das Kunstwerk als für den Sinn des Menschen dem Sinnlichen entnommen' (xiii, 52–64); 'The Work of Art, as being for Apprehension by Man's Senses, is drawn from the Sensuous Sphere' (Knox, pp. 32–41).
87.

> Aber diese Seite äußerlicher Existenz ist es nicht, welche ein Werk zu einem Produkte der schönen Kunst macht; Kunstwerk ist es nur, insofern es, aus dem Geiste entsprungen, nun auch dem Boden des Geistes angehört, die Taufe des Geistigen erhalten hat und nur dasjenige darstellt, was nach dem Anklange des Geistes gebildet ist.
>
> [But this aspect — external existence — is not what makes a work into a product of fine art; a work of art is such only because, originating from the spirit, it now belongs to the territory of the spirit; it has received the baptism of the spiritual and sets forth only what has been formed in harmony with the spirit.] (Hegel, xiii, p. 48; Knox, i, p. 29)

88. The Kapellmeister speaks highly of Mozart's *Don Giovanni* (iii, 158).
89. Egger, p. 103.
90. See also Ulrich Schönherr's reading of the link between the embedded and the frame narratives of *Das Sanctus* as Hoffmann's attempt to map the fifteenth-century code of the blasphemous versus the sacred onto an early nineteenth-century tension between bourgeois and Romantic conceptions of art in 'Social Differentiation and Romantic Art: E.T.A. Hoffmann's *The Sanctus* and the Problem of Aesthetic Positioning in Modernity', *NGC*, 66 (1995), 3–16. Egger also notes that while Zulema is distracted from pure music by the sounds of the zither, Bettina is open to the dangers posed by the secularization of church music (p. 105).
91. Al-Taee, p. 126.
92. Substantial parts of this chapter were published as an article: '*Alla Turca* versus the Romantic East: E.T.A. Hoffmann and Oriental-Style Music', *German Life and Letters*, 67:2 (2014), 139–58 (© 2014 John Wiley & Sons Ltd). I am grateful to the editors for their permission to reproduce this material here.

CHAPTER 5

Knowing the Orient: Scholars, Sages, and the Limits of Cultural Transfer

da sehe ich denn zu meinem Leidwesen, wie wenig die himmlische Weisheit deinen verstockten irdischen Sinn zu durchdringen vermag!
[and so I see to my great disappointment just how scarce is the heavenly wisdom that can penetrate your stubborn, earthly mind!][1]

'Wunderbar ist dieser Zug aller Deutschen in unserer Zeit nach dem Indischen' [The way India attracts every German today — it's wondrous].[2] These words, spoken by Achim von Arnim's prince in the 1810 novel, *Armut, Reichtum, Schuld und Buße der Gräfin Dolores* [*Poverty, Wealth, Guilt, and Penance of Countess Dolores*], encapsulate the sheer extent of the public as well as scholarly preoccupation with the Orient which spread through Romantic-era Germany. India was not the only focus of this obsession. The years leading up to the Romantic movement witnessed a burgeoning interest in scholarly Orientalism which took hold of academia. This encompassed the study of not only Sanskrit but also of Arabic, Syriac, Persian, Hebrew, Chinese, and even Egyptian hieroglyphs, and evolved from the study of languages into an examination of ancient religions and mythology. Despite the lack of an actual colonial interest in the East, it was German scholars who led the field in Europe, and their fascination for this subject lasted well into the nineteenth century.

The advancement of the discipline of comparative philology played a major part in this phenomenon. Initially an important area for biblical exegesis, the study of oriental languages became significant for scholars seeking to understand the original meaning of the Scriptures.[3] The philosopher Johann Georg Hamann (1730–88), for example, sought in oriental languages the kernel of an original divine revelation. As Tuska Benes states, 'As the oldest languages for which evidence supposedly existed [...] Oriental tongues were the most poetic and spiritually symbolic and thus promised to bring Hamann closer to the divine truth.'[4] In the late eighteenth century the quest for an authentic interpretation of the Scriptures continued, and its connection to ancient eastern languages was established in a number of scholarly journals produced at leading German universities. Examples include the *Magazin für die biblisch-orientalische Litteratur und gesammte Philologie* [*Magazine for Biblical-Oriental Literature and for all Philology*] (1788–89), edited by J. G. Hasse, Professor of Oriental

Languages at Königsberg, and the *Neues Repertorium für biblische und morgenländische Litteratur* [*New Repertory for Biblical and Oriental Literature*] (1790–91), edited by the Jena Professor of Philosophy and Oriental Languages, H. E. G. Paulus. A survey of the essays in this field reveals that scholars were divided over the question of which oriental languages would best serve their purpose, and the resulting breadth of intellectual enquiry characterized the field of scholarly Orientalism. The Halle journal, *Magazin für Alte, besonders morgenländische und biblische Litteratur* [*Magazine for Ancient, and particularly Oriental and Biblical Literatures*] (1787–90), provides a case in point, with contributors investigating such diverse languages as Arabic, Hebrew, Persian, Syriac, and Armenian in order to ascertain the original sources of the Bible. In the same journal, conflicting opinions appear on the original language of the Gospels, with a 1789 anonymous writer contesting that St Matthew's Gospel was originally written in the Syriac-Chaldean language, while a 1790 contributor attests that the Gospel of Mark first appeared in Coptic.[5] While it has thus been established that German orientalists of the Age of Goethe were generally rooted in the field of theology, the increasing study of oriental languages also served a nationalist purpose, as part of the search for 'the cultural starting point of the German nation'.[6] Sanskrit in particular was appropriated for this aim. Following Herder's location of the origins of humanity in India,[7] Friedrich Schlegel's 1808 study, *Über die Sprache und Weisheit der Indier* [*On the Language and Wisdom of the Indians*], identified a developmental link between the German language and Sanskrit. The tradition begun by Herder therefore aimed at identifying the German people as the modern descendants of the first civilized race in India, boosting the nationalist cause. This perhaps explains the ongoing academic enthusiasm for India: in 1816 Franz Bopp added to Schlegel's work with *Über das Conjugationssystem der Sanskritsprache* [*On the Conjugation System of the Sanskrit Language*], and in 1818 the first German Chair in Indology was established and given to August Wilhelm Schlegel at Bonn University.

This new expertise in oriental languages functioned not only as a means to serve religious and nationalistic purposes, but also initiated a European-wide search for ancient literary texts from the East. This was of particular significance for the German Romantic movement, which blossomed just as this 'Oriental Renaissance', as Raymond Schwab famously termed it, was reaching its peak. Within the context of the 'neue Mythologie', theorized by Friedrich Schlegel and practised by Novalis, these oriental texts were thought of as 'sources for rejuvenating the spiritual life of a disenchanted present'.[8] Such discoveries were largely due to the British colonial presence in India, as enthusiasm for the study of Sanskrit began in earnest in the 1770s with the efforts of Sir William Jones of the East India Company.[9] Jones's translation of the ancient Hindu play *Sakuntala* was in turn translated into German by Georg Forster in 1791, and the orientalist Friedrich Majer relied on the English of Jones's colleague, Charles Wilkins, for his 1802 German translation of the *Bhagavat-Gita*, published in Julius Klaproth's *Asiatisches Magazin* [*Asiatic Magazine*].[10] Majer, in turn, was influential in persuading Friedrich Schlegel to learn Sanskrit in order that he might access these texts in their original language and translate them directly.[11] Meanwhile, the importance of other oriental languages continued to be upheld as a means of discovering the literature that might further the 'neue Mythologie' project. Anquetil-Duperron, for example, urged the study of Persian so that the reception of ancient Persian poetry might be based on a full knowledge of the original texts, rather than skewed by a partial understanding gleaned from translated fragments, and published an essay on this topic in German in 1789.[12] Furthermore, Napoleon Bonaparte's 1798 expedition to Egypt helped to crystallize an already pronounced European interest in Egyptology. Linguists had already been drawn to the mysteries of the Egyptian hieroglyphs, such as the Göttingen scholar Georg Christoph Meiners, for example, who published an essay on the hieroglyphic writing system in the 1788 *Göttingisches historisches Magazin* [*Göttingen Historical Magazine*].[13] Adding to the existing work, scholars accompanying the expedition produced a compendious series of volumes entitled *Description de L'Égypte* [*Description of Egypt*], an exhaustive scientific and cultural history of the Egyptian people. The first of these appeared in 1809, followed a year later by the Heidelberg academic Georg Friedrich Creuzer's *Symbolik und Mythologie der alten Völker* [*Symbolism and Mythology of the Ancient Peoples*], which deals extensively with the Egyptian people as well as Greek and Indian mythology.

The influence of these scholarly trends on German Romantic fiction was dependent not only upon the scores of studies produced in universities, but also on the relationships between Romantic writers and the scholars themselves, as well as the literary reception of these scholars. Some orientalists were, of course, also writers of fiction, the most obvious example being Friedrich Schlegel. Additionally, close personal relationships developed between scholars and writers, as in the case of Creuzer and Karoline von Günderrode, whose poetry and plays are marked by oriental themes.[14] Many Romantic authors attended universities where Orientalism was flourishing, for example Arnim and Tieck at Halle and Göttingen, Novalis at Jena, and indeed Hoffmann at Königsberg. Joseph von Eichendorff's comment on the timely interaction of scholars and writers reinforces the notion of the Romantics as a loose collective, sharing intellectual and imaginative discoveries:

> Da standen unerwartet und fast gleichzeitig mehrere gewaltige Geister in bisher ganz unerhörter Rüstung auf: Schelling, Novalis, die Schlegels, Görres, Steffens und Tieck [...] Es war, als sei überall, ohne Verabredung und sichtbaren Verein, eine Verschwörung der Gelehrten ausgebrochen, die auf einmal eine ganz neue wunderbare Welt aufdeckte.
>
> [Unexpectedly and almost simultaneously there emerged a number of powerful minds, in battalions never seen before: Schelling, Novalis, the Schlegels, Görres, Steffens and Tieck [...] It was as if a conspiracy between scholars had arisen everywhere, with neither arrangement nor visible association, discovering all at once a new, wondrous world.][15]

A further example of the spirit of exchange between scholar and poet is Tieck's acceptance of Majer's essay 'Über die mythologischen Dichtungen der Indier' [On the Mythological Poetry of the Indians] for his *Poetisches Journal* [*Poetic Journal*], published in Jena in 1800.[16] Furthermore, even those orientalists who were not established academics influenced literary production. Heinrich Friedrich von Diez (1751–1817) and Joseph von Hammer-Purgstall (1774–1856) each had an actual rather than imagined experience of the Orient, as ambassadors to Constantinople. As they were translators of oriental languages, Goethe consulted them both as trusted advisers in the production of his *West-Östlicher Divan* [*West-Eastern Divan*] (1819).

Such interaction, perhaps inevitably, had an impact on the literary reception of Orientalism, in that the scholar became a key figure in imaginative depictions of the Romantic search for insight into eastern mythology and magic. Goethe's humorous wordplay when he referred to Majer as 'Magier' [magician] was as much connected to Majer's interest in mythology as to the curious spelling of his surname.[17] The cross-over between the oriental magus and the scholar of Orientalism developed in an imagined conflation of the two, and this supposed connection worked both ways, as the magus is often portrayed as a bookish figure. In Hoffmann's oeuvre, the most obvious example is found in *Der goldene Topf* (1814), in which Lindhorst's extensive library is presented to the reader in detail. *Prinzessin Brambilla* (1820) provides a further example, when Celionati, who claims allegiance with the Indian magician Ruffiamonte, is said to have studied at Halle and Jena (III, 896). Hoffmann's portrayals of scholars also suggest that the Orient's transformative potential for the seeker of mythological origins and divine harmony is not simply intuitively experienced but arises from sustained studious engagement. Anselmus's transcription of Coptic and Arabic scripts, reminiscent of Friedrich Schlegel's toils in a Parisian library, is the means by which he ultimately enters a mythological world. Indeed, as shall be discussed later, there is the suggestion that scholars of the Orient have the desire, if not the ability, to become oriental, an aim which is, however, often parodied by Hoffmann. This desire is present in Baron Exter of *Das steinerne Herz*, a German official who has learned Turkish and plays the role of an oriental sorcerer. Furthermore, historical figures who were scholars of the Orient appear, implicitly or explicitly, as fictional characters in Hoffmann's texts. In *Die Irrungen*, Heinrich Friedrich von Diez is mentioned by name and is referred to as an expert on the Koran whom a learned Jewish scholar wishes to consult regarding a particularly difficult passage. The same text provides another example, when Baron von S. receives his astounded uncle while sitting cross-legged on a sofa, wearing an oriental-style dressing gown and a turban, in a room with a Turkish rug. As noted above (pp. 30–31), the orientalized images of Greece in *Die Irrungen* were partly inspired by the travel-writing of J. L. S. Bartholdy, to whom Hoffmann paid a visit on 6 July 1807. Hoffmann's description of the scene awaiting him in Bartholdy's home is comically familiar: 'Bartholdy empfing mich gestern in einem angenehm dekorierten Kabinett nach türkischer Art mit übereinander geschlagenen Beinen auf einem Sopha sitzend' [Yesterday Bartholdy received me in a pleasantly decorated gallery in the Turkish style, sitting on a sofa with his legs crossed] (I, 168). Hoffmann imaginatively documents not only the intellectual and literary search for the Romantic Orient, but also the attempts of scholars to transfer their claimed knowledge of foreign cultures into a German context, and the German reception of this alleged wisdom.

Hoffmann's would-be oriental sages appear in tales which have specifically German settings. They typify the hybrid scholar/magus figure in that they practise, with varying degrees of success, the eastern magic which they are studying, and relate their knowledge of the Orient to the possession of exceptional powers. Baron Exter in *Das steinerne Herz*, Dapsul von Zabelthau in *Die Königsbraut*, Major O'Malley in *Der Elementargeist*, and Irenäus Schnüspelpold in *Die Irrungen* and *Die Geheimnisse* all reside in German locales for the narrative present. In most cases they have travelled outside of Europe, to a country or countries deemed in Hoffmann's time to fall into the broadly constructed Orient, which includes Greece, northern Africa, Turkey, and India. If they have not actually travelled to the East, they have invariably enjoyed an unconventional education comprising elements such as the study of oriental languages, traditions, or magic rituals. Their formative experiences, therefore, are steeped in a tradition outside of the European, and as a result they are generally outsider figures even though they are often originally Europeans. What unites these sages is their attempt to practise oriental rituals and to impart their knowledge of the East to others who are at best confused by such behaviour and at worst resistant or even hostile to it. Their success at what we might now term 'cultural transfer' is questionable, for in attempting to relate their experiences of the Orient for the benefit of European observers, they are hampered both by their own subjectivity and by an uncomprehending audience. Cultural theorists explain such difficulties as arising from the mutual exclusivity of separate 'system[s] of significations', in other words, cultures.[18] These systems provide the means by which particular societies understand themselves and their interaction with the world, but are often alien to outside groups familiar with a completely different set of significations.[19] The particular difficulty experienced by those who wish to mediate, or translate, between two cultures is summed up succinctly by Gershon Shaked's description of an audience observing portrayals of a foreign culture:

> we [...] translat[e] unfamiliar relations to ones familiar to us. When we attempt to fill the gaps deriving from our misunderstanding of a text or spectacle, we try to translate an alien subjective experience (which, on the theatrical level, takes on a quasi-objective dimension, appearing as reality in its own right) to a close subjective experience. That process creates a gap between the original and the translation, and, moreover, within the process of translation, various intermediaries stand between us and absolute misunderstanding or partial understanding, seeking to bring the distant closer and put the near at a distance.[20]

Hoffmann's German orientalists are the 'intermediaries' in question, and their efforts 'to bring the distant closer', are carried out either by showcasing the allegedly magical powers they claim to have learned from the study of oriental religions, or by attempting to teach the uninitiated.

Das steinerne Herz

Baron von Exter in *Das steinerne Herz* is a key example of a German figure attempting to convey to a German audience his close link to, and understanding of, the perceived mysteries of the Orient, in this case specifically Turkey. Exter's role as intercultural mediator finds its basis in his former position as ambassador to Turkey, and once this position has expired, he continues in his now self-appointed role as mediator between East and West, attempting to convey the mysteries and charms of the Orient to a German public. Even though he has returned to Germany, he retains an obsessive fascination with the Orient which manifests itself in his choice of clothing, words, and behaviour. The story is set in the first decade of the nineteenth century, approximately forty years after Exter held his diplomatic post, and yet he continues to produce rather ostentatious displays of the oriental lifestyle he has tried to assimilate. Perhaps most strikingly, he claims to have magical powers, partly derived from a magic ring which he received in Turkey as a gift of thanks after rescuing a woman's child from the Bosphorus. When he attends a costume party, however, all but one of the guests find him ridiculous, and his oriental posturing, for example when he reclines on a sofa wearing his turban, smoking a pipe and drinking coffee, goes largely unnoticed. Only the Hofrat Reutlinger, the host whose fixation on the past is as strong as Exter's preoccupation with Turkey, is persuaded by Exter's claimed authority, to such an extent that on Exter's suggestion, he insists that his unwilling nephew must travel to Constantinople before he may marry.

Exter's orientalism is purely performative, and it reveals more about his infatuation with the Orient that it ever can about Turkish life. This is evident not only in his clothing (he is, after all, at a costume party) but in the manner in which he is greeted by friends — '"Salama milek!" sprach der Hofrat, den Baron Exter umarmend' ["Salama milek!" said the Councillor, embracing the Baron] (III, 327) — and in descriptions of his former life in Turkey: 'Seine Beschreibung des Pallastes, den er in Pera bewohnte, erinnert an die diamantnen Feen-Palläste in "Tausend und einer Nacht"' [His description of the palace in which he lived in Pera reminded one of the diamond fairy-tale palaces of "The Thousand and One Nights"] (III, 326).[21] According to Röder, European orientalists create a paradox which stems from their efforts to deconstruct and rationalize, and thereby understand, something which they in fact insist is mysterious and unknowable — the Orient itself.[22] The situation is further exacerbated by characters such as Exter who attempt the impossible and try actually to become oriental, claiming in the process a wisdom superior to that of their fellow Germans. Insisting on his supreme authority, Exter claims that the only way to educate oneself is to travel to Turkey as he did, 'da lernst du alles was du brauchst für's Leben' [there you will learn everything that you need for life] (III, 344). This statement is not at all vindicated by the conclusion of the tale, however, as having returned from Constantinople, Reutlinger's nephew Max continues his life as he had previously planned, marrying his sweetheart Julie and having several children, a life, indeed, so ordinary that it is parodied by the narrator's refusal to bore the reader with its details: '[du] verlangst wohl nicht noch zu wissen, wie die Braut geputzt war und wieviel Kinder das Paar bis jetzt erzeugt hat' [surely you won't want to know what the bride wore, and how many children the couple have had up until now] (III, 344). Exter's attempts to infuse others with his passion do not, therefore, inspire the reaction for which he is hoping. As cultural mediators might be likened to translators, we can view Exter's shortcomings with reference to the following discussion of translation practice:

> An awareness of the translator's role as a mediator can [...] explain the often-quoted advice that the translator should step into the original writer's shoes and act out the sender's part on the stage provided by the target language [...] this amounts to asking for the impossible.[23]

Exter attempts through his clothing, gestures, and words to become entirely a representative of the foreign culture which he, as a German, can never fully understand. He thereby both fails to give a convincing representation of the East, and loses his connection with the German observers who can only interpret his actions as those of a fantasist, a point of view made clear by his old friend General Rixendorf, who tells Reutlinger, 'ihr verderbt euch beide das Leben mit euern Fantastereien, du und Exter' [You and Exter both ruin your lives with your fantasizing] (III, 338). His failure lies partially in his exaggerated sense of self-worth and of his capacity to understand the mysterious 'Other', but also in an inherently flawed attempt to transfer a culture to a foreign context.

Exter's failure to convince and find acceptance as an 'oriental' in Europe may reflect Hoffmann's attitude towards the orientalist scholars of his time, even those who were genuinely lauded for their expertise. *Das steinerne Herz* in particular contains a veiled parody of a well-known German scholar of oriental history and languages, a connection which has thus far gone unnoticed by Hoffmann critics. Goethe's adviser on matters oriental, Heinrich Friedrich von Diez (1751–1817), although largely unknown today, was a famous orientalist in his lifetime.[24] A diplomatic official rather than an established scholar, Diez nevertheless wrote a substantial history of oriental people and customs entitled *Denkwürdigkeiten von Asien* [*Notable Elements of Asia*] (1811–15), and translated Turkish poetry as well as the Persian *Buch des Kabus* [*Book of Kavus*] in 1811.[25] On his death he bequeathed his collection of over 800 oriental manuscripts to the Königliche Bibliothek in Berlin, a donation which survives today in the Staatsbibliothek's *Dieziana* collection. Hoffmann's Berlin years overlapped with those of Diez, who lived in the city from 1807 until his death, and his familiarity with Diez's work may be assumed from the above-mentioned episode in *Die Irrungen*, in which it is claimed that a character has travelled from Smyrna to Berlin to consult the Geheimerat Diez on an ambiguous passage in the Koran, only to arrive in the city and find that Diez has died (V, 507). This reference is in keeping with a real-life time frame, as *Die Irrungen* was written in 1821, four years after Diez's death.

Although Diez is not mentioned by name in *Das steinerne Herz*, aspects of his life and character, which Hoffmann chooses to parody, are mirrored in the figure of the Baron Exter. Like Exter, Diez was appointed Ambassador to Turkey in 1784 and lived in Constantinople. He remained in his post for seven years, and his recall to Germany caused him much anguish. His description of his departure exhibits a sense of self-worth not far from that displayed by Hoffmann's fictional ambassador:

> Mein Schiff ist seit vorgestern von Türken nicht leer geworden, welche zu mir gekommen sind, um zu weinen und Abschied zu nehmen. Alle haben nur diese Worte im Munde: ein solcher Gesandter, wie der, war niemals hier, und es wird auch kein zweiter nach ihm kommen.

> [Since the day before yesterday, my ship has not been free of Turks, who have come to me in order to cry and bid me goodbye. Each of them has only these words to say: such an Ambassador as he has never been here before, and there will not be a second like him again.][26]

In later life, Diez became something of an eccentric recluse but was well known for his oriental proclivities, which were apparent in his home as well as his style of dress. Like Exter, in his later years he continued to assume an ambassadorial lifestyle despite having retired from the post:

> [Er] hatte sich die Räume des Hauptgebäudes in morgenländischem Stile ausgeschmückt und besaß ein türkisches, persisches und chinesisches Zimmer, in denen er nach Weise der Gesandtschaften offene Tafel hielt und fast täglich Berühmtheiten des Geistes und der Gesellschaft bei sich sah. Diez war unverheiratet und hatte sich allmählich zu einem Sonderling entwickelt [...] Eine mächtige Gestalt, meist orientalisch gekleidet, dazu ein breites Gesicht und eine gewaltige, Mark und Bein erschütternde Stimme gaben der Erscheinung des Gelehrten etwas überaus Achtunggebietendes.
>
> [He had decked out the rooms of the main building in oriental style and had a Turkish, a Persian, and a Chinese room, in which he held an open house, as ambassadors tend to do, and received famous intellectuals and fashionable types in his home almost every day. Diez was unmarried and had gradually become an eccentric [...] A powerful figure, usually in oriental clothes, with a broad face and a strong voice that shook its hearers to the core: the bearing of this scholar commanded complete respect.][27]

Diez devoted much of his time after his retirement to the study of eastern languages and customs, and his contribution to the field in Germany is significant. The type of behaviour he exhibited in his endeavours to achieve an at least partly oriental identity for himself, however, contributed to his reputation as an eccentric outsider. Likewise, the Baron von Exter's return to Europe and subsequent mimicking of an oriental lifestyle, an endeavour which ultimately fails, suggests that oriental customs do not easily translate to a western sphere without becoming distorted or even ridiculous.

Die Königsbraut

The comic story *Die Königsbraut* focuses on the failed attempt by an equally eccentric figure to introduce oriental magic to a German setting. Set in the fictional German village of Dapsulheim, the tale portrays the character Dapsul von Zabelthau, a German scholar of the Cabbala who focuses primarily on the art of communication with the spirit world. This mysterious activity was prominent in French and German literary portrayals of the Cabbala in the late eighteenth and early nineteenth centuries. The trend arose largely due to the enduring appeal of a popular text from 1670, the Abbé de Villars's *Comte de Gabalis, ou, Entretiens sur les sciences secrètes* [*Count Gabalis, or Conversations on the Secret Sciences*].[28] Villars's work presents a series of fictional conversations with the mysterious Comte de Gabalis, a Cabbalist who breaks the strict rules of secrecy enforced by his religion in order to reveal the ways of the spirit world to the narrator. A central concern of this work is the communication between mankind and the elemental spirits, and it remained popular well beyond its initial publication, with a German translation appearing in 1782. The common notion of the Cabbala as a secret religion, open only to the initiated, was readily appropriated by the Romantic quest to engage with the mysteries of the Orient, and found its counterpart in the Romantic veneration of mysterious symbols, such as the hieroglyph or the veil of Isis, which reveal the path to wisdom only to the chosen few.[29] In the late eighteenth and early nineteenth centuries, however, this relatively positive reception was overshadowed by a growing view that the Cabbala was not only connected to, but interchangeable with, the occult. In literary works this perception of the Cabbala is central to the fictional treatment of spirit-conjuring.[30] Hoffmann's awareness of this aspect of Cabbala reception is made clear by his intertextual references to Villars's text, which he read in both the original French and in translation,[31] and also to Jacques Cazotte's *Le Diable Amoreux* [*The Devil in Love*] (1772) and Friedrich Schiller's *Der Geisterseher* [*The Ghost-Seer*] (1787–89). Cazotte and Schiller consider Cabbalistic engagement with the elemental world within a framework of black magic, and these particular works are mentioned by name in Hoffmann's *Der Elementargeist*. Besides these, Goethe's *Die neue Melusine* [*The New Melusine*] (1807), in which a magic ring has the power to bind humans to elemental spirits, has been named as an additional influence for *Die Königsbraut*.[32] Goethe's influence is prominent in Hoffmann's tale, as Zabelthau dedicates his life to developing a lasting spiritual relationship with a sylph, or air spirit.[33] Meanwhile, his daughter Ännchen inadvertently realizes her father's dream when she puts on a ring she unearths whilst digging carrots, forming an instant and seemingly unbreakable bond with an earth spirit.

Zabelthau conforms to the scholar/magus model because he attempts to practise magic arts following both intellectual and actual voyages of discovery. Like the Baron Exter, he returns from travels to the Orient convinced of his own aptitude for oriental magic, and he insistently holds onto the notion of his own exceptionalism. His outsider status developed under his childhood tutor, who harboured a passion for the secret arts, taught Zabelthau oriental languages, encouraged his foible for mysticism, and bequeathed to him a library of books on the Cabbala. Later on, Zabelthau confirms his position as an outsider with voluntary withdrawals from German society, first of all when he travels to Egypt and India, and then when he returns home and marries, only to ignore his wife and retire to an astrological tower to spend the rest of his life reading the stars. This academic pursuit develops into a desire actually to become a magus, for Zabelthau is incapable of separating intellectual endeavour from an attempted mastery of magic. In particular, he devotes his time to cultivating a level of wisdom worthy of the sylph, Nehahilah, who, he believes, wishes to form a union with him. He attempts to bring Nehahilah closer to him by means of Cabbalistic practices, following the Comte de Gabalis's pronouncement that sylphs may gain immortality through marriage to a sage. One condition for such a union, which Hoffmann again lifts from *Comte de Gabalis*, is the renunciation of all earthly matters, in particular carnal relations with women.[34] This self-denial might be read as a parallel to the plight of the Romantic artist who must disregard the appeal of earthly love in order to achieve poetic fulfilment. In

Zabelthau's case, however, the gravity of this undertaking is undermined by a rather more mundane sin of the flesh: he has a frustrating but highly comical inability to give up the enjoyment of food for more than a few hours at a time: 'Jeden Morgen nehme ich mir vor zu fasten [...] aber wenn dann der Mittag kommt [...] ich fresse erschrecklich!' [Every morning I resolve to fast [...] but when midday comes [...] I eat uncontrollably!] (iv, 1155). Zabelthau's years of dedicated study are no match for his appetite, and the comic irony of this failure is reinforced by the fact that it is his prosaic daughter who succeeds, albeit unintentionally, in forming a union with the spirit world. The effectiveness of Zabelthau's endeavours to harness magical powers is tested when he discovers that Ännchen has unwittingly entered into a binding engagement to the Vegetable King, Daucus Carota der Erste, a malevolent gnome who wishes to drag her down to his underground realm for all eternity. Although he calls on his Cabbalistic learning to rescue his daughter, ultimately his attempts at magic do little to improve the situation, and Carota's comical defeat comes about when he cannot bear listening to the terrible poetry of Ännchen's fiancé, Amandus von Nebelstern, and sinks into the ground. Zabelthau's desired transition from scholar to magus therefore proves to be a failed mission.

Zabelthau's practice of magic is marked by a semiotic system whose meaning is not always clear to its observer. According to Patrice Pavis, in order to portray a foreign culture successfully, one must '[put] systems of signs together and [organize] them from a semiotic point of view'. Additionally, one must ensure that these signs have 'productive and receptive pertinence'.[35] In Zabelthau's case, magic becomes a performance lacking in 'receptive pertinence', so that he fails to communicate his intentions to his daughter. When he becomes aware of Ännchen's involvement with the spirit world, he summons her to his astrological tower, in order to explain to her the ways of the elemental spirits. The role he takes on as an initiate of Cabbalistic knowledge is compromised, however, by his daughter's inability to draw the right conclusion from his appearance. Surrounded by apparently magical props and dusty books, Zabelthau also dresses for the part: 'Er hatte eine hohe, spitze, graue Mütze auf dem Kopfe, trug einen weiten Mantel von grauem Kalmank und hatte einen langen weißen Bart am Kinn, so daß er wirklich aussah wie ein Zauberer' [He had a tall, pointed grey hat on his head, wore a wide cloak of grey calamanco, and had a long, white beard on his chin, so that he truly looked like a sorcerer] (iv, 1152). Ännchen's reaction, once she overcomes her initial shock, is to interpret what she sees according to her own framework of understanding, which results in a comical error: 'Fräulein Ännchen [lachte] recht herzlich und fragte: ob's denn schon Weihnachten sei und ob Papachen den Knecht Ruprecht spielen wolle?' [Miss Anna laughed heartily and asked if it was already Christmas and Papa was playing Knecht Ruprecht] (iv, 1152). Zabelthau's rather dramatic staging of his magical enterprise misses its mark because he fails to provide an adequate frame of reference for his observer, and without this, Ännchen falls back on an example drawn from German culture in order to explain her father's appearance.

Zabelthau's failure to convince his audience is largely related to the linguistic as well as semiotic expression of his art. His insufficient explanations of the Cabbala mean that his credibility as an oriental scholar is called into question. Pavis's theory of intercultural translation states that:

> the real situation of enunciation (that of the translated text in its situation of reception) is a transaction between the source and target situations of enunciation that may glance at the source, but that has its eye chiefly on the target.[36]

Zabelthau reverses the practice of intercultural translation, barely glancing at his target audience while he immerses himself in a source culture entirely foreign to his daughter. The combination of his exclusively metaphysical concerns and Ännchen's highly practical mind exacerbate this problem. Zabelthau reveals to his daughter his desire to unite with the sylphide, and draws on the Cabbalistic history of such bonds when he tells Ännchen that Zoroaster was said to be born of a union between a woman and a salamander.[37] Ännchen's literal perspective cannot, however, be changed and she meets her father's statements with intractable incomprehension, writing to Amandus that her father wishes to marry 'eine Frau, die in den Lüften schwebt' [a woman who floats about in the air] (IV, 1169). Furthermore, Zabelthau's intensive study of oriental languages is of little help when he tries to communicate the beauty of the spirit world in German. Speaking of a noble earth spirit named Tsilmenech, he notes that this is 'ein Chaldäischer Name, der in echtem reinen Deutsch so viel heißt als Grützkopf' [a Chaldean name which, in pure and simple German, means Porridge-for-Brains] (IV, 1166), and his beloved sylph's Syriac name, Nehahilah, translates into German as 'Spitznase' [Pointy Nose] (IV, 1168). These comical names hardly convey the higher spiritual plane which Zabelthau wishes to describe. Thus the mysterious beauty of the Orient becomes compromised by his misguided attempts to transfer it to a German location, as he neglects to address the cultural context of the setting in which he speaks.

Zabelthau's inability to make himself understood may also be attributed to his failure to abide by one of the main tenets of Hoffmann's Romanticism: an engagement with the real world. Refusing to make any meaningful connection with the physical world he inhabits, Zabelthau is aware of the events of earthly life only in so far as they relate to prophecies and stargazing. This results both in a naïve reaction to the real, physical world, and in an unsympathetic attitude towards human emotions and problems. Like Peregrinus Tyss, Zabelthau leads a reclusive life and has limited knowledge of the everyday world. This means that others may attempt to take advantage of his inexperience. Upon his return from his travels, for example, he finds that a relative has taken possession of the whole of his extensive land and property except for the village of Dapsulheim. Zabelthau's unexpected reaction is one of guileless gratitude that the watchtower, so suited to astrological observations, has been left for him to enjoy. Moreover, the birth of his daughter and the subsequent early death of his wife go largely unnoticed while he sits in his tower, and his consciousness of the sad event of his wife's burial is raised only by his observation of a mysterious shooting star which suggests to him the curse of misfortune (IV, 1142). His close engagement with fortune-telling and astrology becomes absurd, for example when his very first action upon meeting a friendly stranger is to read his palm, and when he agrees with his daughter's prediction of a good crop of lettuce by claiming there is a metaphysical explanation. Zabelthau's obstinate refusal to follow any conventionally practical reason is best illustrated at the end of the tale, when Ännchen accidentally hits Amandus with a spade and he falls to the ground, unconscious. Instead of checking for signs of life, Zabelthau immediately rushes to his tower to consult the stars on whether or not Amandus is dead. His passion for the mysteries of the Cabbala overrides all common sense, a fact which severs any intellectual or personal connection he might have had with the other inhabitants of Dapsulheim. His efforts to communicate his knowledge are therefore abortive, as he cuts himself off from the daughter whom he wishes to educate. As a comical counterpart to Hoffmann's frustrated artist figures, he also serves to illustrate the perils of complete detachment from worldly life, as the result is invariably a failure to achieve the artistic ideal of meaningful expression.

Der Elementargeist

Der Elementargeist comments on the challenge of encouraging a positive reception of oriental magic in the modern age, even when it is successfully practised. Unlike Zabelthau, the central magical figure in the story, Major O'Malley, is adept at oriental magic and successfully puts his reading into practice by engaging in the act of spirit-conjuring. Although O'Malley has an everyday official identity which acts as a disguise — he is an Irish Major in a German regiment during the Napoleonic wars — he views himself primarily as a scholar and magician, situating his work within a long tradition of men who studied and wrote on hermeticism, alchemy, and the most fantastical elements of the Cabbala. Andreas B. Kilcher and Myriam Burkhard's contextualization of this tale notes that following Villars's *Comte de Gabalis*, anyone who attempted to forge links with the elemental spirit world was inaccurately but automatically labelled a Cabbalist.[38] Popular views on the Cabbala in Hoffmann's time would therefore mark out O'Malley as a part of this tradition. Drawing on this reception, *Der Elementargeist* places significant emphasis on the responses of other characters to O'Malley. The reader is privy not only to the opinions of the narrator, a soldier and nobleman named Viktor who comes under O'Malley's influence, but also to those of Viktor's Christian servant, Paul Talkebarth, and his military colleague, Captain von T. Their reactions to O'Malley arise in the context of two ideological debates which have to date failed to attract detailed scholarly attention in relation to the story. Both the split between accepted religion and magic, and the conflict between magic and Enlightenment rationalism become focal points for O'Malley's treatment in German society, and, unusually for Romantic fiction, religion and superstition work alongside Enlightenment reason in order to ensure his marginalization.

O'Malley's knowledge of spirit-conjuring, and more importantly, the responses he elicits in other characters, are shaped within the very real context of a burgeoning literary market. This made hermetic texts, as well as popular fiction on the theme of magic, widely available. Sabine Doering-Manteuffel notes that one unintended effect of the Enlightenment project to improve literacy was to reshape the previously oral folk magic tradition into a 'literary culture'.[39] The growing information culture and public demand for printed media contributed to the wide distribution of 'mass-produced literature on magic and the occult' by the end of the eighteenth century, so that such subjects became available topics for the educated reader.[40] O'Malley's wide-ranging study of the writings of such figures as the Egyptian sage and alleged founder of the hermetic tradition Hermes Trismegistus, the Rosicrucian Heinrich Nollius, the alchemist Robert Fludd, the mystic Wilhelm Postel, and the Alexandrian Jews Josephus and Philo bears witness to this development. Furthermore, he expounds on the value of reading as a valuable means of accessing the spiritual wisdom which is not taught at military schools.[41]

Moreover, Viktor's appetite for literature with a mystical theme strongly influences his perception of O'Malley as a mysterious oriental figure, despite his Irish roots. Viktor has read both Schiller's *Geisterseher* and Cazotte's *Le Diable Amoreux*, translated into German in 1780 as *Teufel Amor*, texts also enjoyed by Hoffmann prior to the writing of *Der Elementargeist*.[42] The basic plot of Hoffmann's text follows Cazotte and Schiller: all three stories deal with soldiers, who are also noblemen, tempted to dabble in the art of spirit-conjuring under the influence of an older, sinister figure with mystical knowledge of an unearthly realm. Despite initial misgivings, the protagonists voluntarily become involved with the spirit world: Schiller's Prince had a youthful desire, 'mit der Geisterwelt in Verbindung zu stehen' [to be connected to the spirit world], which he later indulges, and the young Viktor in *Der Elementargeist* feels a 'Hang zum Mystischen' [tendency towards the mystical] (v, 676), which he follows up when he becomes the pupil of the uncanny O'Malley, and is initiated into the world of black magic.[43] The similarities between Schiller's mysterious Armenian spirit-conjurer and O'Malley provide sufficient evidence for Viktor to associate the Major with the Armenian as a liminal figure who has connections with an oriental belief system. Schiller's Armenian has 'ein gewisser Schnitt des Gesichts, der nicht europäisch war' [a face with a certain shape that was not European], and his impressive stature and dark eyebrows single him out as an unusual figure.[44] Similarly, O'Malley is tall and is described as having dark, bushy eyebrows that lend him the countenance of a comic mask (v, 678). The comparison of O'Malley's face to a mask references the Armenian once more, as he first appears in Schiller's text as a mysterious masked figure during the Venice carnival. These similarities lead Viktor to view O'Malley as 'eine Art Armenier' [a sort of Armenian] (v, 679). His theory is given further weight by the illustration of a man with a strong resemblance to O'Malley in the pages of a book of magic named 'Excorporationen' [Excorporations], which has come into disrepute among an enlightened readership (v, 679). O'Malley's reception, therefore, is determined in advance by existing knowledge of a literary type.

The prevailing interpretation of O'Malley in the text as a dangerous threat to the social and moral order arises from a religious perspective. He is consequently sidelined by the Christian figures who continue to thrive even within an Enlightenment society that considers superstition and irrational beliefs to be outdated. Jacob Neusner explains this apparent paradox:

> 'Rationality' refers to what makes self-evidently valid 'sense' to the participants in a society and a culture. Within that definition, distinctions become possible between truth and falsehood, but also between what is acceptable and what

> is disruptable in knowledge and practice alike. Throughout the history of humankind, societies have claimed to distinguish between true religion and magic [...] both science and religion [...] [enjoy] the standing of a socially acceptable form of activity and knowledge, and both stand against magic as disreputable and unacceptable.[45]

One example of how the distinction is drawn between a socially acceptable religion and magic is the tendency among Christian believers to 'designat[e] one act and its result as a miracle, and another as the work of the devil'.[46] In the context of this tradition, O'Malley is brought into disrepute as his practices are regarded as belonging to a false religion whose followers form an unholy alliance in rejecting the Christian god. His purported link to the spiritual realm is misunderstood as a diabolical pact by the soldiers who claim 'der Major sei ein Doppeltgänger und stehe überhaupt mit dem Teufel im Bunde' [the Major is a Doppelgänger and is certainly in league with the devil] (v, 680). This suspicion is shared by Viktor's faithful servant Paul Talkebarth, a pious Christian who enjoins Viktor to resist O'Malley's power. Far from viewing magic as rationally impossible, Talkebarth is a survivor from a superstitious age and not only believes in, but seems to understand O'Malley's magical powers. As Owen Davies explains, a belief in black magic, or witchcraft, was not necessarily contradictory to Christian teaching, for although after the dawn of the Enlightenment 'many [...] considered witchcraft to be a vulgar notion bred of ignorance and credulity', '[t]here was certainly a conflict between the perceived absurdity and irrationality of witchcraft and the evident ubiquity of the belief in every known culture going back to antiquity, together with the irrefutable word of the Bible on the subject.'[47] When O'Malley creates a teraphim for Viktor, and conjures up a female salamander to breathe life into it, Talkebarth understands the process but interprets it in a Christian rather than a Cabbalist context. O'Malley's decision to conjure a female salamander, or fire-spirit, is based on the observation that Viktor's horoscope shows Mars in the first house, an indication, in astrology, of a fiery spirit. This corresponds directly to an extract from Villars's text, in which Gabalis suggests that the narrator should contact a salamander spirit for the same reason.[48] Transferred from a pseudo-Cabbalist context to a Christian one, however, this pact is viewed as diabolical, with the fiery region of the salamander indicating a hellish realm. Talkebarth tells Viktor: 'Die Salamander seien die schlimmsten Dinge, deren sich der Teufel bediene, um eine arme Menschenseele ins Verderben zu locken, weil sie gewisse Begierden — nun! man müsse nur standhaft bleiben, und Gott fest im Herzen behalten' [Salamanders are the worst of the creatures used by the devil to tempt a lowly human soul into ruin, because certain desires — well! We must simply remain steadfast, and keep God firmly in our hearts] (v, 703). Within this Christian belief system, O'Malley and the salamander cannot be allowed to survive, and they flee before Talkebarth's steadfast faith, according to which they are 'der Herr Major Satan und die Mamsell Beelzebub' [Major Satan and Lady Beelzebub] (v, 704). The Cabbalistic interpretation and the Christian reading are necessarily mutually exclusive, for as Neusner notes, 'one group's holy man is another group's magician', and in this sense O'Malley fits the definition of 'magician', a term 'reserved for the outsider deemed an enemy'.[49]

The representatives of Enlightenment rationalism work in tandem with those of a religious faith to exclude O'Malley from the mainstream. In keeping with their rejection of superstition, the characters representing the Enlightenment tend to ridicule rather than fear him. Stephen Sharot explains how a society increasingly interested in self-improvement and education, such as that of Enlightenment Europe, might support the continued presence of religion while rejecting magic as a false science. In brief, if religion and science are fundamentally different, then they need never compete, but magic must be either a false religion or an attempt at science. Consequently, science and magic have both 'a crucial similarity, which makes [them] alternatives or competitors, and a crucial difference, which results in science replacing magic'.[50] This is explained as a 'partial secularization thesis', which allows for the survival of mainstream religion, as non-falsifiable, but rejects magic as 'a survival among the uneducated of a previous stage of civilization'.[51] One indication of this trend in *Der Elementargeist* is an outright refusal by some characters to acknowledge the mystical elements with which they are confronted. Instead, the magical becomes banal and figures representing the spiritual realm are judged on their adherence or otherwise to modern fashion. For example when Viktor describes O'Malley to his friend Albert, he tells him, 'Was aber bei der pedantischen Formkrämerei jener Zeit ganz unerhört scheinen mußte: O'Malley trug — keinen Zopf' [But in that time of pedantic attention to form, this must certainly have been outrageous: O'Malley did not wear a plaited wig] (v, 679). Later on, Albert's response to Viktor's description of the salamander's red hair and fiery silk dress is intentionally prosaic: '"Ei," sprach Albert lachend, "deine Salamandrin hat keinen sonderlichen Geschmack — rötlichbraunes Haar, und dazu sich in feuerfarbne Seide zu kleiden"' ['Well,' said Albert with a laugh, 'your salamander doesn't have much taste — auburn hair, and she dresses herself in fire-coloured silk'] (v, 698). Magic is thus reduced from an object of fear to one of mockery, a development which negates its influence on the collective and reinforces O'Malley's status as an eccentric outsider.

As a competitive alternative to nineteenth-century religion and science, O'Malley's magic must be rejected as either morally wrong or simply nonsensical. Therefore even when the 'rational' characters acknowledge the practice of magic, they almost immediately dismiss it. This is illustrated by a debate which arises between O'Malley and Viktor's colleague, Captain von T., when the Captain presses O'Malley to relinquish his belief in magic, claiming that it is a remnant of an era that should be forgotten in the enlightened age:

> Im Ernst wolle er aber jetzt den Major fragen, ob er nicht gut tun würde, das alberne Gerücht, daß er wirklich über unheimliche Mächte gebiete, zu widerlegen, und so auch seiner Seits dem dummen Aberglauben zu steuern, der nicht mehr in das aufgeklärte Zeitalter passe. (v, 681)
>
> [He now wanted to ask the major, in all seriousness, whether it wouldn't be best for him to refute the absurd rumour that he had uncanny powers, and thus do his part in stemming the idiotic superstition that was no longer appropriate in this enlightened age.]

In keeping with the epistemological shift of his era, the Captain gives voice to a 'shifting intellectual interpretation of folk magic from being a very real and implicitly satanic offence to being a merely fraudulent and morally reprehensible crime'.[52] When O'Malley proves his ability to conjure up a figure from the spirit world, the Captain faints in shock, unable to bear what he cannot rationally explain.

O'Malley's reasoning, on the other hand, follows the Romantic call to question the primacy of empirical thought, and explains the Captain's inability to understand him as the result of a clash between opposing belief systems:

> [S]eht Ihr wohl, Hauptmann! Weil Euer Geist unfähig ist, Göttliches zu empfangen und zu gebären, ja weil Eure Natur nicht einmal von der Beschaffenheit sein mag, sich auch nur zur Erkenntnis zu entzünden, deshalb müßtet Ihr eigentlich leugnen, daß aus irgend einem Menschen sich dergleichen gestalten könne. (v, 682)
>
> [[Y]ou see, Captain! Just because your mind is incapable of receiving and reproducing the divine, yes, because your nature is not of the sort that can be ignited to realize insight, you are obliged to deny that any other person could develop in this way.]

The seemingly diabolical O'Malley therefore exhibits an understanding of the Romantic world-view which denies that empirical investigation is the only reliable means of gaining knowledge, suggesting divine revelation as an alternative. His understanding of 'göttlich' [divine], however, does not adhere to the standard Christian interpretation which remains acceptable in enlightened Germany. On the contrary, O'Malley's beliefs are deemed obsolete, and are decidedly non-European, as his scholarly study is partially based on Egyptian hermeticism. His attempt to prove his superior knowledge to modern German observers is doomed to failure, for their entrenchment in a rational education makes them unwilling and indeed unable to tolerate any expression of a faith which may be construed as superstitious, outdated, or even foreign.

Die Irrungen/Die Geheimnisse

Hybrid identities become increasingly blurred in the double narrative *Die Irrungen/Die Geheimnisse*, most notably in the case of Irenäus Schnüspelpold. His multiple identities, which resist clear definition, reflect the social standing of not only the oriental Other, but also of Jewish Germans in Hoffmann's society. A Cabbalist scholar and magus of unspecified heritage, Schnüspelpold has travelled through the Orient in pursuit of wisdom. The stories are set in Berlin, however, and when in the Prussian capital, Schnüspelpold attempts to conceal his background by claiming a German identity that fits in with his surroundings: that of a retired Chancellery Assistant. Mirroring real-life officials who travelled to Constantinople and then returned to the German-speaking states, such as Diez and Hammer-Purgstall, Schnüspelpold travels to Turkey as well as Greece, the Arabian peninsula, Egypt, and other unspecified lands 'wo sich den Kundigen die Schachten tiefer Weisheit öffnen' [where the wells of profound wisdom open up to the enlightened] (v, 542). He later continues to study oriental wisdom in Berlin, and as a Cabbalist his primary interests are alchemy and teraphim creation. His oriental identity is both complicated and reinforced by claims that he is Jewish. The character Amalia Simson states that he is a Jewish scholar from Smyrna who has come to Berlin with the intention of working with Diez, and he is also the double of Amalia's father, the Jewish banker Nathanael Simson. The liminal position of Jews in Europe from the late eighteenth century onwards is perhaps best demonstrated by Herder's description of the Jewish people as the 'Asiatics of Europe'.[53] This common perception was connected to the association of the Jews with the eastern biblical lands, and as a result, German representations of Jewish people and their religion and traditions became one facet of Germany's 'parallel Orientalisms'.[54] As Ivan Davidson Kalmar and Derek J. Penslar note, 'Jews were often subjected to the same orientalizing gaze which was turned on the Islamic Other.'[55] For Jews living in Europe, however, the position was more complicated as they were deemed to be both European and eastern, or as some critics argue, neither quite fully the former nor the latter.[56] This fuelled a growing number of orientalist depictions in the Romantic period, some of which explicitly associated Jewish characters with the Orient, as in Achim von Arnim's *Isabella von Ägypten* [*Isabella of Egypt*] (1812). *Die Geheimnisse* provides a striking example of the orientalist gaze in its description of the gaping German crowds who gather outside Schnüspelpold's home hoping to see evidence of his magic powers, even as he insists that he is nothing but a respectable retired official. Schnüspelpold is not only a hybrid scholar/magus, therefore, but is perceived as a liminal figure because of his Jewish associations, and both his German and his oriental identities remain unstable throughout the texts.

In an additional role as the alleged King of Crete, Schnüspelpold uses magic in a bid to help the 1820s cause for Greek independence, but ultimately fails in his undertaking precisely because he attempts to apply oriental magic to a German subject. Prior to the events narrated, this process has begun in Greece, where Schnüspelpold has read the princess's horoscope and foreseen the possibility of Greek victory through her marriage to a Greek prince, Teodoros Capitanaki, who would become the saviour of his people. Schnüspelpold's first impulse is to create a teraphim, following his Cabbalist belief that it could be animated by spirits to bring Teodoros into being. When this enterprise fails, he searches for a human subject who might be transformed into the prince, and in the mistaken belief that this person is Baron Theodor von S., he travels with the princess to Berlin to find him and begin the transformation. Danny Praet's detailed analysis of the texts reveals how the narrative parallels the alchemical process.[57] The union of the prince and princess can be likened to the 'chemical wedding', the stage of the alchemical process in which two opposing principles come together within the 'materia prima', or base material, in order to effect its transformation into gold.[58] On a symbolic level, these two principles may relate to the blending of male and female in marital union. The plan to turn the Baron into a brave Greek prince exemplifies the positive transformation of the self, for which the alchemical process was a popular metaphor in Hoffmann's time.[59] The Baron undergoes only a superficial change, however, which leads Praet to state that 'the main theme of *Die Irrungen* and *Die Geheimnisse* is the Baron's failing process of transmutation'.[60] The reason for this failure is his entrenchment in the superficial culture of upper-class Berlin society. His adoption of Greek dress is related to the popular support for Greek independence, but this support does not extend to practical help, and he is prepared to wear Greek-style clothes only as long as they are in fashion and will not provoke ridicule.[61]

Schnüspelpold's inability to effect a lasting change in the Baron lies in his misguided effort to bring oriental wisdom into a German context. The materials for his experiments, in other words the human subjects who might be open to the spiritual transformation represented by alchemy, are nowhere to be found in Berlin society, where the main concerns are fashion, popular tea parties, and superficial politics. Schnüspelpold's eventual recognition of his failure supports this reading: 'unerachtet aller meiner cabbalistischen Wissenschaft sah ich doch nicht ein, daß ein fantastischer Elegant zum Höheren eben so wenig zu brauchen ist als ein Korkstöpsel' [despite all my Cabbalist knowledge, I didn't realize that an outlandish fop is of as little use for higher purposes as a cork] (v, 565). The narrator humorously implies that this is indeed the case when he parodies an alchemical recipe, reducing it to the banal in his formula for the perfect Berlin tea party. Equating the fashionable ladies to tea, the young men to lukewarm water, the poets to sugar and the intellectuals to rum, he notes, 'so mag die psychische Mischung des Zirkels verglichen werden mit der physischen Mischung des Tees' [in this way the psychological mixture of the circle may be equated with the physical mixture of the tea] (v, 532). As products of 1820s Berlin, the Baron and his acquaintances are excluded from communion with the heavenly, and Schnüspelpold is defeated in his mission because he attempts to carry it out in a setting which is closed to oriental spiritualism and its transformative potential.

The cultural gap between Hoffmann's orientalized Greece and modern Germany cannot be closed by attempts to transfer eastern wisdom to the West, and this explanation for Schnüspelpold's failure is strengthened by a consideration of a character who has thus far gone largely unnoticed in Hoffmann criticism. At the conclusion of *Die Geheimnisse*, the wise woman Aponomeria appears as a sort of *deus ex machina* to prevent the princess from declaring her love to the Baron and thereby marrying the wrong man.[62] It is Aponomeria who confirms the presence of Teodoros Capitanaki in Greece rather than Germany, showing the princess a vision of the prince before spiriting her back to her homeland, where she can await him. Like Schnüspelpold, Aponomeria is an initiate of Cabbalist wisdom who lives in Greece, but she has refused to accompany him on the journey to Berlin as she realizes it is a doomed mission. Indeed, Aponomeria does not leave Greece except to appear momentarily in Berlin in order to fetch the princess. Herein lies the secret to her success: by remaining in Greece Aponomeria is able to find the genuine prince, and the Baron consequently stays in Germany and returns to his favourite pastime of acquiring clothes in the latest fashion. Aponomeria's recognition of the unlikelihood that modern Berlin could be the home for the true prince shows up Schnüspelpold's short-sightedness in conducting his search in Germany. The removal of the princess from Berlin at the end of the tale serves to emphasize her point, one which Schnüspelpold ultimately concedes when he realizes the error of his ways.

Conclusion

The ubiquity of oriental magic as a theme in Hoffmann's work, as well as the blurred line between scholar and magus, is indicative of the growing German trend towards sustained scholarly study of the Orient in a culture which nevertheless continued to view the East as mysterious and magical. Hoffmann joins his contemporaries in thematizing oriental traditions and rituals, but he also parodies the attempt to transfer eastern wisdom to the West, and the German reception of this scholarly enterprise. The challenges presented to the scholar/magus who tries to explain his knowledge in a German setting are related both to his own limitations and to the limited receptivity of his audience. The clash between the scholars of oriental wisdom and their German observers arises, on the whole, from the different systems to which they subscribe. These may be semiotic systems, systems of religious belief, or philosophies of education, but the result is invariably a missed opportunity for genuine communication between two cultures. In Hoffmann's work, the fault can lie with those Germans who claim a superior scholarly insight afforded by intellectual enlightenment, yet choose to undermine the value of the foreign, as in the case of Captain von T. Another flaw is to be found in the would-be scholarly authorities such as Exter and Zabelthau. These characters fail to transmit convincingly their knowledge of foreign cultures to their German observers, either because of a pomposity which renders them ridiculous, or because they have distanced themselves from their own German cultural heritage to such an extent that they can no longer understand the apparently familiar audience to whom they speak. In either case, the representatives of oriental culture make references which seem irrelevant, outdated, or even nonsensical to modern Germans, and the resulting misunderstandings mean that the potential insights of oriental wisdom remain, on the whole, inaccessible.

Notes to Chapter 5

1. Hoffmann, *Die Königsbraut*, IV, 1167.
2. Achim von Arnim, *Armut, Reichtum, Schuld und Buße der Gräfin Dolores*, in *Sämtliche Romane und Erzählungen*, ed. by Walther Migge, 3 vols (Munich: Hanser, 1962), I, 378.
3. See also Suzanne L. Marchand, *German Orientalism in the Age of Empire: Religion, Race, and Scholarship* (New York: Cambridge University Press, 2009), pp. 38–52 and pp. 57–58.
4. Tuska Benes, 'Comparative Linguistics as Ethnology: In Search of Indo-Germans in Central Asia, 1770–1830', *Comparative Studies of South Asia, Africa and the Middle East*, 24:2 (2004), 117–32 (p. 119).
5. See 'Von der Grundsprache des Evangelium Matthäi' [On the Original Language of the Gospel of Matthew], *Magazin für Alte, besonders morgenländische und biblische Litteratur*, 2 (1789), 57–78, and 'Koptisches Original von Markus Evangelium' [The Coptic Original of the Gospel of Mark], *Magazin für Alte, besonders morgenländische und biblische Litteratur*, 3 (1790), 8–20 (both anonymous contributors).
6. See Andrea Polaschegg, *Der andere Orientalismus: Regeln deutsch–morgenländischer Imagination im 19. Jahrhundert* (Berlin and New York: Walter de Gruyter, 2005), p. 161 and Benes, p. 117.
7. Herder claims that Asia was the first part of the earth to be habitable, because the mountains rise to a level which the sea never could have reached: 'Hier war also nach aller Wahrscheinlichkeit irgend in einem glückseligen Tal am Fuß und im Busen der Gebürge der erste erlesene Wohnsitz

der Menschen' [Here, in all probability, was mankind's first exquisite home, in a blissful valley at the foot of, and in the heart of, the mountains] (Johann Gottfried Herder, *Werke*, ed. by Wolfgang Pross, 3 vols (Munich: Hanser, 1984–2002), III/i (2002), p. 37). See also A. Leslie Willson, 'Herder and India: The Genesis of a Mythical Image', *PMLA*, 70 (1955), 1049–58.

8. Benes, p. 120.
9. See Todd Kontje, *German Orientalisms* (Ann Arbor: The University of Michigan Press, 2004), p. 63.
10. See A. Leslie Willson, 'Friedrich Majer: Romantic Indologist', *Texas Studies in Literature and Language*, 3:1 (1961), 40–49 (p. 46).
11. Ibid., p. 42.
12. Anquetil-Duperron, 'Bemerkungen über den Nuzzen, den das Lesen der Orientalischen Schriftsteller gewährt', *Magazin für Alte, besonders morgenländische und biblische Litteratur*, 2 (1789), 1–26.
13. Georg Christoph Meiners, 'Geschichte der hieroglyphischen Schrift', *Göttingisches historisches Magazin*, 3 (1788), 456–85.
14. For example, the poems 'Mahomets Traum in der Wüste' [Mohammed's Dream in the Desert] (1804), 'Die malabarischen Witwen' [The Widows of Malabar] (1805), 'Eine persische Erzählung' [A Persian Tale] (1805), and the drama *Udohla* (1805).
15. Joseph von Eichendorff, *Erlebtes* [*Experiences*], in Joseph von Eichendorff, *Werke*, ed. by Ansgar Hillach, 3 vols (Munich: Winkler, 1970), I, 926–27.
16. Friedrich Majer, 'Über die mythologischen Dichtungen der Indier', *Poetisches Journal*, 1 (1800), 165–216.
17. See Willson, 'Friedrich Majer', p. 41.
18. Patrice Pavis, 'Introduction', in *The Intercultural Performance Reader*, ed. by Patrice Pavis (London and New York: Routledge, 1996), pp. 1–21 (p. 2).
19. Ibid.
20. Gershon Shaked, 'The Play: Gateway to Cultural Dialogue', trans. by Jeffrey Green, in *The Play Out of Context: Transferring Plays from Culture to Culture*, ed. by Hanna Scolnicov and Peter Holland (Cambridge: Cambridge University Press, 1989), pp. 7–24 (p. 7).
21. See also Röder, who describes Exter as a 'Pseudo-Orientaler'. Birgit Röder, '"Fort in die Welt! — Nach Konstantinopel!": Das Orientbild im literarischen Werk E.T.A. Hoffmanns', *GLL*, 64:4 (2011), 501–20 (p. 501).
22. Ibid., p. 520.
23. Albrecht Neubert, 'Translation as Mediation', in *Babel: The Cultural and Linguistic Barriers between Nations*, ed. by Rainer Kölmel and Jerry Payne (Aberdeen: Aberdeen University Press, 1989), pp. 5–12 (p. 7).
24. See Franz Babinger, 'Ein orientalischer Berater Goethes: Heinrich Friedrich von Diez', *Goethe-Jahrbuch*, 34 (1913), 83–100.
25. See ibid., pp. 95–96.
26. Letter from Heinrich Friedrich von Diez to Christoph W. von Dohm, 20 May 1790. Cited in Babinger, p. 92.
27. Babinger, p. 94.
28. Nicolas-Pierre-Henri de Montfaucon de Villars, *Comte de Gabalis, ou, Entretiens sur les sciences secrètes* (Amsterdam: Pierre de Coup, 1715).
29. See also Christoph Schulte, 'Kabbala in der deutschen Romantik: Zur Einleitung', in *Kabbala und Romantik*, ed. by Eveline Goodman-Thau, Gerd Mattenklott, and Christoph Schulte (Tübingen: Max Niemeyer, 1994), pp. 1–19 (p. 1). Schulte argues that its focus on magic, mystical language, mysterious symbolism, and *Naturphilosophie* made the Cabbala an ideal vehicle in the Romantic struggle to combat Enlightenment rationalism.
30. Ibid., pp. 7–8.
31. See Andreas B. Kilcher and Myriam Burkhard, 'Die Königsbraut', in *E.T.A. Hoffmann: Leben — Werk — Wirkung*, ed. by Detlef Kremer (Berlin and New York: Walter de Gruyter, 2009), pp. 325–32 (p. 325).
32. Ibid., p. 327.
33. According to Gabalis, the elemental spirit world is composed of four realms and their representative spirits: fire is represented by salamanders, air by sylphs, water by nymphs, and earth by gnomes. See Villars, pp. 35–36.

34. 'Considérez meurement, si vous aurez le courage, & la force de renoncer à toutes les choses, qui peuvent vous être un obstacle à parvenir à l'élévation pour laquelle vous êtes né?' [Consider carefully whether you have the courage and strength to renounce all the things that could hinder you from reaching the heights for which you were born] (Villars, p. 20). The specific renunciation of pleasures of the flesh is later elaborated upon: 'Les Sages ne vous admettront jamais à leur Compagnie, si vous ne renoncez dès-à present à une chose, qui ne peut compâtir avec la Sagesse [...] il faut renoncer à tout commerce charnel avec les Femmes' [The sages will never admit you to their company, if you do not renounce immediately one thing which is incompatible with wisdom [...] you must renounce all carnal relations with women'] (Villars, p. 21).
35. Patrice Pavis, *Theatre at the Crossroads of Culture* (London and New York: Routledge, 1992), p. 6.
36. Ibid., p. 138.
37. This is also stated in *Gabalis*, p. 88.
38. Andreas B. Kilcher and Myriam Burkhard, 'Der Elementargeist (1821)', in *E.T.A. Hoffmann: Leben — Werk — Wirkung*, ed. by Detlef Kremer (Berlin and New York: Walter de Gruyter, 2009), pp. 371–77 (pp. 372–73). This observation also bears out Schulte's claim, above (see notes 29 and 30).
39. Sabine Doering-Manteuffel, 'The Supernatural and the Development of Print Culture', in *Beyond the Witch Trials: Witchcraft and Magic in Enlightenment Europe*, ed. by Owen Davies and Willem de Blécourt (Manchester and New York: Manchester University Press, 2004), pp. 187–94 (pp. 187–88).
40. Ibid.
41.

> Hättet Ihr aber nur etwas Weniges in tüchtige Bücher geguckt, kenntet Ihr den Cardanus, den Justinus Martyr, den Lactanz, den Cyprian, den Clemens von Alexandrien, den Macrobius, den Trismegistus, den Nollius, den Dorneus, den Theophrastus, den Fludd, den Wilhelm Postel, den Mirandola, ja nur die kabbalistischen Juden, Joseph und Philo, Euch wäre vielleicht eine Ahnung aufgegangen von Dingen, die jetzt Euern Horizont übersteigen, und von denen Ihr daher auch gar nicht reden solltet.
>
> [If only you had looked even briefly in proper books, if you knew about Cardano, Justin Martyr, Lactantius, Cyprian, Clement of Alexandria, Macrobius, Trismegistus, Nollius, Dorneus, Theophrastus, Fludd, Wilhelm Postel, Mirandola, or even the Cabbalist Jews Joseph and Philo, perhaps you would have some idea about those things that currently are beyond your limits, and of which you should therefore not speak at all.] (v, 681–82)

42. Kilcher and Burkhard note that Hoffmann borrowed a copy of *Teufel Amor* from a library in January 1821. See Kilcher and Burkhard, 'Der Elementargeist', p. 372.
43. Friedrich Schiller, *Sämtliche Werke*, ed. by Gerhard Fricke and Herbert G. Göpfert, 5 vols (Munich: Carl Hanser, 1960), v, 59.
44. Ibid., p. 145.
45. Jacob Neusner, 'Introduction', in *Religion, Science and Magic: In Concert and in Conflict*, ed. by Jacob Neusner, Ernest S. Frerichs, and Paul Virgil McCracken Flesher (New York and Oxford: Oxford University Press, 1989), pp. 3–7 (pp. 3–4).
46. Ibid., p. 4.
47. Owen Davies, *Witchcraft, Magic and Culture, 1736–1951* (Manchester and New York: Manchester University Press, 1999), pp. 7–8.
48. 'Je suis d'avis que vous commenciez par les Salamandres: car vous avez un Mars au haut de ciel dans vostre figure; ce qui veut dire qu'il y a bien de feu dans toutes vos actions' [In my opinion you should start with the salamanders, because your face shows you have Mars in the ascendancy; which means that there is fire in everything you do] (Villars, p. 76).
49. Neusner, pp. 4–5.
50. Stephen Sharot, 'Magic, Religion, Science and Secularization', in *Religion, Science and Magic: In Concert and in Conflict*, ed. by Jacob Neusner, Ernest S. Frerichs, and Paul Virgil McCracken Flesher (New York and Oxford: Oxford University Press, 1989), pp. 261–83 (p. 262).

51. Ibid., p. 262 and p. 263.
52. Owen Davies and Willem de Blécourt, 'Introduction: Beyond the Witch Trials', in *Beyond the Witch Trials: Witchcraft and Magic in Enlightenment Europe*, ed. by Owen Davies and Willem de Blécourt (Manchester and New York: Manchester University Press, 2004), pp. 1–8 (p. 3).
53. Citation and translation from Ivan Davidson Kalmar and Derek J. Penslar, 'Orientalism and the Jews: An Introduction', in *Orientalism and the Jews*, ed. by Ivan Davidson Kalmar and Derek J. Penslar (Lebanon, NH: Brandeis University Press, 2005), pp. xiii–xl (p. xiv).
54. Ibid., p. xvi.
55. Ibid., p. xiii.
56. '[t]he Jews, the Asiatics of Europe, straddled both worlds but were understood by everyone to stem from "oriental stock"' (ibid., p. xxix).
57. Danny Praet, 'Kabbala Iocularitер Denudata: E.T.A. Hoffmann's Ironical Use of Rosicrucianism, Alchemy, and Esoteric Philosophy as Narrative Substructures in *Die Irrungen* and *Die Geheimnisse*', *DVjs*, 79 (2005), 253–85.
58. See Kurt Stiasny, *E.T.A. Hoffmann und die Alchemie* (Aachen: Shaker Verlag, 1997), pp. 16–17.
59. Praet discusses Goethe's unfinished poem, 'Die Geheimnisse', within this tradition, pointing to the significance of the shared titles of Goethe's and Hoffmann's works.
60. Praet, p. 277.
61. 'Er [...] wäre, hätte er nicht das Aufsehn und den Spott anglomanischer Grafen und Barone gefürchtet, von Stund' an nicht anders als neugriechisch gekleidet einhergegangen' [Had he not feared a sensation, and the mockery of counts and barons who favoured English styles, he would have gone around in nothing but modern Greek clothing from that time onwards] (v, 475).
62. Danny Praet and Mark Janse have speculated, convincingly, on the meaning of Aponomeria's name, noting that it refers to her occupation as a midwife, but they do not reflect on her role in finding the Greek prince. See Danny Praet and Mark Janse, '"Dem Namen nach": Greek and Jewish References and Word Play in the Character Names of E.T.A. Hoffmann's *Die Irrungen* and *Die Geheimnisse*', *HJb*, 13 (2005), 78–97. Otherwise she is an overlooked character in secondary literature.

CONCLUSION

The reception of Hoffmann as a cynical Romantic has been challenged by critics who call for due consideration of his interest in the assimilation of the fantastical into modern life. To date, this very positive step forwards in Hoffmann criticism has not extended to his treatment of the Orient, with scholars choosing to focus on the problematic nature of attempts by the self-declared 'rational' West to explain the 'mysterious' East, or indeed the seemingly unbridgeable gap between Christianity and Islam.[1]

Moreover, Willson's early reading of Hoffmann's Orients as the dying embers of the 'mythical image', while justified in part, robs this theme in his work of a great deal of its richness. Hoffmann certainly affirmed the power of the imagination even as he acknowledged bleak situations: his final short story, *Des Vetters Eckfenster* [*My Cousin's Corner Window*] (1822), in which a bed-bound invalid gains artistic inspiration by observing day-to-day human interaction in the marketplace below his window, is testament to a more modest evaluation of the redemptive nature of artistic fancy. With this approach in mind, one could certainly read Hoffmann's imaginative flights to the Orient as symptomatic of an escapism that is nevertheless aware of its own limitations. Indeed, Ritchie Robertson makes this claim with regard to the imagined Dresden of *Der goldene Topf.* For all its seeming relationship to reality, it is the fictional product of wishful thinking: a peaceful city representing a relative paradise compared to the war-torn Dresden of the Napoleonic Wars in which Hoffmann lived at the time of writing.[2] This dark reality underlies many of Hoffmann's flights into fantasy. In *Der Dichter und der Komponist* (1813), the composer Ludwig completes the writing of a symphony and proceeds to lose himself in thoughts about the higher nature of music even as the city of Dresden outside is overrun with French soldiers. Similarly, *Der Elementargeist* begins with grim reflections on the war. As German soldiers retreat to Liège, Albert reflects on the loss of life by way of a highly stylized comparison of the earth to a grisly bride welcoming her groom — the bloodied corpses of the soldiers (v, 660). This experience is imaginatively transferred to the territory of oriental magic when the Cabbalist O'Malley urges the union of man with the elemental spirits. Even in the light-hearted work on the same oriental theme, *Die Königsbraut*, the threat of death lurks beneath Carota's unsettling promise to welcome Ännchen to his underground palace for all eternity. Meanwhile, the rarely considered *Erscheinungen* [*Visions*] (1817) portrays an Anselmus who has not made the transition to the oriental paradise of Atlantis but remains in a Dresden occupied by soldiers and is visibly shaken by his experiences.[3] Such material affirms the perceived need to escape into the imagination, and the transformative potential offered by the paradise Atlantis might indeed appear as the last refuge of characters plagued by the horrors of the present.

Pointing out Hoffmann's cynicism towards the idealized image of the Orient, however, suggests a lack of differentiation between a key part of Hoffmann's artistic goal, and the distant dream of Romantic universalism. Hoffmann certainly responded to the idea of universalism, and as I have argued, the employment of oriental models in *Der goldene Topf* and *Prinzessin Brambilla* is characteristic of a desire to explore the possibility, if not probability, of achieving a harmonious existence based on the teachings of Naturphilosophie. As critics have long been aware, however, Hoffmann is interested not only in the aesthetics of Universalpoesie, but in the problem of how to reconcile this worthy aim with the realities of modern life. Transcendence of the world is simply not possible while one lives in it, but Hoffmann's acknowledgement of this fact does not weaken the significance of his relationship to the Romantic Orient, but strengthens it. His writing does not simply contain 'glimmerings of the mythical image', but rather responds in a constructive way to the model set up by the earlier Romantics.[4] Hoffmann shows how the Orient can serve to inspire art in modern Germany, while also giving several implicit warnings about how its image might become distorted and meaningless. Indeed, critical depictions of characters' responses to the Orient within his work, whether Romantic or otherwise, form a set of guidelines relating to both the problems of subjectivity and the flaws inherent in the Romantic project itself. The above reading of *Die Automate* (pp. 60–63) proves that even Romantic souls can fall prey to the lure of perceived oriental mystery, as it is constructed by the German public, and thereby lose their connection to the genuinely Romantic. Furthermore, Hoffmann's artists, scholars, and musicians must learn to do away with the merely decorative in order to transcend the particular and reach for the universal. Yet again, various ways in which the oriental image is appropriated serve to emphasize this aspect of Hoffmann's thought. The ostentatious donning of oriental garb, the performative practice of alleged oriental magic, and the use of pipes, triangles, and drums to create an eastern flavour in music are all exposed as empty gestures that never elevate art but instead parrot a trend. Hoffmann's apparent cynicism, then, might instead be read as a useful response which points the way forwards for the Romantic poet or musician who wishes actually to create art in the objectively real world of the nineteenth century, even as he looks to an imagined Orient for inspiration.

This very practice of course leaves open the question of Romantic cosmopolitanism versus self-interest. Hoffmann is not entirely innocent of the charge levelled by Said against the Romantics, in so far as he turns to the Orient to strengthen his claims about Romantic aesthetics. This is particularly true of his response to the new mythology project, as well as his elucidation of what constitutes Romantic music. Indeed, one might even suggest that he falls victim to his own criticism in this regard, for the empty oriental cipher he rejects in favour of the inspiration afforded by a Romanticized Orient is surely present in his own exclamation that the unknown realm of music is a charming Dschinnistan.[5] Nevertheless, Hoffmann's use of the Orient owes something to the Enlightenment tradition of criticizing the self through the Other, and the very practice of essentializing the oriental to make it fit a selfish purpose is exposed as a flawed practice, most obviously in *Das Sanctus*. Moreover, the oriental characters Lindhorst and Rosabelverde are more than capable of resisting and, in the case of the latter, even profiting from normative practices of German society, and on the whole Hoffmann's apparently enlightened characters or docile German women come off less favourably by comparison.

Finally, with a very few exceptions, and unlike his predecessors, Hoffmann does not travel east in his tales. Novalis's apprentices go to Sais, Heinrich von Ofterdingen was to enter the land of the Saracens, and Tieck's young knight Peter finds himself on 'heathen' shores, hosted by a sultan. But Hoffmann's protagonists stay firmly within European, mainly German, settings. *Der Renegat* is an exception, but in the case of this libretto Hoffmann goes to Algiers because he is following an operatic trend dominant in the German-speaking lands, and the music for *Dirna*, set in India, was an accompaniment to someone else's creation. Even in *Das Sanctus*, the Moorish setting is mediated through a German speaker on German soil. It is this feature of Hoffmann's Orientalism that allows him to examine in such critical detail the mechanisms that shape the German engagement with the Orient. Paradoxically, Hoffmann's reluctance to 'go east' is precisely what makes his analysis of this Romantic obsession so penetrating, and his treatment of the subject so rich. His writing is central to both the construction, and critical appraisal, of the Romantic Orient.

Notes to the Conclusion

1. See Birgit Röder, 'Das Sanctus', in Röder, *A Study of the Major Novellas of E.T.A. Hoffmann*, pp. 142–52, and James Hodkinson, 'Moving Beyond the Binary? Christian–Islamic Encounters and Gender in the Thought and Literature of German Romanticism', in *Encounters with Islam in German Literature and Culture*, ed. by James Hodkinson and Jeffrey Morrison (Rochester, NY: Camden House, 2009), pp. 108–27.
2. Ritchie Robertson, 'Introduction', in E.T.A. Hoffmann, *The Golden Pot and Other Tales*, trans. by Ritchie Robertson (Oxford: Oxford University Press, 1992), pp. vii–xxxii (pp. xii–xiii).
3. 'Gedachte man der letzten Belagerung von Dresden, so wurde Anselmus noch blässer als er schon sonst war' [Whenever someone recalled the last siege of Dresden, Anselmus would become even paler than he already was] (IV, 1038).
4. A. Leslie Willson, *A Mythical Image: The Ideal of India in German Romanticism* (Durham, NC: Duke University Press, 1964), p. 227.
5. Hoffmann, *Don Juan* (I, 708).

BIBLIOGRAPHY

Primary Texts

Arnim, Achim von, *Sämtliche Romane und Erzählungen*, ed. by Walther Migge, 3 vols (Munich: Hanser, 1962)

Creuzer, Friedrich, *Symbolik und Mythologie der alten Völker, besonders der Griechen* (Leipzig and Darmstadt: Heyer & Leske, 1st edn 1810–12; 2nd edn 1819–22; 3rd edn 1837–42).

Eichendorff, Joseph von, *Aus dem Leben eines Taugenichts*, in Joseph von Eichendorff, *Werke*, ed. by Ansgar Hillach, 3 vols (Munich: Winkler, 1970), II, 565–647

—— *Erlebtes*, in Joseph von Eichendorff, *Werke*, ed. by Ansgar Hillach, 3 vols (Munich: Winkler, 1970), I, 926–27

Fichte, Johann Gottlieb, *Grundlage der gesammten Wissenschaftslehre, als Handschrift für seine Zuhörer*, in *Johann Gottlieb Fichtes Sämmtliche Werke*, ed. by J. H. Fichte, 8 vols (Berlin: Veit und Comp., 1845–46), I (1845), pp. 83–328

Fouqué, Friedrich de la Motte, *Lalla Rukh, oder die mongolische Prinzessin: Romantische Dichtung aus dem Englischen in den Sylbenmassen des Originals* (Berlin: Schlesinger, 1822)

Goethe, Johann Wolfgang von, *Werke, Hamburger Ausgabe*, 14 vols, ed. by Erich Trunz (Munich: dtv, 1998)

—— *Erotic Poems*, trans. by David Luke (Oxford: Oxford University Press, 1997; repr. 2008)

Grimm, Jacob and Wilhelm Grimm, *Deutsches Wörterbuch* <http://woerterbuchnetz.de/DWB/> [accessed 27 January 2013]

Hegel, Georg Wilhelm Friedrich, 'Vorlesungen über die Ästhetik', in Hegel, *Werke*, ed. by Eva Moldenhauer and Karl Markus Michel, 20 vols (Frankfurt: Suhrkamp, 1970), XIII–XV

—— *Aesthetics: Lectures on Fine Art*, trans. by T. M. Knox, 2 vols (Oxford: Oxford University Press, 1975)

Herder, Johann Gottfried, *Werke*, ed. by Wolfgang Pross, 3 vols (Munich: Hanser, 1984–2002)

Hoffmann, E.T.A., *Sämtliche Werke*, ed. by Hartmut Steinecke and Wulf Segebrecht, 6 vols (Frankfurt am Main: Deutscher Klassiker Verlag, 1985–2004)

—— *The Golden Pot and Other Tales*, trans. by Ritchie Robertson (Oxford: Oxford University Press, 1992)

—— *Prinzessin Brambilla*, ed. by M. M. Raraty (Oxford: Blackwell, 1972)

Kant, Immanuel, *Kritik der reinen Vernunft*, ed. by Jens Timmermann (Hamburg: Felix Meiner, 1998)

—— *Critique of Pure Reason*, trans. and ed. by Paul Guyer and Allen W. Wood (Cambridge: Cambridge University Press, 1998; repr. 2000)

Kleist, Heinrich von, *Das Käthchen von Heilbronn*, in *Werke und Briefe*, ed. by Siegfried Streller, 4 vols (Berlin: Aufbau, 1978), II, 122–237

Novalis, *Schriften: Die Werke Friedrich von Hardenbergs in vier Bänden und einem Begleitband*, ed. by Paul Kluckhohn and Richard Samuel (Stuttgart: Kohlhammer, 1960–88)

Schelling, F. W. J., *Ideen zu einer Philosophie der Natur, als Einleitung in das Studium dieser Wissenschaft: Erster Theil* (Landshut: Philipp Krüll, 1803)

SCHILLER, FRIEDRICH, *Sämtliche Werke*, ed. by Gerhard Fricke and Herbert G. Göpfert, 5 vols (Munich: Carl Hanser, 1960)

SCHLEGEL, FRIEDRICH, *Kritische Friedrich-Schlegel-Ausgabe*, ed. by Ernst Behler, 35 vols (Munich: Ferdinand Schöningh/Zurich: Thomas, 1958-)

SCHUBERT, GOTTHILF HEINRICH, *Ansichten von der Nachtseite der Naturwissenschaft* (Dresden: Arnold, 1808; repr. Darmstadt: Wissenschaftliche Buchgesellschaft, 1967)

——*Die Symbolik des Traumes* (Bamberg: C. J. Kunz, 1814; repr. Heidelberg: Lambert Schneider, 1968)

SONNINI, C. S., *Travels in Greece and Turkey, undertaken by Order of Louis XVI. and with the Authority of the Ottoman Court*, 2 vols (London: T. N. Longman & O. Rees, 1801)

STURLUSON, SNORRI, *The Prose Edda*, trans. by Jesse L. Byock (London: Penguin, 2005)

TIECK, LUDWIG, *Werke*, ed. by Marianne Thalmann, 4 vols (Munich: Winkler, 1963)

VILLARS, NICOLAS-PIERRE-HENRI DE MONTFAUCON DE, *Comte de Gabalis, ou, Entretiens sur les Sciences Secrètes* (Amsterdam: Pierre de Coup, 1715)

WACKENRODER, WILHELM HEINRICH, *Ein wunderbares morgenländisches Märchen von einem nackten Heiligen*, in Wilhelm Heinrich Wackenroder, *Werke und Briefe*, ed. by Gerda Heinrich (Berlin: Union Verlag, 1984), pp. 304–08

WACKENRODER, WILHELM HEINRICH, and LUDWIG TIECK, *Herzensergießungen eines kunstliebenden Klosterbruders*, in Wilhelm Heinrich Wackenroder, *Werke und Briefe*, ed. by Gerda Heinrich (Berlin: Union Verlag 1984), pp. 139–247

ZIGLER UND KLIPHAUSEN, HEINRICH ANSELM VON, *Die Asiatische Banise*, with an afterword by Wolfgang Pfeiffer-Belli (Munich: Winkler, 1965)

Theoretical Works

BACHELARD, GASTON, *The Poetics of Space*, trans. by Maria Jolas (Boston: Beacon Press, 1994)

BHABHA, HOMI K., *The Location of Culture* (London and New York: Routledge, 1994)

FOUCAULT, MICHEL, 'Of Other Spaces', trans. by Jay Miskowiec, *Diacritics*, 16 (1986), 22–27

LACAN, JACQUES, *The Four Fundamental Concepts of Psycho-Analysis*, ed. by Jacques-Alain Miller, trans. by Alan Sheridan (London: The Hogarth Press and the Institute of Psycho-Analysis, 1977)

NEUBERT, ALBRECHT, 'Translation as Mediation', in *Babel: The Cultural and Linguistic Barriers between Nations*, ed. by Rainer Kölmel and Jerry Payne (Aberdeen: Aberdeen University Press, 1989), pp. 5–12

PAVIS, PATRICE, 'Introduction', in *The Intercultural Performance Reader*, ed. by Patrice Pavis (London and New York: Routledge, 1996), pp. 1–21

——*Theatre at the Crossroads of Culture* (London and New York: Routledge, 1992)

SAID, EDWARD W., *Orientalism*, 3rd edn (London: Penguin, 2003)

SHAKED, GERSHON, 'The Play: Gateway to Cultural Dialogue', trans. by Jeffrey Green, in *The Play Out of Context: Transferring Plays from Culture to Culture*, ed. by Hanna Scolnicov and Peter Holland (Cambridge: Cambridge University Press, 1989), pp. 7–24

SPELMAN, ELIZABETH V., *Inessential Woman: Problems of Exclusion in Feminist Thought* (London: The Woman's Press, 1990)

SPIVAK, GAYATRI CHAKRAVORTY, 'Can the Subaltern Speak?', in *Marxism and the Interpretation of Culture*, ed. by Cary Nelson and Lawrence Grossberg (London: Macmillan, 1988), pp. 271–313

Secondary Literature on E.T.A. Hoffmann

ALLROGGEN, GERHARD, 'E.T.A. Hoffmanns Musik zur Dirna', *MHG*, 15 (1969), 31–39

BERGSTRÖM, STEFAN, *Between Real and Unreal: A Thematic Study of E.T.A. Hoffmann's 'Die Serapionsbrüder'* (New York: Peter Lang, 2000)

BROWN, HILDA MELDRUM, *E.T.A. Hoffmann and the Serapiontic Principle: Critique and Creativity* (Rochester, NY: Camden House, 2006)

CHALUPA, CYNTHIA, 'Re-imaging the Fantastic: E.T.A. Hoffmann's *The Story of the Lost Reflection*', *Marvels & Tales*, 20 (2006), 11–29

CHAMBERS, ROSS, 'Two Theatrical Microcosms: *Die Prinzessin Brambilla* and *Mademoiselle de Maupin*', *Comparative Literature*, 27:1 (1975), 34–46

CHANTLER, ABIGAIL, *E.T.A. Hoffmann's Musical Aesthetics* (Aldershot and Burlington, VT: Ashgate, 2006)

CHARLTON, DAVID (ed.), *E.T.A. Hoffmann's Musical Writings: Kreisleriana, The Poet and the Composer, Music Criticism*, trans. by Martyn Clarke (Cambridge: Cambridge University Press, 1989)

DAEMMRICH, HORST S., *The Shattered Self: E.T.A. Hoffmann's Tragic Vision* (Detroit: Wayne State University Press, 1973)

DICKSON, SHEILA, 'E.T.A. Hoffmann: Mind, Mythology and Meaning', *FMLS*, 32:3 (1996), 251–63

DOBAT, KLAUS-DIETER, *Musik als romantische Illusion: Eine Untersuchung zur Bedeutung der Musikvorstellung E.T.A. Hoffmanns für sein literarisches Werk* (Tübingen: Max Niemeyer, 1984)

DOLAN, EMILY I., 'E.T.A. Hoffmann and the Ethereal Technologies of "Nature Music"', *Eighteenth-Century Music*, 5 (2008), 7–26

DUNKER, AXEL, 'Die schöne Insulanerin: Kolonialismus in E.T.A. Hoffmanns Südsee-Erzählung *Haimatochare*', *DVjs*, 76 (2002), 386–402

DUTCHMAN-SMITH, VICTORIA, *E.T.A. Hoffmann and Alcohol: Biography, Reception and Art* (London: Maney Publishing for the Modern Humanities Research Association, 2010)

EGGER, IRMGARD, 'Krieg der Töne — Konkurrenz der Diskurse: Dissonanz und Konsonanz bei E.T.A. Hoffmann', *HJb*, 16 (2008), 98–108

ELLINGER, GEORG, *E.T.A. Hoffmann: Sein Leben und seine Werke* (Hamburg and Leipzig: Verlag von Leopold Voß, 1894)

FISCHER, STEPHAN, 'E.T.A. Hoffmann's *Prinzessin Brambilla*: Auf der Suche nach der verlorenen Lust', *MHG*, 34 (1988), 11–34

HARPER, ANTHONY and OLIVER NORMAN, 'What Really Happens to Anselmus? "Impermissible" and "Irrelevant" Questions about E.T.A. Hoffmann's *Der goldne Topf*', *New German Studies*, 11 (1983), 113–22

HELFER, MARTHA B., 'The Male Muses of Romanticism: The Poetics of Gender in Novalis, E.T.A. Hoffmann, and Eichendorff', *GQ*, 78:3 (2005), 299–319

HERD, RUDOLF, 'Hoffmanns "Dirna" wieder aufgetaucht!', *MHG*, 15 (1969), 2–3

HODKINSON, JAMES, 'Moving Beyond the Binary? Christian–Islamic Encounters and Gender in the Thought and Literature of German Romanticism', in *Encounters with Islam in German Literature and Culture*, ed. by James Hodkinson and Jeffrey Morrison (Rochester, NY: Camden House, 2009), pp. 108–27

HÖRMANN, YVONNE, *Die Musikerfiguren E.T.A. Hoffmanns: Ein mosaikartiges Konglomerat des romantischen Künstlerideals* (Würzburg: Königshausen & Neumann, 2008)

JOSHUA, ELEOMA, 'Misreading the Body: E.T.A. Hoffmann's *Klein Zaches, genannt Zinnober*', *EGY*, 4 (2010), 39–56

KEIL, WERNER, 'E.T.A. Hoffmann, Dirna: Ein indisches Melodrama', essay in inlay booklet of E.T.A. Hoffmann, *Dirna*, Martin Herrmann, Werner Klockow and Angelika Krautzberger, Deutscher Kammerakademie Neuss, cond. by Johannes Goritzki (Classic Produktion Osnabrück, 999 607–2, 2001), pp. 5–8

—— 'E.T.A. Hoffmann als Komponist', in *E.T.A. Hoffmann: Leben — Werk — Wirkung*, ed. by Detlef Kremer (Berlin and New York: Walter de Gruyter, 2009), pp. 425–48

KILCHER, ANDREAS B., and MYRIAM BURKHARD, 'Der Elementargeist (1821)', in *E.T.A. Hoffmann: Leben — Werk — Wirkung*, ed. by Detlef Kremer (Berlin and New York: Walter de Gruyter, 2009), pp. 371–77

——'Die Königsbraut', in *E.T.A. Hoffmann — Leben — Werk — Wirkung*, ed. by Detlef Kremer (Berlin and New York: Walter de Gruyter, 2009), pp. 325–32

KOHLENBACH, MARGARETE, 'Women and Artists: E.T.A. Hoffmann's Implicit Critique of Early Romanticism', *MLR*, 89 (1994), 659–73

MCCLAIN, WILLIAM H., 'E.T.A. Hoffmann as Psychological Realist: A Study of "Meister Floh"', *Monatshefte*, 47:2 (1955), 65–80

MCGLATHERY, JAMES, 'The Suicide Motif in E.T.A. Hoffmann's "Der goldne Topf"', *Monatshefte*, 58:2 (1966), 115–23

MARKX, FRANCIEN, *E.T.A. Hoffmann, Cosmopolitanism, and the Struggle for German Opera* (Leiden: Brill, 2016)

MATALA DE MAZZA, ETHEL, 'Romantic Politics and Society', trans. by Julia Ng and Ladislaus Löb, in *The Cambridge Companion to German Romanticism*, ed. by Nicholas Saul (Cambridge: Cambridge University Press, 2009), pp. 191–207

MOORE, ANNELIESE W., 'Hawaii in a Nutshell: E.T.A. Hoffmann's *Haimatochare*', *Hawaiian Journal of History*, 12 (1978), 13–27

PETERS, DIANA STONE, 'E.T.A. Hoffmann: The Conciliatory Satirist', *Monatshefte*, 66:1 (1974), 55–73

PRAET, DANNY, and MARK JANSE, '"Dem Namen nach": Greek and Jewish References and Word Play in the Character Names of E.T.A. Hoffmann's *Die Irrungen* and *Die Geheimnisse*', *HJb*, 13 (2005), 78–97

PRAET, DANNY, 'Kabbala Ioculariter Denudata: E.T.A. Hoffmann's Ironical Use of Rosicrucianism, Alchemy, and Esoteric Philosophy as Narrative Substructures in *Die Irrungen* and *Die Geheimnisse*', *DVjs*, 79 (2005), 253–85

PUKNUS, HEINZ, 'Dualismus und versuchte Versöhnung: Hoffmanns zwei Welten vom "Goldenen Topf" bis "Meister Floh"', *Text und Kritik: Sonderband E.T.A. Hoffmann* (1992), 53–62

REDDICK, JOHN, 'E.T.A. Hoffmann's "Der Goldne Topf" and its "Durchgehaltene Ironie"', *MLR*, 71:3 (1976), 577–94

ROBERTSON, RITCHIE, 'Introduction', in E.T.A. Hoffmann, *The Golden Pot and Other Tales*, trans. by Ritchie Robertson (Oxford: Oxford University Press, 1992), pp. vii–xxxii

RÖDER, BIRGIT, *A Study of the Major Novellas of E.T.A. Hoffmann* (Rochester, NY: Camden House, 2003)

——'"Fort in die Welt! — nach Konstantinopel!": Das Orientbild im literarischen Werk E.T.A. Hoffmanns', *GLL*, 64:4 (2011), 501–20

RUPRECHT, LUCIA, *Dances of the Self in Heinrich von Kleist, E.T.A. Hoffmann and Heinrich Heine* (Aldershot and Burlington, VT: Ashgate, 2006)

SCHAFER, R. MURRAY, *E.T.A. Hoffmann and Music* (Toronto: University of Toronto Press, 1975)

SCHMIDT, RICARDA, *Wenn mehrere Künste im Spiel sind: Intermedialität bei E.T.A. Hoffmann* (Göttingen: Vandenhoek & Ruprecht, 2006)

——'Schmerzliches Sehnen und böser Hohn: Ambivalenzen in Hoffmanns Darstellungen von Künstlern', *HJb*, 17 (2009), 20–36

SCHMITZ-EMANS, MONIKA, 'Naturspekulation als "Vorwand" poetischer Gestaltung: Über das Verhältnis E.T.A. Hoffmanns zu den Lehren G.H. Schuberts', *MHG*, 34 (1988)

SCHNAPP, FRIEDRICH, 'Die Quellen von Sodens Melodram *Dirna*', *MHG*, 15 (1969), 4–6

SCHÖNHERR, ULRICH, 'Social Differentiation and Romantic Art: E.T.A. Hoffmann's *The Sanctus* and the Problem of Aesthetic Positioning in Modernity', *NGC*, 66 (1995), 3–16

SCOTT, WALTER, 'On the Supernatural in Fictitious Composition; and Particularly on the Works of Ernest Theodore William Hoffmann', *The Foreign Quarterly Review*, 1 (1827), 60–98

SLESSAREV, HELGA, 'E.T.A. Hoffmann's "Prinzessin Brambilla": A Romanticist's Contribution to the Aesthetic Education of Man', *Studies in Romanticism*, 9:3 (1970), 147–60

STIASNY, KURT, *E.T.A. Hoffmann und die Alchemie* (Aachen: Shaker Verlag, 1997)

TATAR, MARIA M., 'Romantic "Naturphilosophie" and Psychology: A Study of G. H. Schubert and the Impact of his Works on Heinrich von Kleist and E.T.A. Hoffmann' (unpublished doctoral thesis, Princeton University, 1971)

——'Mesmerism, Madness and Death in E.T.A. Hoffmann's *Der goldne Topf*', *Studies in Romanticism*, 15 (1975), 365–89

VAS, LAURA TERÉZIA , 'Orbis Pictus: Intermedialität zwischen Berliner Stadtmalerei und literarischer Stadterfahrung dargestellt anhand der Werke von E.T.A. Hoffmann und Wilhelm Raabe' (unpublished doctoral thesis, University of Cincinnati, 2008)

WOLFGANG-WÜHRL, PAUL, *E.T.A. Hoffmann, Der goldne Topf: Die Utopie einer ästhetischen Existenz* (Paderborn, etc.: Ferdinand Schöningh, 1988)

Other Secondary Sources

AL-TAEE, NASSER, *Representations of the Orient in Western Music: Violence and Sensuality* (Farnham and Burlington, VT: Ashgate, 2010)

ANONYMOUS, 'Koptisches Original von Markus Evangelium', *Magazin für Alte, besonders morgenländische und biblische Litteratur*, 3 (1790), 8–20

ANONYMOUS, 'Von der Grundsprache des Evangelium Matthäi', *Magazin für Alte, besonders morgenländische und biblische Litteratur*, 2 (1789), 57–78

ANQUETIL-DUPERRON, ABRAHAM-HYACINTHE, 'Bemerkungen über den Nuzzen, den das Lesen der Orientalischen Schriftsteller gewährt', *Magazin für Alte, besonders morgenländische und biblische Litteratur*, 2 (1789), 1–26

ARAVAMUDAN, SRINIVAS, *Enlightenment Orientalism: Resisting the Rise of the Novel* (Chicago: University of Chicago Press, 2012)

BABINGER, FRANZ, 'Ein orientalischer Berater Goethes: Heinrich Friedrich von Diez', *Goethe-Jahrbuch*, 34 (1913), 83–100

BARKHOFF, JÜRGEN, 'Female Vampires, Victimhood, and Vengeance', in *Women and Death: Representations of Female Victims and Perpetrators in German Culture 1500–2000*, ed. by Helen Fronius and Anna Linton (Rochester, NY: Camden House, 2008), pp. 128–43

——'Romantic Science and Psychology', in *The Cambridge Companion to German Romanticism*, ed. by Nicholas Saul (Cambridge: Cambridge University Press, 2009), pp. 209–25

BENES, TUSKA, 'Comparative Linguistics as Ethnology: In Search of Indo-Germans in Central Asia, 1770–1830', *Comparative Studies of South Asia, Africa and the Middle East*, 24:2 (2004), 117–32

BERNSTEIN, J. M., 'Recognition and Embodiment (Fichte's Materialism)', in *German Idealism: Contemporary Perspectives*, ed. by Espen Hammer (Abingdon and New York: Routledge, 2007), pp. 183–205

BOWLES, EDMUND A., 'The Impact of Turkish Military Bands on European Court Festivals in the 17th and 18th Centuries', *Early Music*, 34:4 (2006), 533–60

BRANSCOMBE, PETER, and DAVID J. BUCH, 'Dumme Gärtner aus dem Gebirge, Der [*Der dumme Gärtner aus dem Gebirge, oder Die zween Anton* ('The Dumb Gardener from the Mountains, or The Two Antons')]', in *The New Grove Dictionary of Opera*, <www. oxfordmusiconline.com> [accessed 8 February 2013]

COLVIN, SARAH, *The Rhetorical Feminine: Gender and Orient on the German Stage, 1647–1742* (Oxford: Clarendon Press, 1999)

COWAN, ROBERT BRUCE, 'Fear of Infinity: Friedrich Schlegel's Indictment of Indian Philosophy in *Über die Sprache und die Weisheit der Indier*', *GQ*, 81:3 (2008), 322–38

DAVIDSON KALMAR, IVAN, and DEREK J. PENSLAR, 'Orientalism and the Jews: An Introduction', in *Orientalism and the Jews*, ed. by Ivan Davidson Kalmar and Derek J. Penslar (Lebanon, NH: Brandeis University Press, 2005), pp. xiii–xl

DAVIES, OWEN, and WILLEM DE BLÉCOURT, 'Introduction: Beyond the Witch Trials', in *Beyond the Witch Trials: Witchcraft and Magic in Enlightenment Europe*, ed. by Owen Davies and Willem de Blécourt (Manchester and New York: Manchester University Press, 2004), pp. 1–8

DAVIES, OWEN, *Witchcraft, Magic and Culture, 1736–1951* (Manchester and New York: Manchester University Press, 1999)

DOERING-MANTEUFFEL, SABINE, 'The Supernatural and the Development of Print Culture', in *Beyond the Witch Trials: Witchcraft and Magic in Enlightenment Europe*, ed. by Owen Davies and Willem de Blécourt (Manchester and New York: Manchester University Press, 2004), pp. 187–94

DOLAN, EMILY, 'The Idea of Timbre in the Age of Haydn' (unpublished doctoral thesis, Cornell University, 2006)

EPSTEIN NORD, DEBORAH, *Gypsies and the British Imagination, 1807–1930* (New York: Columbia University Press, 2006)

FARRELL, GERRY, *Indian Music and the West* (Oxford: Clarendon Press, 2007)

FISHER, BURTON D., *Mozart's 'The Magic Flute'* (Boca Raton, FL: Opera Journeys Publishing, 2001)

FRANK, MANFRED, 'Philosophy as "Infinite Approximation": Thoughts Arising out of the "Constellation" of Early German Romanticism', in *German Idealism: Contemporary Perspectives*, ed. by Espen Hammer (Abingdon and New York: Routledge, 2007), pp. 291–308

FRANKS, PAUL, 'All or Nothing: Systematicity and Nihilism in Jacobi, Reinhold, and Maimon', in *The Cambridge Companion to German Idealism*, ed. by Karl Ameriks (Cambridge: Cambridge University Press, 2000), pp. 95–116

GOER, CHARIS, and MICHAEL HOFMANN, 'Einleitung', in *Der Deutschen Morgenland: Bilder des Orients in der deutschen Literatur und Kultur von 1770 bis 1850*, ed. by Charis Goer and Michael Hofmann (Munich: Wilhelm Fink, 2008)

GUTHENKE, CONSTANZE, *Placing Modern Greece: The Dynamics of Romantic Hellenism, 1770–1840* (Oxford: Oxford University Press, 2008)

HEAD, MATTHEW, *Orientalism, Masquerade and Mozart's Turkish Music* (London: Royal Musical Association, 2000)

HEITNER, ROBERT R., *German Tragedy in the Age of Enlightenment* (Berkeley and Los Angeles: University of California Press, 1963)

HENNING, JOHN, 'Goethe and "Lalla Rookh"', *MLR*, 48:4 (1953), 445–50

HODKINSON, JAMES, *Women and Writing in the Works of Novalis: Transformation beyond Measure?* (Rochester, NY: Camden House, 2007)

HOFMANN, MICHAEL, 'Humanitäts-Dikurs und Orient-Diskurs um 1780: Herder, Lessing, Wieland', in *Der Deutschen Morgenland: Bilder des Orients in der deutschen Literatur und Kultur von 1770 bis 1850*, ed. by Charis Goer and Michael Hofmann (Munich: Wilhelm Fink, 2008), pp. 37–55

HOGAN, DESMOND, 'Kant's Copernican Turn and the Rationalist Tradition', in *The Cambridge Companion to Kant's* Critique of Pure Reason, ed. by Paul Guyer (New York: Cambridge University Press, 2010), pp. 21–40

HORSTMANN, ROLF-PETER, 'The Early Philosophy of Fichte and Schelling', in *The Cambridge Companion to German Idealism*, ed. by Karl Ameriks (Cambridge: Cambridge University Press, 2000), pp. 117–40

IRWIN, ROBERT, *The Arabian Nights: A Companion* (London: Allen Lane, 1994; repr. London: I. B. Tauris, 2005)

KING, RICHARD, 'Orientalism, Hinduism and Feminism', in *Orientalism: A Reader*, ed. by A. L. Macfie (Edinburgh: Edinburgh University Press, 2000), pp. 336–42

KITTLER, FRIEDRICH A., *The Truth of the Technological World: Essays on the Genealogy of Presence*. trans. by Erik Butler (Stanford: Stanford University Press, 2013)

KLINKERT, THOMAS, and WEERTJE WILLMS, 'Romantic Gender and Sexuality', in *Romantic Prose Fiction*, ed. by Gerald Gillespie, Manfred Engel, and Bernard Dieterle (Amsterdam, Philadelphia: John Benjamins Publishing Company, 2008), pp. 226–48

KONTJE, TODD, *German Orientalisms* (Ann Arbor: The University of Michigan Press, 2004)

LA VARR BYRD, VANCE, 'Ausblick und Einblick: German Literary Responses to Early Panoramas (1787–1844)' (unpublished doctoral thesis, University of Pennsylvania, 2008)

MCGLATHERY, JAMES, 'Madness in German Romanticism', in *Thematics Reconsidered: Essays in Honor of Horst S. Daemmrich*, ed. by Frank Trommler (Atlanta: Rodopi, 1995), pp. 187–99

MACKENZIE, JOHN M., *Orientalism: History, Theory and the Arts* (Manchester and New York: Manchester University Press, 1995)

MAJER, FRIEDRICH, 'Über die mythologischen Dichtungen der Indier', *Poetisches Journal*, 1 (1800), 165–216

MARCHAND, SUZANNE L., *Down from Olympus: Archaeology and Philhellenism in Germany, 1750–1970* (Princeton: Princeton University Press, 2003)

—— *German Orientalism in the Age of Empire: Religion, Race, and Scholarship* (New York: Cambridge University Press, 2009)

MEINERS, GEORG CHRISTOPH, 'Geschichte der hieroglyphischen Schrift', *Göttingisches historisches Magazin*, 3 (1788), 456–85

NEUSNER, JACOB, 'Introduction', in *Religion, Science and Magic: In Concert and in Conflict*, ed. by Jacob Neusner, Ernest S. Frerichs, and Paul Virgil McCracken Flesher (New York and Oxford: Oxford University Press, 1989), pp. 3–7

NIEKERK, CARL, 'The Romantics and Other Cultures', in *The Cambridge Companion to German Romanticism*, ed. by Nicholas Saul (Cambridge, Cambridge University Press, 2009), pp. 147–61

PNEVMONIDOU, ELENA, 'Veiled Narratives: Novalis' "Heinrich von Ofterdingen" as a Staging of Orientalist Discourse', *GQ*, 84:1 (2011), 21–40

POLASCHEGG, ANDREA, *Der andere Orientalismus: Regeln deutsch–morgenländischer Imagination im 19. Jahrhundert* (Berlin and New York: Walter de Gruyter, 2005)

—— 'Von chinesischen Teehäusern zu hebräischen Melodien: Parameter zu einer Gebrauchsgeschichte des deutschen Orientalismus', in *Orientdiskurse in der deutschen Literatur*, ed. by Klaus-Michael Bogdal (Bielefeld: Aisthesis, 2007), pp. 49–80

PRAGER, BRAD, *Aesthetic Vision and German Romanticism: Writing Images* (Rochester, NY: Camden House, 2007)

RICE, JOHN A., 'Axur, re d'Ormus', in *The New Grove Dictionary of Opera* <www.oxfordmusiconline.com> [accessed 13 June 2012]

—— 'Tarare', in *The New Grove Dictionary of Opera* <www.oxfordmusiconline.com> [accessed 13 June 2012]

RINGER, A. L., 'On the Question of "Exoticism" in 19th Century Music', *Studia Musicologica Academiae Scientiarum Hungaricae*, 7 (1965), 115–23

SAUL, NICHOLAS, *Gypsies and Orientalism in German Literature and Anthropology of the Long Nineteenth Century* (London: Legenda, 2007)

—— 'Love, Death and *Liebestod* in German Romanticism', in *The Cambridge Companion to German Romanticism*, ed. by Nicholas Saul (Cambridge: Cambridge University Press, 2009), pp. 163–74

SCHMIDT, RICARDA, 'From Early to Late Romanticism', in *The Cambridge Companion to German Romanticism*, ed. by Nicholas Saul (Cambridge: Cambridge University Press, 2009), pp. 21–39

SCHNÄDELBACH, HERBERT, 'Hegel', in *Music in German Philosophy: An Introduction*, ed. by Stefan Lorenz Sorgner and Oliver Fürbeth, trans. by Susan H. Gillespie (Chicago and London: The University of Chicago Press, 2010), pp. 69–93

SCHULTE, CHRISTOPH, 'Kabbala in der deutschen Romantik: Zur Einleitung', in *Kabbala und Romantik*, ed. by Eveline Goodman-Thau, Gerd Mattenklott, and Christoph Schulte (Tübingen: Max Niemeyer, 1994), pp. 1–19

SCHWAB, RAYMOND, *The Oriental Renaissance: Europe's Rediscovery of India and the East, 1680–1880*, trans. by Gene Patterson-Black and Victor Reinking (New York: Columbia University Press, 1984) [First published in French as *La Renaissance orientale* (Paris: Éditions Payot, 1950).]

SHARAFUDDIN, MOHAMMED, *Islam and Romantic Orientalism: Literary Encounters with the Orient* (London and New York: I. B. Tauris, 1994)

SHAROT, STEPHEN, 'Magic, Religion, Science and Secularization', in *Religion, Science and Magic: In Concert and in Conflict*, ed. by Jacob Neusner, Ernest S. Frerichs, and Paul Virgil McCracken Flesher (New York and Oxford: Oxford University Press, 1989), pp. 261–83

SORGNER, STEFAN LORENZ, and OLIVER FÜRBETH, 'Introduction', in *Music in German Philosophy: An Introduction*, ed. by Stefan Lorenz Sorgner and Oliver Fürbeth, trans. by Susan H. Gillespie (Chicago & London: The University of Chicago Press, 2010), pp. 3–25

STAFFORD, BARBARA MARIA, *Body Criticism: Imaging the Unseen in Enlightenment Art and Medicine* (Cambridge, MA and London: MIT Press, 1991)

STAMM, ULRIKE, 'Die hässliche Orientalin: Zu einem Stereotyp in Reiseberichten des 19. Jahrhunderts', in *Orientdiskurse in der deutschen Literatur*, ed. by Klaus-Michael Bogdal (Bielefeld: Aisthesis, 2007), pp. 141–62

STANDAGE, TOM, *The Mechanical Turk: The True Story of the Chess-Playing Machine that Fooled the World* (London: Penguin, 2002)

SWANN, KAREN, 'Harassing the Muse', in *Romanticism and Feminism*, ed. by Anne K. Mellor (Bloomington and Indianapolis: Indiana University Press, 1988), pp. 81–92

TAUTZ, BIRGIT, 'From Text to Body: The Changing Image of "Chinese Teachers" in Eighteenth-Century German Literature', *EGY*, 1 (2007), 27–45

THIHER, ALLEN, *Revels in Madness: Insanity in Medicine and Literature* (Ann Arbor: The University of Michigan Press, 1999)

THORNTON, LYNNE, 'Frauenbilder: Zur Malerei der "Orientalisten"', in *Europa und der Orient 800–1900*, ed. by Gereon Sievernich and Heinrich Budde (Berlin: Bertelsmann Lexikon, 1989), pp. 342–55

—— *Women as Portrayed in Orientalist Painting* (Paris: ACR, 1994)

TZOREF-ASHKENAZI, CHEN, 'India and the Identity of Europe: The Case of Friedrich Schlegel', *Journal of the History of Ideas*, 67:4 (2006), 713–34

—— *Die indogermanische Verbindung: Friedrich Schlegels Suche nach den indischen Ursprüngen der Deutschen*, trans. by Markus Lemke (Göttingen: Wallstein, 2009)

WALTER, HUGO G., *Sanctuaries of Light in Nineteenth-Century European Literature* (New York: Peter Lang, 2010)

WILLIAMSON, GEORGE S., *The Longing for Myth in Germany: Religion and Aesthetic Culture from Romanticism to Nietzsche* (Chicago and London: The University of Chicago Press, 2004)

WILLSON, A. LESLIE, 'Herder and India: The Genesis of a Mythical Image', *PMLA*, 70 (1955), 1049–58

—— 'Friedrich Majer: Romantic Indologist', *Texas Studies in Literature and Language*, 3:1 (1961), 40–49

—— *A Mythical Image: The Ideal of India in German Romanticism* (Durham, NC: Duke University Press, 1964)

WILSON, W. DANIEL, *Humanität und Kreuzzugsideologie um 1780: Die 'Türkenoper' im 18. Jahrhundert und das Rettungsmotiv in Wielands 'Oberon', Lessings 'Nathan' und Goethes 'Iphigenie'* (New York: Peter Lang, 1984)

WINKLE, SALLY A., *Woman as Bourgeois Ideal: A Study of Sophie von La Roche's Geschichte des Fräuleins von Sternheim and Goethe's Werther* (New York: Peter Lang, 1988)

INDEX

www.ingramcontent.com/pod-product-compliance
Lightning Source LLC
LaVergne TN
LVHW061327060426
835511LV00012B/1895